The Derbyshire Returns
to the
1851 Religious Census

Edited by
Margery Tranter
in collaboration with
David A. Barton and Paul S. Ell

Derbyshire Record Society
Volume XXIII, 1995

Published by the Derbyshire Record Society
9 Caernarvon Close, Chesterfield S40 3DY

First published 1995

ISBN 0 946324 19 0

**The Derbyshire Record Society acknowledges with gratitude the
generous financial assistance of the Aurelius Trust towards the cost of
producing this volume.**

Printed by Technical Print Services Ltd
Brentcliffe Avenue, Carlton Road, Nottingham NG3 7AG

CONTENTS

LIST OF MAPS

PREFACE

During the 1970s both David Barton and I were examining differing aspects of nonconformity in Derbyshire. The 1851 Religious Census formed the starting point for his examination of urban-based dissent in the period 1850 to 1920 and provided the *terminus ad quem* for my own study of rural nonconformity. The transcripts of selected material from the microfilm held in the Local Studies Library at Matlock which we had made in the course of that research were subsequently expanded to include all the information given in the census and were checked with the originals at the Public Record Office.

The entire project has benefitted from the facilities available in the Department of English Local History at the University of Leicester and in particular from the interchange of ideas made possible by the work on religious pluralism (initially funded by the Leverhulme Trust) based in the department.

David Barton's special contribution has been the analysis of the background to the census and his knowledge of the minutiae of nonconformity in Derbyshire; evidence of the latter may be found throughout the volume as well as in the denominational notes in Appendices 2 and 3. Without Paul Ell's experience and expertise in producing computerised maps of religious data and his analysis of national patterns of worship at registration district level the volume would have been the poorer.

Responsibility for any errors and omissions resulting from entering the returns on the word-processing and mapping programs used here, or in the analysis derived therefrom, is mine alone.

Department of English Local History
University of Leicester

Margery Tranter
December 1994

ACKNOWLEDGEMENTS

This volume owes much to help and advice from many different sources. The staff of the Public Record Office, where the documents published here are held (Class HO 129), as well as those of the Derbyshire, Leicestershire and Staffordshire record offices, and the Derbyshire Local Studies Library at Matlock, from whose microfilm copies the initial transcripts were made, have been unfailingly courteous and helpful. We owe especial thanks to Victoria Launders of the University of Leicester Computer Centre, whose patience in designing a program, correcting numerous errors and answering innumerable queries has been inexhaustible. Matt Matthews has given advice on the mapping program. We are grateful to the University Graphics Department for reproducing Map 1, and we thank Dr Keith Snell of the Department of English Local History who read the first draft of the introduction.

Finally, we are greatly indebted to the Aurelius Trust for a generous grant towards the cost of publishing this book, and to Prof. Charles Phythian-Adams, the head of the Department of English Local History, for his advice on our submission to the trust.

E.M.T.

INTRODUCTION

The National Background

On Sunday 30 March 1851 every person attending a place of worship in England and Wales was counted. This unique and never-repeated procedure was part of the national census which took place on 31 March. The results thereby obtained form what has been called 'one of the most remarkable documents of the 19th century'. Even if we allow some rhetorical exaggeration to Dr Kitson Clark in his Ford Lectures for 1960 this claim is, nevertheless, true.[1] Although later in the century censuses of church attendance in various towns were organised, usually by local newspapers,[2] the 1851 census was the only attempt to measure attendance and accommodation on a national scale. The information obtained has enabled historians to study the variegated pattern of church attendance throughout the country and to distinguish, to some extent, between those who conformed to and those who neglected what Horace Mann, the organiser of the census, called 'the public ordinances of religion'.[3] The results of the census, when published by Mann in 1853, staggered the nation, especially the clerical establishment, which was dismayed at the number of absentees revealed by the figures. Anglicans were horrified to find that attendances at Nonconformist chapels were rather more than those at Anglican churches, while Nonconformists were pleased to see they were beginning to be recognised as a responsible alternative religious force.[4]

The organisation of the Religious Census was entrusted to Horace Mann, solicitor and later barrister and afterwards chief clerk in the General Register Office. The son of Thomas Mann, Horace was born in 1823, educated at the

---

[1] G. Kitson Clark, *The making of Victorian England* (1965), p. 148.

[2] 'Statistics on church and chapel accomodation in Derby, *The Nonconformist* (6 Nov. 1871); 'Church and chapel attendance in Chesterfield', *Derbyshire Courier* (Nov. 1881); 'Nonconformist accomodation in Derby' *Derby Free Churchman*, (Feb. 1904).

[3] H. Mann, *Report on Religious Worship in England and Wales*, (Parliamentary Papers, 1852-3, lxxxix), p. clviii.

[4] I. Sellars, *Nineteenth-century nonconformity* (1977), pp. 8–9; for the Independents' reaction see A. Peel, *These hundred years: a history of the Congregational Union of England and Wales, 1831-1931* (1931), p. 203; see also O. Chadwick, *The Victorian Church* (2nd ed., 1970), I, pp. 367–8.

Mercers' School, London, and entered Lincoln's Inn in 1842. Called to the bar in 1847, Mann practised on the Home Circuit until 1850. He was then placed at the Census Office as an assistant to the Registrar General with responsibility for organising the religious and educational parts of the census.[1]

The information was collected on three standard forms. A blue form printed in black was sent to every Anglican incumbent asking for the location of the church or chapel, date of consecration, endowments, the number of seats and proportions that were free or rented. Respondents were also required to give the numbers of attenders at each service during the day and the average attendance during a stated preceding number of months; in practice this was generally six or twelve. For churches built since 1800 the form asked how it was built, by whom and at what cost. There was also space on the form for the signatory to add additional remarks. A second form, printed in red on blue paper, was sent to those in charge of non-Anglican churches. Similar information on seating and attendance was required but no enquiries were made regarding costs or endowments, although an additional query asked if the building was 'separate and entire' and exclusively used for worship. A third form, printed in black on white paper, was drawn up for the meetings of the Society of Friends (Quakers). This asked for attendance figures but, instead of sittings, the actual floor area of the building and the number of worshippers capable of being accommodated was required.[2]

The timing of the religious census coincided with the educational census (another experiment) and the ten-yearly population census and the same organisation was used for all three. The Census Office in London sent out 31 tons of population forms nationally, with a further 19 tons of religious and educational forms. The forms were distributed locally, collected and checked by enumerators and registrars, who then returned them to the Census Office.

As Edward Higgs observes, 'The mid-century was certainly a period when the almost indiscriminate collection of statistics had become a mania and the [1851] census can be seen as part of this movement to reveal the state of the nation'.[3] The religious census may be seen as an attempt to reveal the

---

[1] K.S. Inglis, 'Patterns of religious worship in 1851', *Journal of Ecclesiastical History*, 11 (1960) pp. 74ff., 75 n. 4., quoting J. Foster, *Men at the Bar: a biographical handlist of the members of the various Inns of Court* (1885), p. 303.

[2] Mann, *Report*, Appendix, pp. clxxii, clxxiv.

[3] E. Higgs, *Making sense of the census: the manuscript returns for England and Wales, 1801–1901* (1988), p. 15.

religiosity of the nation by calculations based on church attendance, which is possibly, as Ieuan Gwynedd Jones observed, 'the only aspect of the religious life of the country which can be studied with a fair degree of accuracy and objectivity'.[1]

At this period the General Register Office was in a state of constant tension, trying to keep its schedules as simple as possible while at the same time attempting to reconcile the demands of those pressure groups, notably the London (later Royal) Statistical Society, who wished questions to be asked on subjects of burning interest to them individually.[2] The Act passed to facilitate the 1851 census empowered the Secretary of State to ask questions on any other matter that he might think advisable and under this heading Sir George Lewis, under-secretary at the Home Office, suggested that it would be useful to gather religious data.[3] In a memorandum of 25 September 1850 George Graham, the Registrar General, suggested to Horatio Waddington, the Under-Secretary of State at the Home Office, that:

> In consequence of a resolution of the Sub-Division of Parishes Commission, it is enacted in the Census Act that the Population of Ecclesiastical Districts as well as parishes be ascertained in the census of 1851 ... [it is] Desirable that Captain Duncan of the Tithe Office can consult maps of ecclesiastical districts and trace boundaries on to Ordnance Maps – Maps of Ecclesiastical districts formed lodged with Registrars of dioceses – Will Sir George Grey issue a circular to the Bishops directing their registrars to forward their maps to the Tithe Office'.[4]

A letter of 2 October 1850 from the Census Office to the parliamentary under-secretary at the Home Office outlines suggestions made by William Farr, head of the statistical department of the General Register Office. In addition to the usual census information, Farr suggested that information be sought on schools, churches and chapels, as well as hospitals and work-houses.[5] Sir George Grey, the Home Secretary, evidently issued the circular, for on 4 October he received a letter from the Archbishop of York, Thomas

---

[1] I.G. Jones, 'Denominationalism in Caernarvonshire in the mid-nineteenth century, as shown in the Religious Census of 1851', *Trans. Caernarvonshire Historical Society*, 31 (1970), p. 78.

[2] Higgs, *Making sense*, p. 11.

[3] Chadwick, *Victorian Church*, I, p. 363.

[4] Public Record Office, HO 45/3251.

[5] PRO, HO 45/3251.

Musgrave, saying that he would send details for York but that he could not answer for the other bishops. The Archbishop of Canterbury, J.B. Sumner, answering on 7 October, said that he did not think that the bishops would object if the proposals were clearly explained to them.[1] The inclusion of the religious enquiries is probably an indication of the unease and disquiet felt about the state of religion in the country; it was to be both a test of church attendance and a check to find out if recent church reforms had improved the religious picture.

The social, economic and political unrest of the first three decades of the nineteenth century and the inter-relationship of the political and ecclesiastical crises have been shown by A.D. Gilbert to underlie reforms proposed or enacted in the 1830s and 1840s.[2] Although efforts had been made to improve the efficiency of the parochial system in the eighteenth century, the financial and legal limitations under which bodies such as Queen Anne's Bounty operated were too restrictive for sufficient change to take place. Hence in 1832 the Ecclesiastical Revenues Commission was established by Parliament with instructions to investigate the financial structure of the Church. Progress, however, was slow and another Commission (later called the Ecclesiastical Commission), with wider powers, was instituted by the Peel administration and eventually became a permanent body. Under the chairmanship of James Blomfield, Bishop of London, the Commission soon became the prime mover behind Church reform. Its composition was enlarged to 49 in 1840 and its powers were increased. The efforts that had already been made to alter the parochial structure had, in the main, been haphazard, partly because the funds available were so limited, while the powers of the Board of Queen Anne's Bounty, which administered them, were quite restricted, in contrast to those of the new commission.

The commission was concerned with the problems of large parishes (in Derbyshire these were found particularly in the north)[3] and with improving spiritual provision for densely populated industrial districts. Endowments which appeared to be excessive were expropriated and the funds thus gained used to supplement stipends in less well-endowed parishes and to support the new ecclesiastical districts made possible by Peel's Act of 1843.[4] Between 1840 and 1855 more than 5,000 parishes benefitted from economies which

---

[1] Ibid.

[2] A.D. Gilbert, *Religion and society in industrial England: church, chapel and social change, 1740–1914* (1976), pp. 125–32. Dr Gilbert summarises both the background and the attempted reforms.

[3] e.g. Hope (36,160 acres), Bakewell (43,020 acres) and Glossop (49,960 acres).

[4] 6 & 7 Victoria, c. 37, quoted in Kitson Clark, *Making of Victorian England*, p. 156.

resulted from the abolition of cathedral offices,[1] and Mann was able to report that 1,255 new ecclesiastical districts and parishes had been formed by 1851.[2] New sees were established at Ripon and Manchester and episcopal salaries were rationalised.[3] On the death of Bishop Ryder in 1836 the see of Coventry and Lichfield was divided and Samuel Butler, formerly Archdeacon of Derby, became Bishop of Lichfield, a diocese which included the Archdeaconry of Derbyshire. Legislation of 1843 created a standard procedure for sub-dividing parishes and the commissioners were able to work towards a target of reducing all parishes to a maximum population of 3,000-4,000. This inevitably produced a heavy demand for new churches and more clergy: the tables constructed by A.D. Gilbert show that in the period after the inauguration of the Ecclesiastical Commission many more new churches were built and old ones rebuilt than at any time in the nineteenth century.[4] The figures also demonstrate that, while the numbers of new Anglican churches and chapels showed a dramatic increase in the period from 1831 to 1851, the recruitment of new priests to serve them was rather slow and the rise in the numbers of Easter communicants for the same period was disappointing.[5] Coinciding with this flurry of Anglican activity in church provision there was a steady increase in the number of Dissenting chapels.[6]

Low church attendance had long been a cause of disquiet, both at parish level and in the higher echelons of Church and State; hence, along with the desire to establish a more equitable provision of church accommodation, went the hope—a rather pious one as the results of the census showed—that more people would be encouraged to attend their parish church. The Elizabethan settlement had assumed one church and maximum regular attendance on the part of the population, under pain of penalty; non-attenders, for example Roman Catholics and Anabaptists, were judged to be religiously unsound and, in the case of the Roman Catholics, probably politically unsound as well. No allowance was made for the irreligious or for those who preferred to spend the Sabbath in other ways. B.I. Coleman has

---

[1] The Cathedrals Act, 1840. This resulted in the reduction of most chapters to a dean and four resident canons while other offices were abolished or became honorary positions. The funds thus saved were re-distributed nationally on a basis of need. Gilbert, *Religion and Society*, pp. 129–30.

[2] Mann, *Report*, p. clxiii.

[3] Gilbert, *Religion and society*, p. 130.

[4] Ibid., p. 130 ,Table 6.1.

[5] Ibid., p. 130 Table 6.2; p. 28, Table 2.1.

[6] Kitson Clark, *Making of Victorian England*, pp. 171–2.

commented that, although the Toleration Act of 1689 allowed only limited toleration to Protestant Dissent, there seems to have been a decline in Anglican observance. He goes on to suggest that after 1714 the Church could no longer expect the wholehearted support of the government, while local justices and churchwardens tended to turn a blind eye to non-attendance at the parish church or unorthodoxy in religion, with the the result that the laws for conformity ceased to operate.[1]

The passing of the Toleration Act did not, however, result in a resurgence of Protestant Dissent. In 1662 Puritanism as a movement had encompassed most classes, including the wealthy, the gentry and the nobility. It formed a political and religious alternative to the establishment but, as the 1662 settlement became tested by time and seemed likely to be permanent, the political and social groupings of the Restoration gradually receded. First the nobility, then the gentry, together with leaders of commerce and industry, seceded to rejoin the Anglican church. This desertion by these important groups was accompanied by a rapid numerical decline, so that by the time of the Methodist Revival many of the Dissenting churches which dated from 1662 were moribund.[2] The example and influence of the Methodist preachers, however, had an invigorating effect, particularly on adherents of the Congregational and Baptist denominations.[3]

Gilbert suggests that non-attendance at church was not uncommon during the eighteenth century.[4] The growth of industry, rapid growth of new towns which stretched Anglican resources to the utmost, or the absence of the social control provided by a squire and a resident clergyman, combined to encourage the intermittent indifference of the working class to settle into a definite pattern. Henry Pelling suggests, with some justice, that the factors quoted as reasons for non-attendance are really excuses for a basically indifferent people: 'If a few miles travel put them off, or if they would only attend at the behest of "gentlemen" or employers, or if they broke off from churchgoing whenever they moved, could they be regarded in any real sense as loyal members of the Church?'.[5] It seems that absence from church worship on Sundays, particularly when those absent were working class, was

[1] B.I. Coleman, *The Church of England in the mid-nineteenth century: a social geography* (1980), p. 4.

[2] Gilbert, *Religion and society*, pp. 15–17.

[3] R. Mansfield, 'History of Congregationalism in Derbyshire from the Methodist Revival to 1850' (Unpublished University of Manchester Ph.D. thesis, 1959) pp. 20–38.

[4] Gilbert, *Religion and Society*, pp. 10–11.

[5] H. Pelling, *Popular politics and society in late Victorian Britain* (2nd ed., 1979), pp. 25–6.

no new phenomenon. As Engels expressed it in 1844, 'All bourgeois writers are agreed that the workers have no religion and do not go to church. Exceptions to this are the Irish, a few of the older workers and those wage-earners who have a foot in the middle class camp—overlookers, foremen and so on'.[1] Similar views were expressed by Andrew Mearns in 1883, while at the end of the century a future Bishop of London, A.F. Winnington-Ingram, remarked rather sadly that 'It is not that the Church of God has lost the great towns: it has never had them'.[2] Further support for this opinion may be found in a 'Statistical report of men who are employed by the Butterley Co. and who are living in the parishes of Langley, Aldercar, Loscoe, Codnor and Eastwood' of 1856. Out of a total of 1,647 employees, there was one communicant in the Church of England, together with 17 regular and 26 occasional attenders at church; 45 were regular attenders at chapel and 150 occasional attenders. Eight people attended 'both church and chapel sometimes'; 82 homes were without a Bible; 443 attended no place of worship.[3] Although the figures are sometimes slightly suspect in this report (which was probably made by Robert Lanham, a 'Scripture Reader' living at Loscoe),[4] it gives a good picture of an industrial community at mid-century and tends to corroborate the frequently expressed opinions on working class 'unconscious secularists'.[5]

It is perhaps too easy for a modern writer to say that a low Anglican attendance in 1851 was predictable, especially in view of the great increase in Nonconformist chapels that had been built since 1800.[6] One feels, however, that the results of the religious census, especially the figures of attendance at Anglican churches, gave statistical support, if of somewhat doubtful validity, to those gloomy remarks Anglican incumbents had been

[1] F. Engels, *The condition of the working class in England*, (trans. W.O. Henderson and W.H. Chaloner) (Oxford 1958), p. 141.

[2] A. Mearns, 'The bitter cry of outcast London', in P. Keating (ed.), *Into unknown England, 1866–1913: selection from the social explorers* (1976), p. 76; A.F. Winnington-Ingram, *Work in great cities* (1896), quoted in K.S.Inglis, *Churches and the working class in Victorian England* (1963), p. 3.

[3] Derbyshire Record Office, D503, Statistical report of men employed by the Butterley Co.

[4] F.A. Peake, 'The "Statistical Report of men who are employed by the Butterley Company ... September 1856": an appraisal', *Derbys. Arch. J.*, 92 (1972), pp. 110–22.

[5] Mann, *Report*, p. cxlviii.

[6] Kitson Clark, *Making of Victorian England*, p. 171; Wesleyan Methodist chapels had increased from 825 in 1801 to 11,007 in 1851, Baptist chapels from 652 to 2,789 and Congregational chapels from 914 to 3,244. Mann, *Report*, p. cxliv, Table 17.

making in visitation returns.[1] What chiefly surprised and reassured *The Times* was that the figures for the Roman Catholics were less than the known number of Irish immigrants. The agitation over 'papal aggression' had been an absurdity and so had the Pope's new hierarchy.[2] What shocked the Anglican establishment was the uncomfortable conclusion that, notwithstanding the debatable nature of some of the statistics,[3] the dissenting churches were supported by nearly half the population of England and Wales. The census finally gave the lie to the belief that the Anglican church was the church of the great majority of the people and consequently entitled to be treated in a privileged fashion.[4]

The census figures were then used in what became known as the 'arithmetical war', which divided on party lines, with the Tory Lord Derby affirming the falsity of many of the statistics, while the Whig Lord Palmerston argued for their reliability.[5] In 1860 the Cabinet, when considering the forthcoming census, planned to repeat the religious enquiry but this time with penalties for refusal to answer. Dissenters raised strong objections to answering religious questions under penalty and the government agreed to make the questions voluntary but with a profession of faith. Dissenting reaction to this was even stronger. Having learnt from the 1851 census that figures based on attendance could be debatable and unreliable, the government suggested that heads of households should state their denomination on the census form. Predictably the dissenters refused to consider this proposal fearing, with some reason, that householders with the most tenuous connection with the Anglican church would nevertheless put 'Church of England' on their form; the proposal was dropped and, despite suggestions, was never revived.[6]

Even after the government had conceded that the religious questions were not to be answered under penalty there was still opposition to the proposal,

---

[1] M.R. Austin, *The Church in Derbyshire in 1823-4: the parochial visitation of the Rev. Samuel Butler, archdeacon of Derby* (Derbys. Arch. Soc. Record Series, 1974). In Ripley, for example, the perpetual curate reported a Methodist school with 200 children and Methodist, Unitarian, Presbyterian and other licensed prayer-houses (p. 144).

[2] Chadwick, *Victorian Church*, p. 367.

[3] Ibid., p. 368 quoting *The Nonconformist*, 27 April 1854. This reported that the Baptist Union could not reconcile Mann's Baptist numbers with their own records and were appointing an official enquiry.

[4] Ibid., p. 368.

[5] Ibid., p. 369.

[6] A. Hume, *Remarks on the Census of Religious Worship for England and Wales, with suggestions for an improved census in 1861* (1860), p. 32 suggested that the returns should not be voluntary but obligatory and that they should be open to inspection for fourteen days before being sent away, giving interested parties a chance to check them.

notably from Samuel Wilberforce, Bishop of Oxford. He presented a petition
to the House of Lords three days before the census claiming that the only
result would be wrong information, and intimating that he was inclined to
advise the clergy not to answer the questions.[1] The Bishop of Lichfield,
John Lonsdale, has left no discernible views on the subject. An outstanding
man, he had been appointed to Lichfield in 1843 after being Archdeacon of
Middlesex and Principal of King's College, London.[2] While his sympathies
were rather with the old high church school, he generally took the liberal
side in any controversy; condemning evangelicals and Puseyites alike, and
distrusting them both, he was known to admit that the Puseyites had far
more learning and ability and would add 'and they are gentlemen'.[3] Thus
it would seem that, if there were any opposition to the census in the diocese,
it was not inspired by the bishop. That there was clerical, or at least
Anglican resentment, in Derbyshire can be gathered from the Tory *Derby
Mercury*, which on 26 March 1851, asserted that:

> Religious and educational statistics of a proper kind and to a
> certain extent may be desirable, by way of addenda to the
> Census, but the manner of obtaining them on the present
> occasion, as also the nature of some of the queries to be
> answered have justly called forth considerable animadversion
> both in and out of parliament. We consider the arrangements
> which have been made for the procuring of these statistics to be
> anything but satisfactory and the returns will, in some degree, be
> open to suspicion.

The correspondence column of the same issue included a letter signed 'T.L.',
claiming that:

> you and your readers are probably not aware of the irregular and
> impertinent proceeding about to be perpetrated. This information
> is to be furnished by *any person* with whom it may please the
> Registrar of the district to leave the schedule for that purpose ...
> I confidently believe that the Secretary of State and the Registrar
> General have assumed powers under this Act which the Act does

---

[1] Chadwick, *Victorian Church*, p. 364; K. Tiller (ed.), *Church and chapel in Oxfordshire,
1851* (Oxfordshire Record Society, 1987), p. xiv.

[2] *DNB*, which rates him the best bishop the diocese ever had; Chadwick, *Victorian Church*,
p. 227, describes him as one of the best bishops of the century.

[3] E. Beckett-Denison, *Life of Bishop Lonsdale* (1868), pp. 207–8.

not give them – viz: the power of deriving information from *any* person, respecting the amount of *property* possessed by every clergyman – and, in short, the powers of demanding answers to any question they may please to put to any person whatsoever, on any question whatever. I say the Act does not give this power and I hope the clergy will resist the exercise of it.

The fact that there were no later letters to support or contradict the writer would appear to imply that feelings were not strong on the matter. That there should have been some resentment among Anglican clergy is not surprising: the questions they were asked were of a more searching nature than those asked of their dissenting colleagues and, moreover, some related to their income, a matter which many might wish to keep to themselves. Nevertheless, the number of returns where the endowments were not given is comparatively few and in some cases, as at Barlborough, Osmaston by Derby or Elvaston, where 'the incumbent was absent on licence on account of illness', they were signed by the curate or churchwardens who would have been ignorant of the stipend.[1]

Providing the exact date for licensing or consecration sometimes proved difficult, even for recent buildings. Thus, Peter French, the minister in charge of the Anglican licensed school room at Winshill, said 'licensed, I think, in 1847', while Richardson Cox, writing of St Giles, Calke, replied 'supposed to be a parish church. Not known when consecrated, under what circumstances consecrated or licensed, supposed to be consecrated'.[2] The dates of licensing were not always easily available, especially when, as in the case of Calke, which was rebuilt in 1826, the benefice was a private peculiar and the co-operation of the owner, Sir George Crewe, was necessary for the question to be answered. Counting the congregation, however, raised more objections. The perpetual curate of Taddington, R.H. Kirby, was actively non-compliant: 'I never count the numbers. Average attendance not counted'; similarly the incumbent of Hayfield, Samuel Welsh, strongly emphasised that he only answered the questions under protest.[3] At St John the Evangelist, Smalley, the registrar complained that 'the minister declined to give me any information on this subject in this return. Have returned the above from information otherwise obtained' (the form is unsigned).[4] Goodwin Purcell, the incumbent of St John the Evangelist at Charlesworth, although objecting

[1] Below, pp. 33, 55, 56.
[2] Below, pp. 21, 30.
[3] Below, pp. 175, 221.
[4] Below, p. 85.

to taking numbers on the Sabbath, supplied an estimate instead. He, in fact, spared no ink in the completion of his form, mentioning the low spiritual state of the parish before his arrival, and the way in which he raised the money to build the church, together with many other details.[1] But it must be emphasised that such objections are isolated cases and in general one is pleasantly surprised at the conscientious way the forms were completed. Joshua Roberts, minister of Alfreton Congregational church, went out of his way to point out that his congregation was enlarged by a funeral sermon that was preached that day, while William Gray, minister of Ripley General Baptist chapel, pointed out that the Sunday School Anniversary was held on Census Sunday and that, as a consequence, the congregation was enlarged.[2]

Several Anglican incumbents commented on the incidence of Methodism in their parishes: the rector of Staveley, J.D. Macfarlane, noted that the 'Mining population here, as generally, chiefly Methodist', while William Dyke, the perpetual curate of Winster, hinted at sinister influences against him: 'the greater portion of the inhabitants of Winster are Professed Dissenters and certain influential persons prevent the children from attending the Church Sunday School and Established Church Service'.[3] Certainly the dice against him were loaded in Winster, which was at the head of a flourishing Primitive Methodist circuit, with a chapel built in 1823 and enlarged in 1850. In addition there was a Wesleyan chapel, built in 1837, and an apparently flourishing Wesleyan Reform group who were to build a chapel in 1852.[4]

Although the government had agreed that the religious questions were purely voluntary, there is no sign of widespread refusal to complete the forms. For 21 places of worship, mainly in the south of the county, the registrar had to fill in the form himself; of these 13 were Anglican. Bearing in mind the total number of returns (787), this hardly represented a concerted rebellion. In general the Derbyshire registrars seem to have been conscientious; in one or two instances, such as Kirk Hallam parish church and Willington Baptist church, they were still writing letters as late as June and August 1852 in attempts to extract the required information.[5]

---

[1] Below, p. 218.

[2] Below, pp. 110, 102.

[3] Below, pp. 163, 184.

[4] C.F. Stell, *An inventory of nonconformist chapels and meeting houses in central England* (1986), p. 57.

[5] Below, pp. 64, 9.

Economic and Social Change in Derbyshire

'No looms here, no Dissent':[1] the description of the fictitious village of
Lowick in George Eliot's *Middlemarch* which ends with these words
encapsulates both a perceived control exercised by squire and church, and an
apparent connection between industry and nonconformity which has all too
often been accepted as true. More recently, however, historians of nineteenth-century religion have called into question these and other broad
generalisations, whether they are concerned with the strengths and
weaknesses of the Established Church and of Dissent, with the perception of
their relationships one with another, or with the extent to which regular
attendance was, in fact, habitual among the bulk of the population, in either
an urban or rural setting. Local studies have examined the effect of such
factors as parish size, type of settlement, landholding, occupational structure
and residency of clergy.[2]

A wealth of statistical information is provided by the 1851 religious
census, but, as Coleman has pointed out, 'the study of religion at this period,
perhaps more than any other, requires some sense of social geography, of
region and of locality, and of the various forces operating on people's
behaviour in each'.[3] It is, therefore, against an understanding of the *local* as
well as the national, background that the information in the census must be
assessed. A deeper understanding of the distribution and practice of religious
belief in Derbyshire in the mid-nineteenth century, and hence of the trends
and attitudes which have either continued or withered in the course of the
succeeding 140 years, can only evolve from an appreciation of social and

---

[1] George Eliot, *Middlemarch* (Penguin ed., 1965), p. 102.

[2] For Derbyshire see the work of M.R. Austin: 'Queen Anne's Bounty and the poor livings
of Derbyshire', *Derbys. Arch. J.*, 92 (1973), 75–89; 'Religion and society in Derbyshire in the
Industrial Revolution', Ibid., 93 (1974), 78–89; 'Enclosure and benefice incomes in Derbyshire',
Ibid., 100 (1980), 88–94; 'Tithe and benefice incomes in Derbyshire', Ibid., 102 (1982), 118–24.
Cf. also D.A. Barton, 'Aspects of nonconformity in six Derbyshire towns, 1850–1914'
(Unpublished University of Sheffield M.A. thesis, 1981) and E.M.Tranter 'Aspects of rural
nonconformity in Derbyshire, 1662–1851' (Unpublished University of Leicester M.A.
dissertation 1974). For the general picture see Coleman, *Church of England*; A.M. Everitt,
'Nonconformity in country parishes', in *Land, Church and People: Essays presented to
Professor H.P.R. Finberg*, (1970), 178–99 ; idem, *The pattern of rural dissent: the nineteenth
century* (University of Leicester Department of English Local History, Occasional Papers, 2nd
series, 4, 1972); R. Gill, *Competing convictions* (1989); K.D.M. Snell, *Church and chapel in
the North Midlands* (University of Leicester Department of English Local History, Occasional
Papers, 4th series, 3, 1991). The latter examines the data provided for the registration districts
of the North Midlands in the religious census and applies statistical methods to test, among
other assumptions, the validity of the hitherto accepted dichotomy between the relative strengths
of Methodism and Anglicanism.

[3] Coleman, *Church of England*, p. 39.

economic factors influential at the time. Some, such as the changing occupational and population structure in both rural and urban areas, were responses to pressures emanating from outside the county, including the growing importance of coal and iron production and the extending railway network in the nation's industrial economy. Others were more purely local, such as differing types of land tenure, tensions in rural areas caused by disputes over tithes or enclosure, and the attitudes and activities of dominant individuals in the community.

The varied economic and social structure of Derbyshire reflects the diversity of its topography and natural resources, but equally this variety precludes broad generalisations as to the factors which may have influenced the practice of organised religious worship in the county. Extractive industries have not been limited to the coalfield areas of the east and south, for in both the Low and High Peak lead-mining and quarrying, whether for limestone, fluorspar, or sandstone for millstones, have a long history, while the exploitation of the gypsum beds of the Trent valley for alabaster was well developed by the fourteenth century. The use of water-power had led to the re-location of textile manufacture, not only around Glossop in the north-west, but also along the valleys of the Derwent and its tributaries in townships such as Edale, Litton and Cressbrook dales, while previously small settlements, such as Belper and Milford, experienced rapid growth. By the mid-nineteenth century, however, competition from steam-driven machinery was already resulting in changes in the location of textile manufacture. Thus at Tissington the 20 per cent decrease in population was due 'to a reduction of hands in the cotton works', while at Edale, Wessington and Darley Abbey the works were closed.[1] Of Duffield it was said that the removal of factory workers and glovers who had found work in Nottingham had caused a decline since the census of 1841.[2]

Although the failure of the lead mines at Foolow, Winster and Snitterton caused a reduction in the number of men employed, it was reported that at Sheldon the immigration of miners from Cornwall explained the increase in the numbers there.[3] On the other hand families from Edale, Eyam and Hope were said to have migrated to the 'manufacturing regions'.[4] Framework-knitting was already well-established as a by-employment in many rural parishes to which it had spread from adjacent areas in Nottinghamshire. The

---

[1] Census of Population, 1851, summary tables, Vol. 1 Pt 2, table 32. Tissington p. 73 n. k; Edale p. 79 n. g; Wessington p. 75 n. g; Darley Abbey p. 71 n. c.

[2] Ibid., p. 71 n. l.

[3] Ibid., Foolow p. 77 n. q; Winster p. 77 n. l; Snitterton p. 77 n. i; Sheldon p. 77 n. b.

[4] Ibid., Edale p. 79 n. g; Eyam p. 77 n. r; Hope p. 79 n.i.

subsequent development of machine-made lace with its concomitant requirement for workers such as lace-runners meant that, by 1851, few parishes, even in the 'agricultural' south, could be classed as wholly rural. It was into these areas and the expanding colliery districts that the bulk of the migration was taking place. At Ockbrook, for example, the increased population was attributed to 'the erection of a lace-thread manufactory', at neighbouring Spondon to the numbers employed in 'stocking and twist-net manufacture', and at Belper and Dethick to an increase in demand for labour in the cotton and worsted works.[1]

The expansion of the collieries and ironworks at Staveley is mentioned and the 60 per cent increase in population between 1841 and 1851 at Clay Lane (now Clay Cross) is also attributed to mining.[2] Set against this growth was the decline of some established occupations, as at Shardlow, where 'the carrying population, formerly considerable, is diverted to the Midland Counties Railway'; at Denby, where 'the colliers migrated consequent on the exhaustion of the mines'; and at Bowden Edge, where fewer men were employed in the quarries.[3] These changes, together with the migration of agricultural labourers and the demolition of houses experienced by such townships as Parwich, Quarndon, Horsley and Mercaston,[4] exemplify the considerable extent to which migration was affecting the county.

By 1851 the population of Derby (40,609) (Map 2) exceeded that of the second largest town in the county, Belper, by 30,000.[5] The population of Chesterfield had risen from 6,212 in 1841 to 7,101 in 1851—the result, according to the census, of the extension of coal-mining and ironworks.[6] The adjacent ecclesiastical district of St Thomas, Brampton, formed in 1832 from parts of two nearby townships, had reached a population of 5,600 due to 'the improvement of trade and inclosure of common land'.[7]

Economic change had a marked effect on the distribution of people in a county in which, apart from Derby itself, urban development had hitherto been limited and where other towns did not comprise separate parishes. These changes posed problems of pastoral care felt particularly by the Anglican church, constrained as it was within a parochial system which had evolved in an earlier age. Derbyshire parishes varied greatly in size from

---

[1] Ibid., Ockbrook p. 69 n. oo; Spondon, p. 69 n. q; Belper p. 71 n. o; Dethick p. 71 n. u.

[2] Ibid., p. 75, nn. q, k.

[3] Ibid., p. 69 n. d, p. 79 n. nn, p. 79 n. e.

[4] Ibid., Parwich p. 73 n. s; Quarndon p. 71 n. h; Horsley p. 71 n. m; Mercaston p. 71 n.k.

[5] The population of Belper had increased from 4,500 in 1801 to 10,082 in 1851.

[6] *Census of Population*, 1851, Vol. 1 Pt 2, Table 32, p. 75 n. l.

[7] Ibid., p. 75 n. o.

small lowland communities which were almost entirely agricultural to the
very large Peak District parishes which contained several chapelries. The
expansion taking place in some of the townships of these large parishes, such
as Hayfield, Mellor and Whitfield in Glossop, or Belper and Heage in
Duffield, was paralleled elsewhere in the county, for example in Alfreton,
Church Gresley, Heanor and Ilkeston.

Industrialisation was not, however, the only factor to influence social
change in the county. In 1813 John Farey, the Board of Agriculture's
Derbyshire reporter, commented not only on the extensive and increasing
estates of large owners such as the Duke of Devonshire, but also on the fact
that very few leases were granted. The example of the Cavendishes, whose
tenants at will he found to be making improvements at their own cost but
without the security of either fixed-term or three-life leases, was being
increasingly followed by others. Very few, among whom, however, he
instanced Edward Coke at Longford, the Earl of Chesterfield at Bretby and
the Stanhopes at Dale and Stanton, were granting twenty-one year leases.[1]

Except on the Cavendish estate in Hope Woodlands few farms were large,
with only twelve above 400 acres. Of these, eight were to be found south of
the Trent. In Ashover, where the average size was 50 acres, Sir Joseph
Banks had 97 tenants and a rent roll of £1,613. Furthermore, Farey commented that most of the small occupiers had some by-employment.[2]
Thirty-five parishes or townships, many of which, like Calke and Somersal
Herbert, were small in area, were held by one owner; but perhaps more
important than ownership, whether by a single landlord or by a dominant
owner among several smaller ones, was the influence of residency.[3] Thus the
influence of the Broadhursts at Church Broughton on 'the lower classes' was
such that it was reported in the Archdeacon's Visitation of 1823–4 that 'they
will not send their children [to the Endowed School] if they are taught the
church catechism', whereas at Scropton 'attendance was better since Mr
Broadhurst left'.[4] In 1851, however, the curate at Church Broughton, W.S.
Vawdrey, was able to report an average congregation of 80 and a Sunday

---

[1] John Farey, *A general view of the agriculture and minerals of Derbyshire*, II (1813), pp.
34–7. A 21-year lease could give more security to tenants than a three-life lease which depended
entirely upon the longevity of the lives and in adverse circumstances could be terminated within
a short space.

[2] Ibid., p. 25.

[3] See Map 3 and E.M. Tranter, 'Landlords, labourers and local preachers: rural nonconformity in Derbyshire 1772–1851', *Derbys. Arch. J.*, 101 (1981), 119–38 for a discussion of the
factors affecting the distribution of rural nonconformity in south and east Derbyshire.

[4] Austin, *Church in Derbyshire*, pp. 147, 63.

School of 81 for a total population of 661.[1] Similarly, at Aston and Weston-on-Trent, the Holdens and Wilmots, although not sole owners, exercised considerable control. In 1766 a letter written on behalf of Anne Holden, sister of the late rector of Weston, to Robert Wilmot asked him not to allow Thomas Fewkes to take over the lease of his parents' tenancy on the grounds that 'he and his wife is such strong Methodist' and 'will do a great deal of hurt in the parish'. Writing to his agent, Wilmot declined to do this, having heard no ill of Thomas, but went on to say 'he may possibly recover ... from this Distraction ... and come to his senses again'. But Fewkes was to be warned that 'if he thinks it incumbent to make converts at Weston or to ramble about the country after the Rogues and Fools of that Profession to the Prejudice of his Family and Fortune, or of my Land and Buildings then his Continuance under me will be but of short duration'.[2] Thus the combination of a relatively small number of parishes dominated by one resident landowner, the impact of fluctuating agricultural prices and a tradition of by-employment may have predisposed the inhabitants of Derbyshire to a greater degree of independence of landlord, church and dissent alike than was to be found in some parts of the country.

Tithe and Enclosure

The support of both church and clergy through the payment of tithe derived ultimately from specific enjoinders in both Old and New Testaments.[3] In England payment of tithe was first enforced by law in AD 900; a quarter of the offerings was intended for the maintenance of the clergy, the remainder was allocated equally to the upkeep of the church fabric, the relief of the poor, and to the bishop for the diocese. This seemingly simple system was rapidly modified in the post-Conquest period by the appropriation of churches for the support of the monasteries, by the building of estate churches whose founders retained the profits of the church themselves, and later, consequent upon the sale of monastic lands at the Dissolution, by the impropriation of tithes by laymen. These were only three of many factors which, by the nineteenth century, had resulted in a complex and varied pattern that elicited responses such as that of the curate of Hognaston who,

---

[1] PRO, HO 129/375/2.

[2] Derbyshire Record Office, Wilmot-Horton papers, DL42/2196/98; 2197/20.

[3] Deut. ch. 14, v. 22. 'Year by year you shall set aside a tithe of all the produce of your seed ... and when the journey is too great for you ... then you may exchange it for silver'; Matt. ch. 10, v. 10; Matt. ch. 23 v. 23.

in 1851, stated that the value of the small tithes was £7 p.a. but that 'the glebe and great tithes are in the hands of a lessee who derives all the benefits of them, subject, however, to an annual payment of £6.9.6d. to the minister. The estimated value of the glebe and tithe is, I believe, about £240'. He then continued:

> It is humbly conceived that a tax of £15 or £20 per cent annually should be levied on all lessees of Church property to be applied exclusively to the support of the minister and for the purposes of education in connexion with the church in the parishes to which the endowment belongs; in as much as the *rights* of the people to such application of that kind of property are more ancient than those of any Lessee can be nor does it appear that any Lessee co[d] have more right to complain of such an arrangement than the purchaser of any stolen property has to demur to the restoration to its rightful owner of that property which does not equitably belong to him.[1]

Inevitably the dependence of the clergy on tithe and the inequities that had evolved bred a resentment that placed a barrier between priest and parishioners and, as both Farey and some of the clergy observed, inhibited improvement of land and crops. No consistency prevailed: in some instances tithes were collected in kind; some lands, especially certain former monastic lands, were tithe-free; elsewhere a modus or fixed composition had been agreed.[2] Farey calculated that in Derbyshire, because of the amount of exonerated land, the value of the tithe overall was only 7¼d on the total county rental,[3] while Dr Austin has drawn attention to the fact that nearly three-quarters of Derbyshire tithes in the 1820s were in the hands of lay impropriators and that even clerical rectors were not necessarily free. At Kedleston, for example, Lord Scarsdale took all the tithes and paid the rector a modus of £90 a year—his sole income.[4] The Archdeacon of Derby, Samuel Butler, commented in his charge in 1833 that lay impropriators were more severe and 'received nearly the full value of the tithes without murmuring; the clergy rarely above two-thirds and grudgingly'.[5] Furthermore, the maintenance of chancels, enjoined by law on the lay rector or

---

[1] Below, p. 138.

[2] Farey, *General View*, II, pp. 29–31.

[3] Ibid., III, pp. 637, 639.

[4] Austin, 'Tithe and benefice incomes', p. 118.

[5] Quoted in ibid., p. 8.

recipient of the great tithes, he found to be all too often inadequate. Austin has calculated that some 60–65 per cent of the total income of benefices was derived from tithe and hence it follows that a fixed modus, while more acceptable to farmers, could be disastrous for clergy stipends and lead to the need for poorly provided benefices to be held in plurality. In 1772 the vicar of Stapenhill stated that a modus of £6 had been fixed in 1676 for the chapelry of Caldwell but that the tithes were currently worth £40 but that he was hoping to have the modus set aside.[1] It would appear that his negotiations were successful since in 1851 the gross commutation was given as £143.[2] Others were not so successful. A protracted dispute between the incumbent, Charles Edward Collins, the impropriator, Eusebius Horton, and the farmers of Lullington continued from 1810 to 1828. A complex situation had resulted from the appropriation of the church of Lullington to Gresley Priory and the subsequent acquisition of the lands and tithes by the Horton family. Here, as at Croxall and Walton, the disputes hinged on the division of the tithes between impropriator and incumbent, on the issue of past payments and their status or otherwise as a modus. The issue could be further complicated by earlier sales, resale and mortgaging of the profits of the rectory.[3] Attempts by the clergy to sort out confused situations such as these without detriment to their successors inevitably aroused antagonism and created an atmosphere in which Dissent or non-attendance could flourish. A note added to the 1823–4 visitation return for Lullington states: 'Some disputes and law-suits between the Vicar and his parishioners ... Mr Collins has been much harassed by his parishioners'.[4] Some indication of the bitterness and disruption to the life of the community caused by these legacies of the past is evinced by the letter of a Joseph Burton to Horton of 26 August 1822 in which a request for the use of the school at Coton for preaching is made 'on account of Mr Collins misconduct ... hitherto we have preached in the street'.[5]

---

[1] Lichfield Record Office, B/V/5, Stapenhill, art. 11.

[2] Below, p. 19.

[3] Derbys. RO, Wilmot-Horton papers, DL42/1975, 42/2014, passim (Catton, Croxall, Walton).

[4] Austin, *Church in Derbyshire*, p. 116.

[5] Derbys. RO, Wilmot-Horton papers, DL42/1992.

Patterns of religious practice

The list of the 39 ecclesiastical districts established in Derbyshire by the Anglican church since 1832 printed in the census report of 1851 gives some indication of the reorganisation that had taken place.[1] The religious census provides far more detailed information but statistical analysis is hampered by a number of problems. Missing data, over-representation caused by multiple attendances, attendance by individuals at more than one denomination, the reliability of the numerical data, and adverse weather conditions in some areas but not others, are among the factors which render comparisons between counties, denominations or districts less than straightforward. Published studies of the census have therefore used various methods to overcome these deficiencies and to establish a methodology whereby the relative strengths and weaknesses of the denominations may be analysed. Professor Everitt used sittings but commented that they probably exaggerate Anglican strength in areas with large medieval churches.[2] This discrepancy also applied to nonconformist chapels—the Quaker meeting house at Shirland had a seating capacity of 64 but only five attenders on Census Sunday, whereas at Hognaston the Primitive Methodists with seats for 30 and standing room for 25, had 65 attenders.[3] The ratio between free and appropriated sittings among both Anglicans and nonconformists also needs consideration. It may be argued that the payment of pew rents in nonconformist chapels indicates a measure of support, but how wholehearted or frequent that support was is not known. In Anglican churches sittings were not only let for money rents but might be appropriated to the use of inhabitants of a particular part of the parish. The fact that only 24 of the 1,300 seats in the parish church of Ashbourne were available for the hamlet of Clifton was seen as a reason for the prevalence of Dissent there.[4] In a study of Methodism in Leeds D.C. Dews used the highest attendance recorded; when considering Methodism in the Leicestershire coalfield, however, C.P. Griffin used evening services, while for Yorkshire D.G. Hey compared highest attendance, total attendance and sittings; and in Notting-

[1] Census of Population, I, pt 2, pp. 641–61.

[2] Everitt, *Pattern of rural dissent*, p. 14.

[3] Below, pp. 148, 138–9.

[4] Below, p. 124.

hamshire, Michael Watts used the best attended service, to which he adds one-third of other services and the best attended Sunday School.[1] For Derbyshire the perceived overall reliability of the information, the number of returns for congregations with only one service and the not infrequent comments made, especially in rural areas, on the numbers who attended only once on Sundays, make it possible to avoid any manipulation of the raw data. Thus the totals of the unmodified figures of sittings and attendances provided by the extant returns form the basis of the maps, tables and text, and only where average attendances alone are given has any substitution been made for missing values. In rural areas it was not unusual for services to be held on alternate Sundays, while in some instances there were specific reasons why no services were held. At Mackworth, for example, the parish church was under repair and therefore neither sittings nor attendance could be given; at Borrowash the opening of a new Primitive Methodist chapel was accompanied by the cancellation of services in neighbouring chapels, including those of other denominations.[2] In whatever way the figures are analysed, however, it must be borne in mind that the census presents a snapshot of one Sunday which may not be representative of the wider picture.

It has been observed earlier that the Derbyshire clergy, ministers and registrars appear to have carried out the requirements of the census conscientiously and that many, like the Anglican priest of the new district of Christchurch, Belper, voluntarily included additional information and explanation. Although four churchwardens and one parish clerk completed returns in the south of the county the majority of Anglican and all Roman Catholic returns were signed by the incumbent, curate or priest-in-charge. By contrast, nonconformist returns were frequently made by a steward, deacon, local preacher or trustee, thus reflecting differences in church organisation, although some circuit ministers do appear to have overseen the returns within their areas. John Frederick England, the superintendent of the Cromford Wesleyan circuit, signed no less than eighteen returns on 31 March for chapels in the Wirksworth, Ashover and South Wingfield district. Since it

---

[1] D.C. Dews, 'Methodist attendances in Leeds as shown by the 1851 Religious Census', *Proc. Wesley Historical Sosicety*, 39 (1974) pp. 113–16; C.P. Griffin, 'Methodism in the Leicestershire and South Derbyshire Coalfield', Idem, 39 (1973) pp. 62–73. The Derbyshire returns show that evening services were by no means universal, especially in rural areas; D.G. Hey, 'The pattern of nonconformity in South Yorkshire 1660–1851', *Northern History*, 8 (1973), pp. 86–118; M. Watts, *Religion in Victorian Nottinghamshire: the 1851 Religious Census for Nottinghamshire* (Nottingham, 1988); Tranter, 'Aspects of rural nonconformity', Appendix II, pp. iii–xiv uses a statistical correlation technique to rank both attendance and sittings.

[2] Below, pp. 78, 63.

was manifestly impossible for him to have visited all the chapels on that day one can only assume that officials from each chapel came to him with information which, in the case of Ashleyhay Bent chapel, he 'corrected'.[1] Similarly, Abimelech Hainsworth Coulson, the Primitive Methodist superintendent minister in Derby, signed ten returns for chapels lying between Dalbury and Kirk Langley in the west and Spondon and Shardlow in the east. Other Wesleyan and Primitive Methodist ministers were responsible for forms for between three and seven separate places of worship.

Nevertheless, in spite of the obvious care taken, there are gaps: no returns are extant for the parish churches of Bakewell, Hartington or Etwall, nor for the chapelries of Drakelow and Snelston, while for Kirk Hallam and West Hallam the completed reply to the registrar's letter in 1852 asking for the number of sittings suggests that completed forms, now missing, had been received. The lack of information for Bakewell is puzzling, for the incumbent, Hubert Kestell Cornish, returned forms for Rowsley and Over Haddon and on the latter stated that, as he had three services on Sunday (two at Bakewell and one at Rowsley), the service at Over Haddon was held on Thursday afternoons, or evenings in the summer months. After nearly a century and a half it is impossible to determine whether such omissions are the result of non-cooperation on the part of the clergy or whether the forms have been lost. That information did go astray is indicated in the bound volumes for Wirksworth sub-district, where inserted slips of paper state that particular enumerators' lists of schools and churches have been mislaid and that three returns are placed there because in each case 'this is the only place it could go', while the Wyaston Wesleyan Methodist chapel 'was not in the enumerator's list'.[2]

The omission of the parish churches of Bakewell, Etwall and Hartington results in the strength of the Anglican church being under-represented not only in the parishes concerned but also in the county overall. It is less easy to estimate the degree to which similar circumstances may have affected the dissenting denominations. The fluidity and fissiparation which characterised the Methodists in particular makes an accurate assessment of the comprehensiveness of the returns difficult, even when they are compared with circuit lists. The informality of much Methodist worship made it easier to establish groups meeting in houses as, for example, in the mill villages of Littondale and Cressbrookdale in Tideswell parish. Oversight of such groups must have proved difficult—four of the seven returns made by the superintendent

---

[1] Below, p. 117.
[2] Below, p. 128.

minister of the Bradwell Wesleyan circuit, David Cornforth, bear a date of 10 May because they 'were omitted to be taken 30 March'—and the permanence of such missionary groups can only be judged in the light of later surviving plans. Moreover, the occurrence of returns apparently submitted by both a steward or class leader and a circuit or other minister, as at Tansley, Egginton or Crich, where comparable but not identical figures are given,[1] implies a degree of duplication where the circuit or superintendent minister did not personally supervise the return of all the forms. An added complication in assessing the strength of the component parts of Methodism arises from the tendency of some Wesleyan Reform groups, as at Ripley, to style themselves as Wesleyans while the status of others, such as the congregations at Shirley and Mapleton, which had withdrawn from the Wesleyan circuit 'because of the arbitrary acts of the circuit minister', is ambiguous.[2]

The clergy of the Church of England, whether bishops, archdeacons or incumbents, were handicapped in their ability to respond to the challenge of a rapidly changing population by the parochial structure and by canon law. In Derbyshire both posed difficult problems. The cumbersome arrangement of large parishes with numerous chapelries, such as Bakewell, Wirksworth and Glossop and the isolated position of parish churches such as Brailsford or Duffield, restricted the flexibility of the Church's ministry. Nevertheless, the details given in the census of new parishes, as at Belper, or new ecclesiastical districts such as Cotmanhay, show that attempts were being made to overcome the problems. Nonconformists, however, were free from such constraints and thus could establish a 'house church' more easily. Nowhere, perhaps, was this more valuable than in those parishes where clusters of settlement lay at a distance from the parish church as at Hilton and Hatton in the parish of Marston-on-Dove.

Indices of attendance and sittings based on the information provided by the individual returns have been calculated for each parish and sample studies of the variations to be found within large parishes have been carried out. The inset maps present the data for the component parts of Bakewell, Duffield and Glossop parishes and for the town of Derby. The method used in this study is that pioneered by K.S. Inglis in 1960.[3] Both this and that subsequently devised by W.S.F. Pickering have been criticised by Michael Watts on the grounds that the former grossly exaggerates the number of

---

[1] Below, pp. 104, 192; 8; 104, 105.

[2] Below, pp. 102, 122, 132.

[3] K.S. Inglis 'Patterns of religious worship in 1851' *Journal of Ecclesiastical History*, 11 (1960), p. 79.

attenders and the latter underestimates them.[1] When, however, the figures for Derbyshire parishes in Nottinghamshire registration districts are calculated on the basis of Inglis's method and then compared with Watts's results the comparability is striking.[2] It seems, therefore, that for Derbyshire the sum of all attenders does not exaggerate attendance to any appreciable degree.

In considering the following analysis, four problems should be borne in mind. First, census data was not collected separately for all the extra-parochial areas, such as Hope Woodlands, Derby Hills and Sinfin Moor; secondly, some chapelries, such as Fernilee, Fairfield, Parwich and Alsop, were several miles distant from their mother parishes of and accordingly, for the purpose of the maps, have had to be treated as separate units. Thirdly, several parishes in the south of the county were divided between Derbyshire, Leicestershire and Staffordshire. Finally, there have been changes to the county boundary since 1851. In the latter case a comprehensive policy has been adopted and all parishes which have at any time prior to 1974 lain wholly or partly within Derbyshire have been included in the returns, analysis and maps.

Piety, Apathy, Disability

An indication of the extent to which the people of Derbyshire availed themselves of the provision for religious worship on Census Sunday may be gleaned from a comparison of the total population with the totals of all the available figures for sittings and attendances (Appendix 1, Tables 1, 2 and 3), but it must be remembered that any attempt to estimate the exact proportion of the population that took part is bedevilled by the vexed question of multiple attendances. Horace Mann suggested in his report that, when the numbers of sick, infirm, children too young to go to church and those restricted by work or other factors were taken into account, only 58 per cent of the total population would be able to attend a service at the same time.[3] Although less credence is sometimes given to this figure today than at the time it does, nevertheless, provide a starting-point from which to consider the Derbyshire figures. The returns provide considerable evidence that in parts of Derbyshire, particularly rural areas where there was

---

[1] W.S.F. Pickering, 'The 1851 religious census — a useless experiment?' *British Journal of Sociology*, 18 (1967), p. 393. Watts, *Religion in Victorian Nottinghamshire*, I, p. xi.

[2] See Appendix 1, Table 5.

[3] Mann, *Report*, pp. cxx–cxxi.

frequently only one Anglican service, or where settlements were distant from the parish church or chapel, attendance more than once on Sunday was not the norm. Although nonconformist meeting-houses might be easier of access for isolated communities it is noticeable that by no means all had more than one service, nor, significantly, are there comments suggesting that it was customary for worshippers to travel long distances to church or chapel. Indeed, it is implied that a distance of two or three miles, particularly in upland areas, was as far as people could be expected to walk, especially in winter months. Several incumbents commented that attendance was better in the summer, winter roads being often impassable, while others took pains to point out that where more than one service was available the congregations were differently constituted. The evidence seems to suggest that, over much of Derbyshire, it may have been common to attend only one service and, furthermore, that dual attendance was frequently interdenominational. It may not, therefore, be grossly inaccurate, in order to attempt a *tentative* estimate of the percentage of Derbyshire folk who attended religious worship, to equate *attendances* with *attenders.*

In spite of the fact that 58 places of worship gave no figures (10 Anglican, 34 Methodist, 14 other), 63 per cent of the county's population *could* be seated at any one time. Anglican churches provided 47 per cent of this accommodation. More important than overall provision, however, is the availability of seating and on this point the census provides the information that 44 per cent was appropriated either by individuals or, in the case of the Church, possibly reserved to particular parts of the parish. Secondly, the distribution of accommodation in relation to population is obviously of vital importance. A brief comparison of Maps 2 and 4 will illustrate this point. From these it can be seen that in the North East, notably in North Wingfield, Chesterfield, Staveley and Eckington — areas of expanding population — accommodation was provided for less than half the population. By contrast, in parts of the Low Peak, the Trent valley and South Derbyshire over 80 per cent could attend simultaneously. The inset maps for Bakewell, Duffield and Glossop depict local differences in these large parishes.[1]

A contrasting pattern is shown by the attendance figures. As the index of 44 per cent for the whole county is not adjusted to compensate for those who attended more than once on 30 March, considerably less than half the total population may be represented. This is substantially lower than that calculated for the whole country by Coleman on the basis of corrected data, but it is important to remember that in this study there is no correction for

---

[1] Mann's percentage figures based on registration districts are: Derbys. 67.5, Notts. 59.7, Leics. 72.5, Staffs., 50.1. Mann, *Report*, Table H, p. cclxxvii.

the 22 places (2 per cent of the total number) for which no figures are available.[1] If double attendances are discounted, for the reasons outlined above, approximately 17 per cent of the population attended an Anglican service and 25 per cent were to be found in dissenting places of worship; in each case, however, the true figure must be somewhat less. But when the totals of actual attendances at the services recorded for 30 March are examined for the county as a whole, 38 per cent of all attenders were at Church services, 25 per cent in Wesleyan chapels and 15 per cent in Primitive Methodist meeting-houses. There are, however, marked differences within the county. Parishes in the north east, like Dronfield, Norton and Eckington, are characterised by low ratings, but so too are Eyam and Peak Forest in the High Peak, and Willington, Church Broughton and Cubley in the largely rural Trent Valley. Indeed, the distribution of parishes with the highest values appears to be unrelated to any specific topographical or economic variable. Some industrialised parishes, like Measham, Donisthorpe and Stretton in the extreme south, have an attendance index of 61 per cent; others in the north, such as Staveley, under 31 per cent.[2]

These broad generalisations can be further refined when attendance figures are more closely examined (Table 3). It was possible to attend an Anglican service in 159 out of the total of 179 parishes and chapelries analysed and mapped, while Methodists were to be found in 134 and Independent and Baptist congregations in 36. In 50 per cent of the 159 parishes Anglican attendance was less than 23 per cent of the population and in a further 25 per cent was no more than 10 per cent higher. Only in a quarter of all parishes was attendance higher than one-third of the population. These figures may be compared with 19 per cent and 29 per cent for all Methodist worshippers; 10 per cent and 15 per cent for the Wesleyans; 9 per cent and 17 per cent for the Primitive Methodists. It must be stressed again that, in terms of actual individuals, these figures are exaggerated; nevertheless, the picture that emerges is one of a definite, albeit divided, challenge to the Church by nonconformity as a whole, but also of an Church still appreciably stronger than any single sect.

---

[1] Coleman, *Church of England*, p. 40, table C, has 58.1 and 60.8 per cent for uncorrected and corrected data respectively. Coleman's maps are not comparable with those in P.S. Ell, 'An atlas of religious worship in England and Wales: an analysis of the 1851 Census of Religious Worship' (Unpublished University of Birmingham Ph.D. thesis, 1992) which maps registration district details within the district boundaries. Coleman's maps, however, show registration district data within the pre-1974 county boundaries, with which they were not co-terminous.

[2] Cf. Coleman's IA of 27.6 for the whole country and 23.7 for the registration county, Coleman, *Church of England*, p. 40, Table C.

The remarks made on the returns provide evidence of some enthusiastic dissenting congregations, such as the Wesleyans at Bentley in Alkmonton parish, where 'we are crowded almost to suffocation the Lord is gracious to us and enlarges our borders. Amen and Amen', or the Primitives at Beeley, who worshipped 'in a low thatched house – some of the people sit on forms ... some sit on the sopha, some on the table, some on the slopstone and some stand behind the door'.[1] Anglican comments are in general more sober, as at Crich ('a much neglected parish now progressively improving') or Christchurch, Belper, where the detailed account submitted by the incumbent stated that, although the Sunday morning congregation was small when teachers and scholars were excluded, 'the evening attendance is very good and the cottage lectures twice a week in various parts of the parish are usually very crowded'.[2] But despite this evidence of personal commitment made by men, women and children in response to the teaching and example of clergy and lay ministers, there appears to have been a widespread disinclination on the part of Derbyshire folk to participate in Sunday worship. Although the forthright comments of the incumbents of Staveley and Brimington focus attention on the north east of the county, this apathy was found throughout; even in rural areas there were few parishes in which more than half the population attended any place of worship.

Although area and distance created problems for Anglican ministers in lowland agricultural parishes like Scropton, where the church was in one corner of the parish 'quite detached from 3/4 of the population which is scattered', it was in upland areas such as Bradley in the Low Peak, with 'no village – a scattered population', or Mellor in the north west, where the church was 'on a hill two miles distant from much of the congregation' with the 'roads impassable in winter', that the problem was most severe.[3] Here parishioners faced long walks in difficult terrain and often inclement weather which militated against regular Sunday attendance at the parish church or parochial chapel and contributed to the success of nonconformist house groups in parishes such as Ashover, where no fewer than ten Methodist groups (five Wesleyan, five Primitive) were returned.

Three themes emerge from this analysis. First, the comments made by some of the clergy, for example the rector of Staveley, on the indifference shown by elements of the population, are substantiated by figures which show that the overall provision for worship exceeded practice by 20 per cent; moreover, in the county as a whole religious observance fell short of the

---

[1] Below, pp. 121, 180.

[2] Below, pp. 104, 92.

[3] Below, pp. 7–8, 129, 223.

national average. It was by no means customary, even for nonconformists, for all members of the congregation to be present every week.[1] In large parishes and rural areas it was sometimes physically impossible to attend church every week, particularly at certain seasons. At Castleton the incumbent stated that 'in the middle of summer the average is something more; particularly in the morning', while at Dronfield the vicar reported that 'the winter congregations are very small – the church being cold and damp';[2] elsewhere in the county comments were made on the stormy conditions of 30 March. Secondly, although when considered against the combined activities of **all** the dissenting congregations Anglicanism appears to be weak, it was, nonetheless, spatially more widely represented. Finally, when compared with any one single denomination—or even the combined forms of Methodism—it can be seen that the Established Church still commanded the highest level of support. These generalisations, however, mask considerable variations between and within parishes.

Landholding, the Church of England and Dissent

The relationship between landholding and dissent has been discussed by writers who have analysed the 1851 Religious Census for other counties. Professor Everitt, for example, has linked the strength of dissent with the freedom found both in market centres and in sub-divided parishes with many freeholders. In contrast, closed parishes where there was one dominant, resident landowner were usually infertile ground for dissenting preachers.[3] Landholding patterns for Derbyshire (Map 3) suggest that sub-division of ownership was found not only in market towns and villages and in the larger parishes of the central and northern areas of the county, but also in much smaller parishes, such as Marston-on-Dove, Gresley, Mickleover and Barrow-on-Trent. Moreover, as the maps for Bakewell, Duffield and Glossop demonstrate, there could be substantial variations in the nature of landholding in the component townships of a single parish. When a broad division into 'estate' and 'freeholder' parishes is adopted an almost equal proportion is found in each—49 per cent in the former, 51 per cent in the latter. Further investigation of parishes in the first group reveals an unequal division between those controlled by one owner (10 per cent) and those with more

---

[1] George Eliot commented on the irregularity of churchgoing among the inhabitants of Ravelo, *Silas Marner* (Penguin ed., 1985), p. 133.

[2] Below, pp. 205–6, 168.

[3] Everitt, 'Nonconformity in country parishes', and *Pattern of rural dissent*.

than one owner (39 per cent). In general, parishes in single ownership were small, two-thirds having a population of under 150 in 1851, while only one exceeded 1,000. Two-thirds of these parishes contained no recorded dissenting congregations, although this is not to say, of course, that they contained no dissenters.

No clear relationship can be seen between the combined index of attendance for all denominations (Map 4) and either topography or landholding. Although the majority of parishes with an index figure of 47 per cent or above are to be found south of a line from Youlgreave to Blackwell, nevertheless the separate chapelry analyses for Glossop and Bakewell emphasise the differences which could occur within extensive parishes. A more interesting complementary distribution may be observed when the Church of England attendances are compared with those of the combined nonconformist denominations. Support for the Church was strongest south and west of a line running from near Parwich and Wirksworth in central Derbyshire to Elvaston and Aston in the Trent valley. Parishes north and east of this line reporting a high level of Anglican support include Blackwell, Shirland, Scarcliffe and Sutton. When those parishes such as Ockbrook, Doveridge, Barrow-on-Trent and Blackwell which show a high degree of support for both dissenters and the Established Church are excluded, the complementary nature of the two patterns is most striking.

Just under 20 per cent of all parishes and townships mapped provided no evidence of dissent and of these 60 per cent could be classed as 'estate' parishes. When these parishes are more closely examined, 17 per cent of those held by a few landowners (category 2 on the map) had no dissent but, at the other end of the spectrum, 36 per cent of these same parishes reported total dissenting attendances of 28 per cent. If, for the reasons explained earlier, double attendances are ignored, attendance at a nonconformist service in 38 per cent of all 'estate' parishes may have represented about 20 per cent of the population. Conversely, in some 'freeholder' parishes, such as Eckington, Bolsover or Norbury only 13 per cent of the people supported nonconformity on Census Sunday.

The individual attendance patterns of the Wesleyan and Primitive Methodists, the Independents and the Baptists (Maps 7, 9, 10, 11) reinforce the impressions outlined above. It is in the strongly freehold agricultural parishes such as Barrow-on-Trent and Sutton-on-the-Hill that the Wesleyans obtained their greatest support while only eight of the much sub-divided parishes of central and northern Derbyshire achieved an index of attendance over 14.6 per cent. Support for the Primitive Methodists was widespread and is found in parishes with all types of landholding, other than those dominated by one owner. Similarly, for both Independents and Baptists the nature of landownership does not appear to be an overriding factor in determining the level of support they enjoyed.

It would seem that, except in a limited number of parishes, small in both area and population and in the hands of one owner, as for example Willesley, Kedleston, Calke and Osmaston by Derby, there is no clear indication of a strong positive link between landholding and support for either the Established Church or nonconformity.

Schism and Evangelism

The pattern of worship portrayed in 1851, although presented in the cold guise of statistics, derived in part from the heat generated by the twin impulses of schism and evangelism. Both depended on the strongly held convictions of individuals, on their tenacity, and on their ability to convince and sustain others in those beliefs. Personality as well as argument has a part to play in conversion.

The doctrinal and legal issues which had resulted in the separation of the early Baptists, as well as the Presbyterians and Congregationalists (the heirs of the Puritan ministers ejected in 1662), from the tenets held by the reformed Church of England appear to have been largely of historical interest in Derbyshire in 1851. Certainly remarks made by the clergy and ministers throw little light upon such questions, apart from the comment aimed at the privileges of the Church made by Joseph Lethbridge, the Congregational minister of Melbourne, that there should be '1. Total and immediate abolition of all Church Rates. 2. Immediate and complete separation of church and state. 3. National Universities to be open to all classes of Her Majestie's subjects'.[1]

More pervasive and possibly of greater immediacy to local communities than differences between the churches were disputes within them, and few denominations in Derbyshire were unaffected. While Methodism as a whole, despite the assertion of the Primitive Methodists at Hathersage that they 'preach the doctrine of the Church of England', bore within itself the seeds of schism, the Established Church was itself no stranger to internal dissension, as can be seen at Winster, where the curate remarked, 'certain influential persons prevent the children from attending...'.[2] In addition to the 589 seats in the church for a population of 928 there was a licensed room in the occupation of Henry Norman with 110 seats. Several factors affected

---

[1] Below, p. 48.
[2] Below, p. 184.

the fissiparation of Methodism in Derbyshire: the proximity of the south and south west of the county to the birthplace of Primitive Methodism in Staffordshire made the agricultural parishes there easily accessible to the travelling preachers, while recession in agricultural prices and the remembrance of tithe disputes no doubt affected the receptivity of farmers and farm workers alike.[1] Thomas Cavendish, vicar of Doveridge, commented on the 'depreciation of agricultural produce' and the further large reductions he would have to make which would reduce the value of the living further. Much of the central part of the county was still difficult of access and there appears to have been a strong feeling among rural Derbyshire Wesleyans, devout but anti-clerical men and women, that Wesleyanism was run by a metropolitan clique.[2] Rural chapels were largely served by local preachers and the only time the more remote ones saw the minister would have been once a quarter when he also collected the money. The minutes of the Cromford Circuit Local Preachers' Meeting seem to indicate lack of pastoral oversight in this very big circuit and a reluctance to preach at Ashover.[3] Furthermore, since the 1820s Wesleyan ministers had become increasingly clerical; they had adopted both clerical dress and the title of 'Reverend', and had accepted ordination by the laying on of hands. In addition the laity were not represented at the Wesleyan Conference until 1869. Members of the more remote chapels might well regard the ministers as an expensive luxury which they could well dispense with. Warrenite agitation in the north west in the years following 1834 had led to secessions from the Wesleyan congregations in Glossop and the founding of the Tabernacle chapel.[4] The Wesleyan Methodists in Matlock had been rent by disagreements even before the expulsion by Conference of three ministers closely associated with Derbyshire over the 'Fly Sheets' controversy in 1849.[5] The many comments which bear witness to the high feelings and extreme positions taken as a result of this dispute are supported by the distribution pattern of the Wesleyan Reform congregations (Map 8), which clearly demonstrates the

---

[1] The tithe claims at Lullington were not prosecuted by Theodore Echalaz, the vicar, in 1851. HO 129/375/67.

[2] D.M. Thompson (ed.), *Nonconformity in the nineteenth century* (1972), pp. 134–5, quoting *Flysheet No 4* (1848); for the unpopularity of Wesleyan ministers see R. Currie, *Methodism divided: a study in the sociology of ecumenalism* (1967), pp. 46ff; for local disaffection see *Tracts for the Times: No 2; being a correspondence between the Rev. J.F. England of Wirksworth and John Cardin of Matlock Bridge* (Birmingham, 1850), p. 7.

[3] Derbys. RO, D1431J/MW/285.

[4] S. Taylor, *Echoes in Glossopdale; being sketches of the rise and spread of Methodism in the Glossop district* (Glossop, 1874), pp. 127–30.

[5] See Appendix 3.

close connection with the Belper and Ripley circuits in which the ejected ministers had served. Nor were the Primitive Methodists unscathed by dissension, for the shortlived Original Methodists were formed in 1839 by secession from within the Belper circuit.[1]

To these national movements must be added smaller, more local and sometimes ephemeral separations. The Particular Baptists in Agard Street, Derby, had been through a period of schism prior to 1851;[2] a doctrinal dispute in the Baptist congregation in St Mary's Gate, also in Derby, had resulted in the founding of a chapel in Sacheverell Street and the subsequent formation of congregations linked with it in Littleover, Mickleover and Chellaston.[3] In Chesterfield the original Presbyterian congregation in Elder Yard had already split into Unitarians and Congregationalists by the late eighteenth century. The Soresby Street Congregational chapel was itself shaken by internal problems when a small group led by one Mary Barry seceded in protest at the 'liberal' theology of the minister William Blandy. After he left in 1852 to join the Anglican church in Nottingham they rejoined the congregation.[4] In Belper, when the co-pastor of the Congregational chapel, F.R. Broadbent, resigned in 1845 and began preaching in a room in King Street, about half the membership followed him. When he too subsequently joined the Anglican Church some returned to the congregational chapel, although the majority also became part of the Christchurch congregation.[5]

The impact of these divisive controversies on the ordinary person, whether a worshipper or non-worshipper, is difficult to perceive. On the one hand the parent body could be seen to have been weakened by schism and the often violent emotions released. On the other, the enthusiasm of firmly held convictions may be infectious and arouse not only curiosity but also an echoing response. What is clearly apparent in the census returns is the increase in the number of churches and chapels during the first half of the century and the evidence of devoted work carried out by clergy and laity alike in order to convey their special message to ordinary folk. A date of

[1] D.M. Grundy, 'The Original Methodists', *Proc. Wesley Hist. Soc.*, 35 (1965–6), 116–21, 149–53, 170–2, 189–95; 36 (1966–7), 22–7, 49–58, 80–5, 115–18, 143–8, 181–6.

[2] B.A.M. Alger, *History of the Derby and district affiliated Free Churches* (Derby 1901), pp. 61–2.

[3] [J.S. Woollard], *The story of Osmaston Road Baptist Church, Derby, 1862–1962* (1962), p. 7.

[4] H.W. Turner, 'A historical sketch of Congregationalism in Chesterfield and district', (MS in Chesterfield Local Studies Library, *c.* 1918), p. 82.

[5] *Belper Congregational Church* (Belper, 1978), pp. 5ff.

erection later than 1800 for buildings in which services were held is given in 441 returns; some of these, however were not specifically built as places of worship, but were private houses.

The process of evangelisation can be most clearly seen in Derby and it is here, too, that the interaction of the two processes is most easily demonstrated. In 1791 William Hutton wrote that 'Derby is strongly tinctured with religious fervour'; sixty years later his observation was still valid.[1] By then Derby had become the head of three Methodist circuits, Wesleyan, New Connexion and Primitive, and had chapels covering every other shade of the nonconformist spectrum, even including the New Jerusalem church (Swedenborgian).[2] The changing character of the town engendered by the advent of the railways and especially the siting of the Midland Railway's headquarters in the town, attracted workers from surrounding areas.[3] Among both them and the leaders of the new industries were many liberal nonconformists who, after the repeal of the Test and Corporation Acts and the passing of the Municipal Corporations Act in 1835, were able to participate in local affairs.[4] Joseph Strutt, a Unitarian and third son of Jedediah, in fact became the town's first nonconformist mayor in the same year.[5] It is, perhaps, not insignificant that, at the foundation ceremony of the Wesleyan Reform chapel, opened in 1857, stones were laid by Derby's two MPs, the mayor and other local dignitaries. The formation of the Wesleyan Reformers' circuit in 1850, with five preaching places and 33 local preachers headed by Everett, Dunn and Griffith, had its origins in schism but ultimately resulted in the establishment in 1855 of a permanent centre of evangelism.[6]

The activities of devoted laymen and the ministers who led them were varied. The Congregational minister of the Victoria Street chapel in Derby, James Gawthorne (appointed in 1801), for example, had founded the Village Preachers Association in 1847 to help country chapels and had formed a new church on London Road in 1844.[7] Meanwhile the General Baptists,

---

[1] William Hutton, *History of Derby* (1791), p. 108.

[2] Below, p. 76.

[3] Barton, Thesis, pp. 17–19.

[4] G.J. Pratt, *Methodist monographs: headlights and sidelights of the movement in Derby* (Derby 1925), pp. 15–20.

[5] R.S. Fitton and A.P. Wadsworth, *The Strutts and the Arkwrights* (Manchester 1958), p. 326.

[6] Derbys. RO, XP/1551, Derby Wesleyan [Reform] circuit plan, Oct.–Dec., 1850; Alger, *History*, pp. 109–10.

[7] J. Robson, *One hundred years: 1847–1947* (Derby District Congregational Lay Preachers' Association, 1947).

themselves an offshoot in 1791 from the Melbourne congregation,[1] had already expanded to found new churches in Belper, Crich, Wirksworth, Ashbourne and Shottle, as well as on Duffield Road, Derby.[2] The latter was described in 1851 as 'an infant cause in a new part of the town'.[3] The evangelical wing of the Methodists at Greenhill chapel, Derby, where the parents of the philosopher Herbert Spencer worshipped, started a new cause in a carpenter's shop in North Street in 1848 which, aided by a grant from the Midland Railway became the London Road chapel.[4] The Unitarian, H.W. Crosskey, later minister of the Church of the Messiah in Birmingham, started the Working Men's Institute.[5] Anglicans meanwhile had founded four churches within the ancient parishes of the town. St Matthew, Darley Abbey, and St Paul, Little Chester, were both in St Alkmund's, Holy Trinity was in St Peter's, and St John, Bridge Gate, in St Werburgh's. Elsewhere in the county similar activity was taking place: offshoots from the Belper congregationalists were found at Heage, Fritchley, Green Bank and Little Eaton; the Chesterfield congregation supported groups at Calow and Wingerworth; and cottage meetings at Matlock had developed into the Matlock Bank Congregational chapel by 1849.[6]

Between 1819 and 1851 a total of 64 Anglican places of worship were built or rebuilt, of which twelve were licensed rooms or schools.[7] The details given on Anglican returns show that the clergy then, as now, were no strangers to the problems of fund-raising. Grants were obtained from national and diocesan church building societies and in three cases a Parliamentary grant is acknowledged. But by far the greatest support came from private benefactors (sometimes, like Thomas West of Brighton, from outside the county), private subscriptions and parochial rates. The most detailed printed account, submitted by the incumbent of Christchurch, Belper, provides an

---

[1] J.B. Radford, 'A charge to keep: the story of Brook St Chapel, Derby' (Unpublished typescript, Derbys. RO, D2670J/MZ7/1), pp. 2–4, 18.

[2] F.G. Hastings, 'The passing of St Mary's Gate', *Baptist Quarterly*, new series, 9 (1938-9), pp. 45–9.

[3] Below, pp. 70–1.

[4] Pratt, *Methodist monographs*, pp. 28, 39 et seq.; B.A.M. Alger, *King St Wesleyan Chapel, Derby: a centenary memorial* (Derby, 1905), pp. 20–22. Spencer's father, William George, later left the Methodists and attended the Friends' Meeting.

[5] E.P. Hennock, *Fit and proper persons: ideal and reality in 19th century urban government* (2nd ed., 1973), pp. 96–7. R.V. Holt, *The Unitarian contribution to social progress in England* (1952), pp. 205, 269.

[6] C. Willott, *Belper and its people* (Belper, 1894), pp. 65ff., 80; Turner, 'Congregationalism in Chesterfield', p. 118; J. Fletcher, *Food for the flock: or scraps of consolation for the spiritual Israel* (Bath and London, 1859), p. 72; Barton, Thesis, p. 248.

[7] Calculated from the returns printed in this volume.

insight into the quite small sums which were donated and the amount of work involved in raising funds to further the work of the Church.[1] Nonconformists were not asked to give financial details of either stipends or building cost, but the voluntary comment for the Langley Mill General Baptist chapel, built in 1839, that 'both school and chapel are out of debt' was evidently considered sufficiently noteworthy to merit inclusion.[2] It was, however, in rural Derbyshire that the Church was most handicapped by its inheritance of large parishes, and hence it was there that the flexibility and homely nature of Methodism had its greatest scope and its divided parts were, at the same time, enabled to proselytise. Out of 218 Wesleyan places of worship 18 per cent were not used exclusively for worship (10 per cent were specifically stated to be dwelling houses); for the Reformers and Primitives the proportion was even greater—43 per cent and 20 per cent respectively. To some extent these figures reflect the impact of schism, as for example at Dethick, Lea and Holloway, where the registrar drew attention to the existence of six places of worship for a total population of 866.[3] Nevertheless they underline a degree of freedom denied the Established Church which had, as at King's Newton, Birchwood (licensed for an evening service only), Calver (a large room over a stable), or Shottle to obtain the bishop's licence before unconsecrated buildings could be used.

Patronage, Paternalism and People

The census captures a static picture, taken on one day in the lives of the individual men, women and children represented by the numbers given. But that record represents only a fragment of a continuum, a gradual development affected by many influences which together led each individual, voluntarily or otherwise, to take part in a service or to be at Sunday School that day. For some, as has been suggested earlier, the determining factors may have resulted from external pressures engendered by practical and social considerations. Others, however, will have been influenced by personal experience or family atmosphere. The Hudson family, where 'religious observance was strict', was described a few years later as attending 'at Twyford Church each Sunday morning and Chapel at nearby Stenson' (a

---

[1] Below, pp. 93–5.

[2] Below, p. 42.

[3] Registrar's report dated 21 Aug. 1852. As well as listing the six chapels the registrar states that the Unitarian chapel at Lea had been re-opened after being closed for 14 years.

Wesleyan chapel nearly two miles distant) in the afternoon.[1] How typical this was in 1851 cannot be ascertained from the census returns.

Impersonal the census may be but there are glimpses within it which give us a deeper understanding of the society it sought to record. On over forty of the returns for nonconformist chapels the signatories included their occupations: twelve were farmers, twelve were small shopkeepers (grocers, tailors, or drapers), while a further eleven carried on a trade such as carpentry, framework-knitting, or basket-making. Among them were three who did not sign but made their mark. Leaders of industry, such as textile and ironworks manufacturers, were also represented. Few of the Anglican returns were signed by anyone other than the clergy, schoolmaster or registrar and no occupational information is given by the few who were either churchwarden or clerk. The Derbyshire signatories range from Joseph Bosworth DD, rector of Sudbury, at one end of the spectrum through the graduate clergy and nonconformist ministers to Sarah Simpkin at Draycott, who made her mark. The equal status given to each in the census summaries masks a diversity of educational and social backgrounds.

Paternalism in Derbyshire came in differing guises. At Ashbourne the Baptist chapel had been bought by the Anglicans for the accommodation of the poor and licensed as St Mary's Chapel. The services held in it were maintained at the expense of the vicar, John Errington. The Anglican evening service at Repton was held in the schoolroom 'for the benefit of the poor'. For the most part, however, the census provides only financial examples of benevolence. The great landowners were naturally involved. The Duke of Devonshire provided over £2,000 for Anglican premises at Handley, Pilsley and Edensor, rebuilt the almshouse chapel at Woodthorpe in Staveley and gave land for a chapel at Biggin; the Duke of Rutland built a licensed room at Rowsley; the Roman Catholic Howards had allowed the medieval chapel of St Mary Magdalene at Glossop to pass to the Congregational successors of the Presbyterians. William Evans MP contributed £450 of the £500 needed for Alkmonton chapel, while Sir John Cave built No Man's Heath chapel. The eccentric John Smedley, for whom hydropathy was a crusade accompanied by piety, was reported by the registrar to have provided not only an undenominational chapel and a school at Lea, but also a tent capable of holding 200 which he took round the surrounding villages.[2] In the course of his evangelistic activities he was said to 'contribute liberally to dissenting places of worship in general while not attaching himself to any'. He does, however appear to have provided money for Wesleyan Reform chapels in the

[1] L.J. Cox, *Over the Hills to Calke* (Derby, 1989) p. 61.
[2] Below, p. 114.

Matlock area. His activities may have helped to foster a peculiarly nonconformist and evangelical ambience which, already evident in Matlock and its
environs by the time of the Compton Census in 1676, may possibly have had
its roots in the activities of and support for the ministers ejected in 1662.[1]
Perhaps the most outstanding example of paternalism is provided by
mill-owning Unitarian Strutt family in Belper. In the earlier part of the
century in addition to well-built houses, they provided coal at cost, milk and
vegetables from their model farms and the occasional ox-roast for their
employees. Although by the middle of the nineteenth century the senior
branch of the family played little part in the mills, a Sunday School was
maintained from which the children were taken to the Unitarian chapel.[2]

Only the Anglican clergy were asked to give specific details of how
building costs were defrayed and it is clear that the examples referred to
above were only a small part of the whole and that much interest and
support was subsumed under the heading 'Private Benefactions'. John
Bannister's list for Christchurch, Belper, gives the names of over 160
contributors whose donations ranged from £10 to one shilling.[3] Goodwin
Purcell, vicar of the new parish of Charlesworth, raised £1,450 by 'personal
appeals to Nobility and Gentry' throughout England.[4] Since a further £227
came from 'written appeals' it would seem he literally presented himself and
his request on the doorstep of many of the contributors! Although the
structure of the forms made it inevitable that more is known about the
Anglican background than those of other denominations we learn, nevertheless, that the Quakers at Heanor held lectures on 'philanthropic subjects'; the
Swedenborgians in Derby held a 'mutual improvement class of Teachers one
evening a week' and had a library, while in the Congregational chapel at
Ilkeston poor people were allowed to occupy sittings without charge.[5]

The census provides little evidence for the use, or misuse, of the
patronage system and sale of advowsons by nobility and gentry, a practice
frequently used to obtain livings for members of their families. In only eight
parishes is there clear evidence of a link between patron and incumbent.
Frederick Curzon, the elder brother of the third Lord Scarsdale, debarred by
illegitimacy from the baronetcy (his birth preceded their parents' marriage),

---

[1] The Compton Census of 1676 records 20 nonconformists in Matlock, 200 in Bakewell:
Anne Whiteman (ed.), *The Compton Census of 1676. A critical edition* (1986), pp. 443–6.

[2] Barton, Thesis, pp. 309–10.

[3] Below, pp. 93–5.

[4] Below, p. 218.

[5] Below, pp. 43, 76, 46.

was vicar of the Scarsdale living of Mickleover;[1] the vicar of Spondon, A.S. Holden, was a brother of William Drury Holden (later Lowe) who succeeded to the Locko estate;[2] while at Stretton-en-le-field, where the Browne (later Cave Browne Cave) family had held the estate and patronage since 1600, the rector was a son of the ninth baronet.[3] At Radbourne, Brailsford, Tissington, Trusley and Doveridge the incumbents had similar links with gentry families. Less easy to discern is the extent to which the sale of advowsons was abused. The market value of the next presentation to the Rectory of Weston on Trent was stated in 1853 to be £4,407 10s. and it was suggested that the asking price for a sale by the Wilmots, who held the advowson, should be 5,000 guineas.[4]

Among the 39 clergy ejected from their livings in 1662 were individuals and family groups like the Hierons, Staniforths and Shelmerdynes, notable for their courage and persistence who continued to serve their people at considerable personal cost.[5] In parishes as far apart as Dronfield, Hognaston, Findern, Turnditch or Little Eaton, where pockets of Old Dissent existed in 1851 and support for Independency is strongest (Map 10), it seems possible that a subtle and pervasive tradition, linked with their personal examples and teaching, may have found expression in the Presbyterian or Congregational congregations of 1851. Most notable of all was William Bagshawe, the 'Apostle of the Peak'. Ejected from Glossop with his curate, Jonathan Twigg, he nevertheless continued to teach and preach and the permanence and extent of his influence is underlined in a letter from Lord George Cavendish of 1874: 'the late Reverend Hubert K. Cornish [vicar of Bakewell in 1851] once said to me that whatever religion existed a few years ago in the High Peak was due to Bagshawe'.[6] A comparable centrifugal conservatism may also be seen in the distribution of Roman Catholic congregations (Map 13) (with the possible exception of an Irish influence in Derby where, as in Glossop, Irish names begin to appear in the 1840s), for the concentration in the north of the county is evident both in 1676 and in the Papist

---

[1] Below, p. 11; cf. L. Mosley, *Curzon: end of an epoch* (1961), pp. 4–5.

[2] *Burke's Landed Gentry* (1952 ed.), p. 1260.

[3] *Burke's Peerage* (1959 ed.), pp. 420–3.

[4] Derbys. RO, DL42/1814. The Revd Robert Nicholas French, rector of Weston-on-Trent, had been certified a lunatic in 1820 at the age of 45 and the emoluments of the living had been used for his maintenance.

[5] A.G. Matthews, *Calamy Revised* (Oxford, 1934), passim.

[6] W.H.G. Bagshawe, *The Bagshawes of Ford* (1886), p. 9n.

Returns of 1705–6.[1] The close connection with the more remote estates of notable recusant families such as the Eyres, the Poles and to a lesser extent the Howards in the north, and with other families such as the Hunlokes of Wingerworth and West Hallam in the east is evident on the map. This mirrors a pattern found in other counties.[2]

The Registration County and the National Pattern

Although this study concentrates on Derbyshire it is important to emphasise that the geography of religion in the county forms part of a national picture which at registration district level has been firmly established.[3]

When the pattern of worship for the Church of England is examined it becomes apparent that, although it was fairly weak in the county, Derbyshire was on the fringe of a large area of Anglican strength which covered much of England south of a line from the Wash to the Bristol Channel, with a notable extension into the West Midlands. This area ran close to the Derbyshire border with, for example, very high Index of Attendance figures in east Leicestershire (52.32 per cent), Rutland (50.61 per cent) and north Warwickshire (53.35 per cent), with quite high values in east Nottinghamshire (41.64 per cent). These may be compared with the mean and median Indices of Attendance for the Church of England for the whole country of 35.11 and 34.99 respectively. The geography of Church of England support in the county, however, seems to be similar to that for much of northern England and Wales, where both the Index of Sittings and Index of Attendance were at or below the national average. The only exception is Ashbourne registration district where the Index of Sittings was above average.

With one or two important exceptions, Derbyshire was not an area of strength for Old Dissent. Presbyterianism, which in England was largely confined to the four northern counties and London, was completely unrepresented in the registration county. Independent strength was below average in all registration districts with the exception of Hayfield in the far

---

[1] In 1676 the following numbers of Papists were noted in the north of the county: Hathersage 140, Bakewell 65, Chesterfield 6, Killamarsh 15, Eckington 32, Tideswell 30, Glossop 4. In the south the distribution, with the exception of West Hallam (40), was much more sporadic. Whiteman, *Compton Census*, pp. 443–6; R. Clark, *The Derbyshire Papist Returns of 1705–6* (Derbys. Record Soc., 1983).

[2] Clark, *Papist Returns*, pp. ix, x; J.A. Vickers, *The Religious Census of Sussex 1851* (Sussex Record Society, 75, 1986–7), p. xxi.; N. Caplan, 'Sussex religious dissent, *c.* 1830', *Sussex Archaeological Collections*, 120 (1982), pp. 196, 203 n. 16.

[3] See Ell, Thesis.

north. This district was one of the southernmost extensions of a zone of Independent strength centred on the Lancashire–West Riding industrial belt. Although the Quakers were represented in five of Derbyshire's eight registration districts their strength in each of them was well below the denomination's national average across a broad range of variables. The Baptists were, perhaps, the most successful of the Old Dissenting denominations. They were strong in two major areas in England and Wales: one covered much of South Wales but another extended into southern Derbyshire. This latter area was centred on Cambridgeshire, south Buckinghamshire and west Hertfordshire but extended through Huntingdonshire and central Northamptonshire into western Leicestershire and southern Derbyshire and Nottinghamshire. Thus in three Derbyshire registration districts, Shardlow, Derby and Belper, the Baptists were of above average strength. Further north their support rapidly declined. It has to be borne in mind, however, that, due to the limitations of data calculated at registration district level, it is impossible to separate the Baptists into their constituent sects: the General Baptists and Particular Baptists who are considered to be Old Dissenting denominations and the General Baptists of the New Connexion, who are considered to belong to New Dissent. It seems probable that the Baptist strength in Derbyshire was a product of the success of the latter since Old Dissent in general was weak in the county.

New Dissent denominations were far stronger in the county. In general, Methodism was strong across a broad swathe of registration districts stretching from southern Northumberland through Durham and Yorkshire to Lincolnshire, Nottinghamshire, Staffordshire and Derbyshire. South of a line from Aberystwyth to the Wash Methodism was much weaker, although there were important exceptions to this in south west England and north Norfolk. Derbyshire lay within this area of Methodist strength but was near its fringe.

When individual Methodist denominations are examined the spatial patterns for the Wesleyan Methodist Original Connexion largely conform to the pattern for Methodism as a whole, with Derbyshire at the southern end of a large band of strength stretching from southern Northumberland. In England and Wales as a whole the Primitive Methodists were the most significant Methodist denomination in terms of spatial spread and intensity after the Original Connexion. In Derbyshire support for the denomination was well above average. The Primitives were strong in three parts of England and Wales: a discontinuous band of districts running south from central Northumberland to the Norfolk–Suffolk border, an area along the Hampshire–Berkshire boundary, and another stretching from Shropshire through north Staffordshire into Derbyshire. It must be remembered that the denomination had its origins in the Potteries and a process of diffusion from this heartland may well explain its strength in the county. The only other

Methodist denomination with above average support in Derbyshire was the Wesleyan Reform movement. In the country as a whole it was to be found in only 122 of the 624 registration districts, and had only one or two congregations in these districts. Only in two areas did the Reformers have a significant impact: one was an area around the Wash and north Norfolk; the other encompassed Derbyshire's six most southerly registration districts and three others in Nottinghamshire. While not as extensive as the Norfolk zone the same level of intensity was found in this area. Other Methodist denominations were also found in Derbyshire, including the Wesleyan Methodist Association, the Methodist New Connexion and the Countess of Huntingdon's Connexion, although none was strong in the county.

Finally, in comparing Derbyshire with the national picture the distribution of the Roman Catholic congregations is interesting. In common with other Midland towns Derby had become the home of Irish immigrants during the first half of the nineteenth century. Largely as a result of their support the Roman Catholic church was of above average strength in that registration district. A similar level was found in Hayfield district, which included Glossop, and formed the furthest extension of the area of Roman Catholic strength encompassing much of Lancashire and parts of the West Riding. Elsewhere in Derbyshire Roman Catholicism either did not exist or was weak.

Editorial method

The returns were initially transcribed from microfilm in the Local Studies Library at Matlock and in the Leicestershire and Staffordshire record offices. The resulting typescript was then checked against the originals in the Public Record Office at Kew (Class HO 129).

The religious and educational data was collected by the same method as that used for the population census, i.e. by registration district. Since these were co-terminous with poor law unions which, in many instances, overlapped county boundaries, the registration counties used for analysis in the Census Office reports differed significantly in some parts of the country from the administrative counties. Even the most cursory glance at Map 1 makes clear the extent to which the historic county of Derbyshire differed from the registration county. Only six registration districts, Bakewell, Belper, Derby, Chesterfield, Chapel and Hayfield lay wholly within it; Shardlow included parishes in Leicestershire and Nottinghamshire, Ashbourne some in Staffordshire. The eastern and northern fringes of Derbyshire lay within poor law unions whose workhouses were in Nottinghamshire and Yorkshire, while the county south of the Trent (Melbourne and Stanton by Bridge excepted) and west of Derby lay within the Ashby, Tamworth, Burton and Uttoxeter unions. The 1851 population census lists 65 townships within the administrative county which were not included in the registration county.[1] Since the registration districts covering the administrative county also fell within different 'divisions' (the primary sub-division of the country used by the Census Office), parts of Derbyshire are subsumed within the analyses for divisions VI (West Midland Counties), VII (North Midlands), VIII (North Western), and IX (Northern) in Mann's Report. The census also draws attention to the difference between the population of the registration county (260,693) and that of the administrative county (296,084). It is, therefore, important to bear in mind that some analyses use the registration county as a starting point, while others, like the present study are based on the administrative county. Thus it follows that indexes of attendance or sittings which have been calculated at registration district level should be mapped within the boundaries of those districts. It is unfortunate that in Coleman's valuable study of the Church of England the registration district data has been mapped within the pre-1974 county boundaries. As a result the patterns shown there for Derbyshire are not comparable either with those of Ell or Gay, nor with those in this volume.[2]

The returns printed here include all those for parishes which lay within the administrative county as it existed in 1851. Thus parishes such as Measham, which was subsequently transferred to Leicestershire, are included. Others which, until the late nineteenth century, were divided between Derbyshire and another county, such as Ravenstone, where the parish church was in Derbyshire, or Appleby Magna and Packington, where the churches were in Leicestershire, have also been included in full. Parishes such as Seal, which have been transferred to Derbyshire since 1851, are also included.

The order in which the returns are printed follows that adopted by the Census Office in their printed volumes. Thus the registration districts are given in numerical order and each return has the official number allocated when they were collated before binding. The PRO official reference for each return consists of the class number (HO 129), the registration district number and the number given to the return. Three districts, Belper, Bakewell, and Shardlow were each divided into two volumes in which the numbering started afresh. Thus, in these districts, there may be two returns bearing the same number, as for example in the case of HO 129/449/17.

---

[1] Census of Population, 1851, II, pp. 86–9.

[2] Coleman, *Church of England*, pp. 20, 21; J.D. Gay, *The geography of religion in England* (1971); Ell, Thesis.

Analysis and presentation of the returns on a parish basis poses a further dilemma—that of the distinction between a civil parish and an ecclesiastical parish. Derbyshire was one of the counties named in the 1662 Settlement Act, which authorised townships and villages within the northern counties 'by reason of the largeness of the parishes within the same' to appoint overseers of the poor to relieve their own inhabitants.[1] The forms sent to Anglican incumbents asked them to state the 'parish, ecclesiastical division or district, township or place' in which the particular place of worship lay. Those sent to non-Anglican respondents asked for the 'parish or place'. The overall impression given by the returns is that the clergy and laity responsible, whether Anglican or nonconformist, assumed that the word 'parish' implied the *ecclesiastical* parish. It is clear, however, that the existence of townships which were, for *civil* purposes, classed as parishes but lay within a larger ecclesiastical unit led to an ambiguity in the returns. There is evidence on the original returns that some difficulty was experienced in ordering them; thus on the return for St Michael, Alvaston, a pencilled note states 'not in the enumerator's list', while the duplicate numbering of some forms implies that some may initially have been mislaid. Birchover church and Ripley General Baptist chapel, for example are numbered 449/57A and 446/11A respectively. This may help to explain the absence of a surviving return for Bakewell parish church noted earlier. The incumbent completed forms for Rowsley and Over Haddon on which he mentioned the services at the parish church and it seems improbable that he omitted to complete the form for Bakewell. In all 787 forms, as opposed to worshipping communities, are extant for Derbyshire and, apart from Bakewell, the only notable omissions are for Hartington and Etwall parish churches and the chapelries mentioned earlier.

The orthography of the originals, including capitalisation, has been retained but some punctuation has been added for clarity. Each church or chapel is listed under the parish or township in which it was situated. Headings printed in bold capitals indicate the map units within which the entries following have been analysed. Population figures from the 1851 census are given for each parish, and, where available, for townships.

---

[1] Michael Nolan, *A treatise of the laws for the relief and settlement of the poor* (1808), II, App. II, p. 53. This gives the text of the Act of 13 and 14 Car. II ch. 12. For the reference to Derbyshire see art. XXI.

The Maps

One of the main problems in the historiography of the 1851 Religious Census is that, even when spatial patterns of worship are described, very few maps depicting those patterns are given. Traditional methods of map-drawing are both time-consuming and expensive. The use of a computer mapping programme helps to resolve these problems in that, once a base map has been produced, maps depicting different variables for comparative purposes can be generated very quickly. As all the distribution maps in this volume were produced by this method it may be worth explaining the processes involved. There are essentially three stages. The starting point is an outline map—in this case of the ecclesiastical parishes of Derbyshire prior to the creation of new ecclesiastical districts in the nineteenth century. Each parish was then assigned a unique code and its boundaries traced using a digitiser. During the tracing co-ordinate data are sent to a computer file and after some editing are read into the cartographic package GIMMS. Within this package a polygon file is created containing the parish outlines in a form accessible to the software. At this point any errors that may have occurred as a result of the mislabelling of parish codes, omission of a boundary or the failure fully to close the outline of a parish can be resolved. The second stage was to provide non-locational data to be represented on the map. The information contained in the Religious Census was entered on to the database Ingres and the variables required abstracted and entered into the general purpose statistical package Minitab. This enabled new variables, such as the indices of sittings and attendance, to be created, edited and filed. The third stage involved bringing together the locational data (the parish boundaries) and the non-locational (religious) data. At this point the scale of the map is set together with the key, legend divisions and any necessary text. By simply changing the non-locational dataset and certain information in the mapping file, such as legend classifications and text, it is possible to produce large numbers of maps quickly.[1]

The criteria for the number of classes and class divisions for all the maps were carefully considered from the wide number of options available in GIMMS. In order to make description and interpretation as straightforward as possible it was decided to adopt a legend based on *five* classes, divided

---

[1] For more information on GIMMS see A.W. Carruthers, *GIMMS Introductory User Guide* (2nd ed., Edinburgh 1987), and A.W. Carruthers and T.C. Waugh, *GIMMS Reference Manual* (Release 5, Edinburgh 1988); for Minitab see B.F. Ryan, B.L. Joiner, and T.A. Ryan, jnr, *Minitab Reference Manual* (Release 7, Boston, Mass., 1989). For details of the application of GIMMS in a study of the geography of religion see P.S. Ell, 'The geography of religious worship in England and Wales', *GIMMS Newsletter*, 12 (1991), pp. 6–7.

at the quintiles, so that for each denomination the same number of observations (parishes) fall into each class. An example may help to clarify this last point. If a denomination was present in 100 parishes then with our five classes 20 observations (parishes) would fall into each category. A sixth (null) class outside this system was created to identify parishes where the denomination was not recorded as being present.

THE MAPS

On Maps 2–13 the detached areas identified by number are as follows:

1   Glossop
2   Bakewell
3   Duffield
4   Derby

An asterisk indicates a detached area of a parish for which no separate information is available. These include (a) extra-parochial areas, (b) detached chapelries, and (c) detached portions of parishes which are subsumed in the Returns within the main part of the parish.

The catgories used in Map 3 (Landholding and Dissenting Attendances) are based on information taken from J.M. Wilson, *The Imperial Gazetteer* (1870), supplemented by contemporary directories, and are as follows:

1   'Estate' parishes held in one hand.
2   'Estate' parishes held in few hands.
3   'Freeholder' parishes in which the land was subdivided.
4   'Freeholder' parishes in which the land was much subdivided.
5   Extra-parochial areas.

THE REGISTRATION COUNTY
(Part of Division VII - The North Midlands)

THE REGISTRATION DISTRICTS OF THE
ADMINISTRATIVE COUNTY

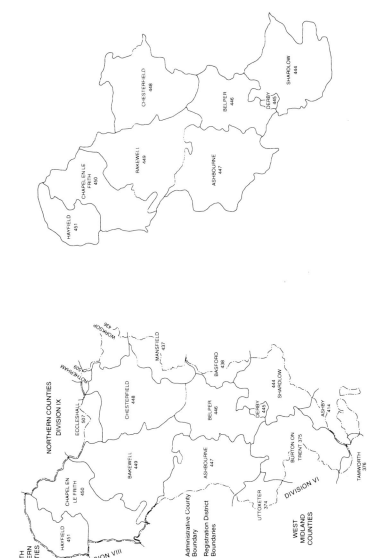

1. The Administrative and Registration County

2. Population

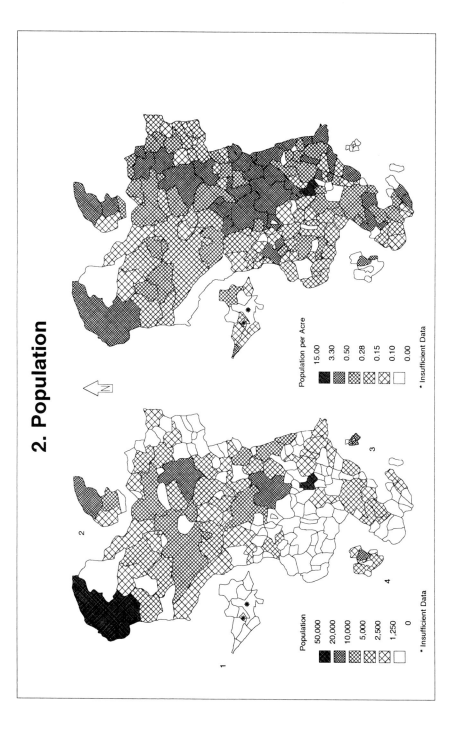

Population

50,000
20,000
10,000
5,000
2,500
1,250
0

* Insufficient Data

Population per Acre

15.00
3.30
0.50
0.28
0.15
0.10
0.00

* Insufficient Data

3. Landholding and Dissenting Attendances

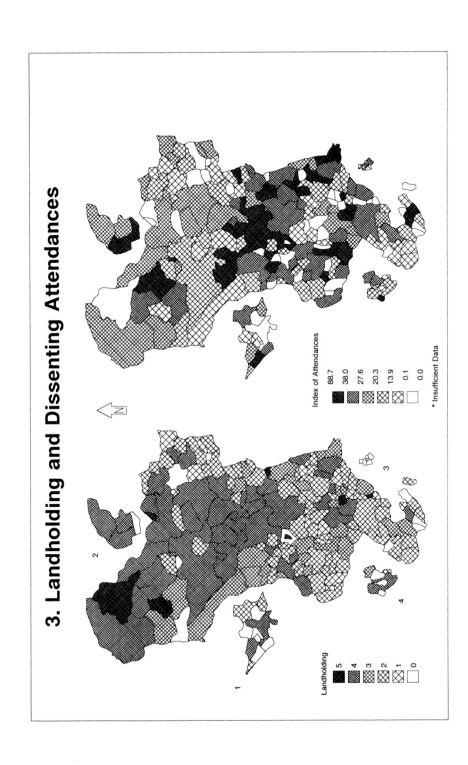

Landholding
- 5
- 4
- 3
- 2
- 1
- 0

Index of Attendances
- 88.7
- 38.0
- 27.6
- 20.3
- 13.9
- 0.1
- 0.0

* Insufficient Data

4. Index of Religious Support: All Denominations

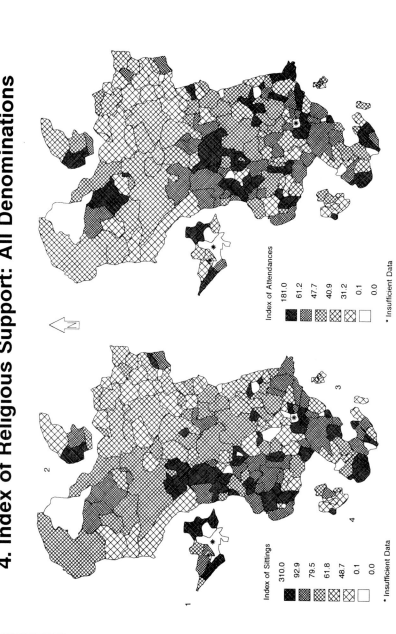

Index of Sittings
- 310.0
- 92.9
- 79.5
- 61.8
- 48.7
- 0.1
- 0.0
- * Insufficient Data

Index of Attendances
- 181.0
- 61.2
- 47.7
- 40.9
- 31.2
- 0.1
- 0.0
- * Insufficient Data

5. The Church of England

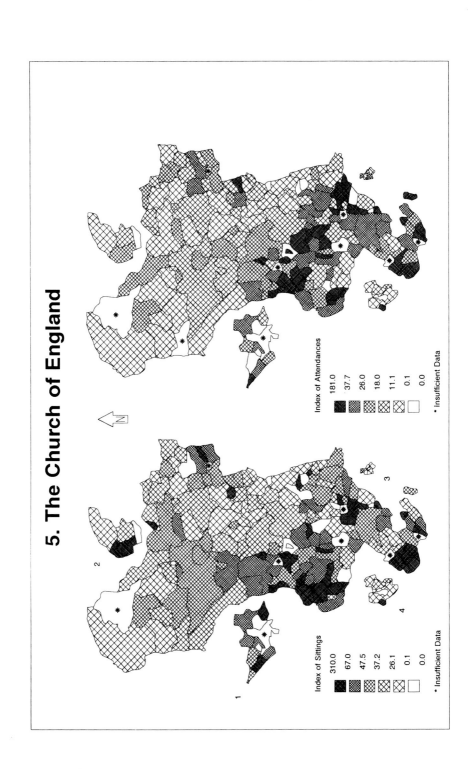

Index of Sittings

- 310.0
- 67.0
- 47.5
- 37.2
- 26.1
- 0.1
- 0.0

* Insufficient Data

Index of Attendances

- 181.0
- 37.7
- 26.0
- 18.0
- 11.1
- 0.1
- 0.0

* Insufficient Data

6. All Methodists

N

Index of Sittings

■	310.0
▨	67.0
▩	47.5
▨	37.2
▨	26.1
▨	0.1
☐	0.0

* Insufficient Data

Index of Attendances

■	181.0
▨	37.7
▩	26.0
▨	18.0
▨	11.1
▨	0.1
☐	0.0

* Insufficient Data

7. Wesleyan Methodists

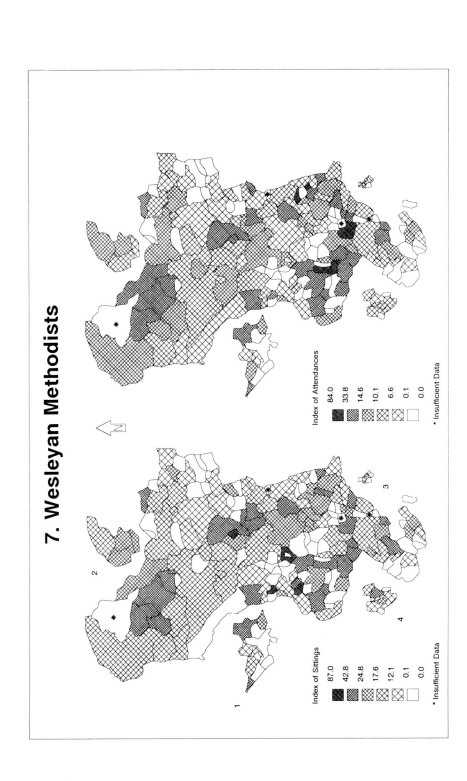

Index of Sittings

- 87.0
- 42.8
- 24.8
- 17.6
- 12.1
- 0.1
- 0.0

* Insufficient Data

Index of Attendances

- 84.0
- 33.8
- 14.6
- 10.1
- 6.6
- 0.1
- 0.0

* Insufficient Data

N

8. Wesleyan Reformers

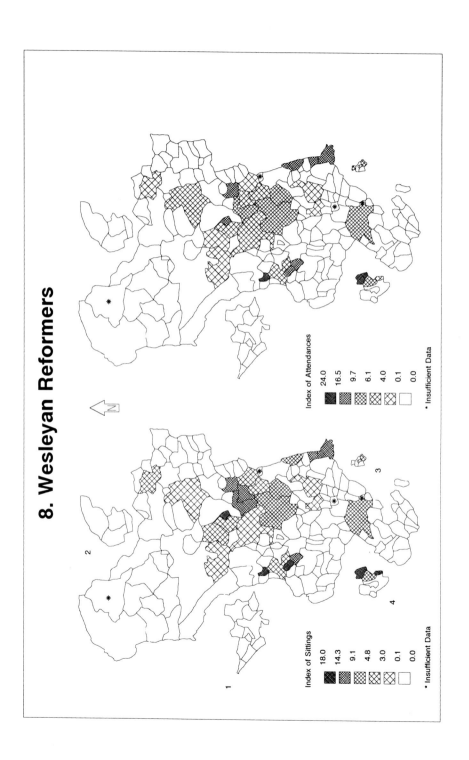

Index of Sittings

- 18.0
- 14.3
- 9.1
- 4.8
- 3.0
- 0.1
- 0.0

* Insufficient Data

Index of Attendances

- 24.0
- 16.5
- 9.7
- 6.1
- 4.0
- 0.1
- 0.0

* Insufficient Data

9. Primitive Methodists

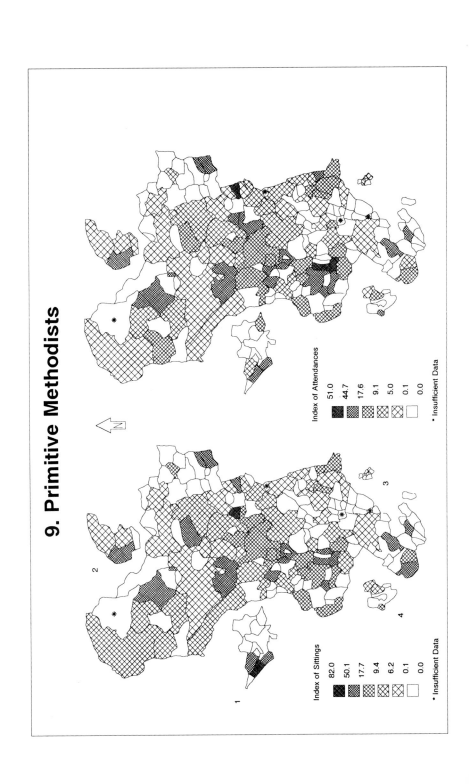

Index of Sittings
- 82.0
- 50.1
- 17.7
- 9.4
- 6.2
- 0.1
- 0.0

* Insufficient Data

Index of Attendances
- 51.0
- 44.7
- 17.6
- 9.1
- 5.0
- 0.1
- 0.0

* Insufficient Data

10. Independents

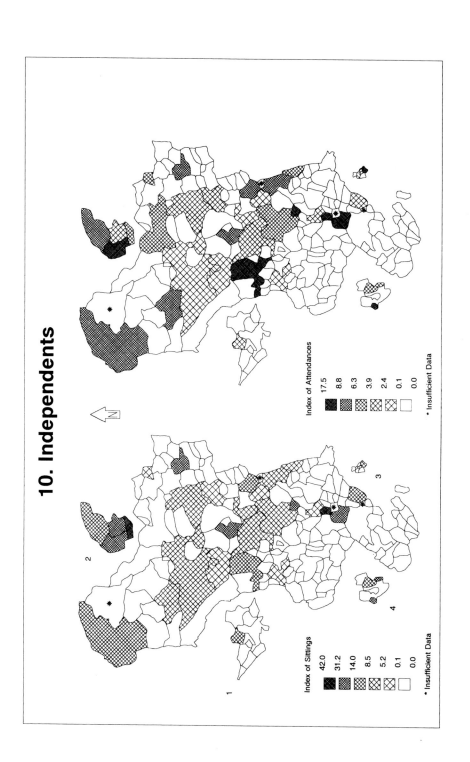

Index of Sittings

■	42.0
▦	31.2
▩	14.0
▨	8.5
▧	5.2
□	0.1
□	0.0

* Insufficient Data

Index of Attendances

■	17.5
▦	8.8
▩	6.3
▨	3.9
▧	2.4
□	0.1
□	0.0

* Insufficient Data

11. All Baptists

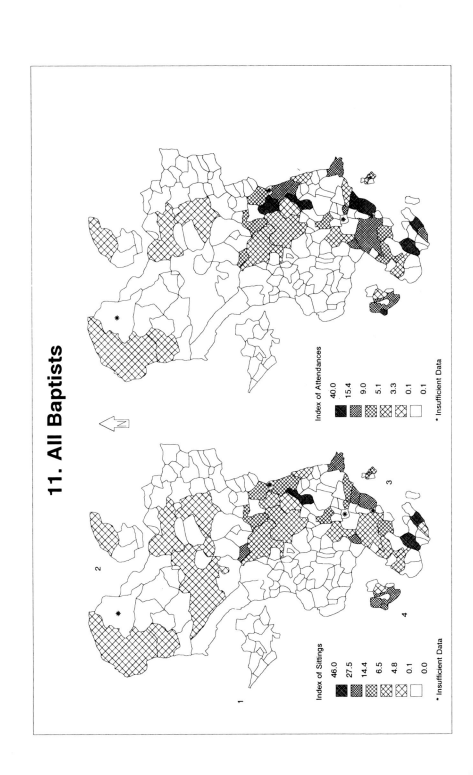

Index of Sittings

- 46.0
- 27.5
- 14.4
- 6.5
- 4.8
- 0.1
- 0.0

* Insufficient Data

Index of Attendances

- 40.0
- 15.4
- 9.0
- 5.1
- 3.3
- 0.1
- 0.1

* Insufficient Data

12. General Baptists

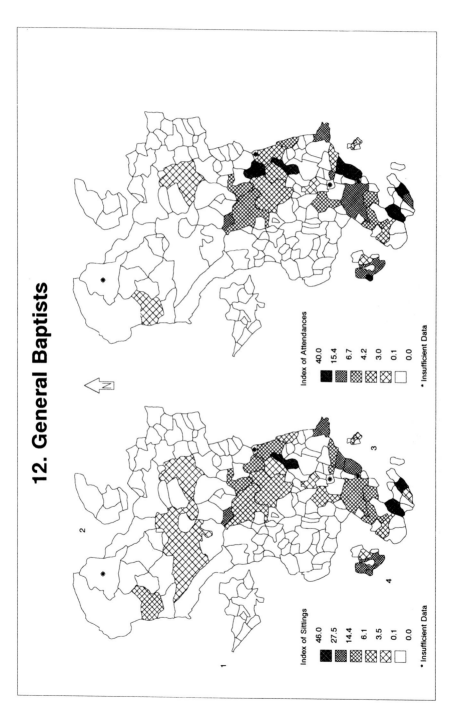

Index of Sittings
46.0
27.5
14.4
6.1
3.5
0.1
0.0
* Insufficient Data

Index of Attendances
40.0
15.4
6.7
4.2
3.0
0.1
0.0
* Insufficient Data

13. The Roman Catholics

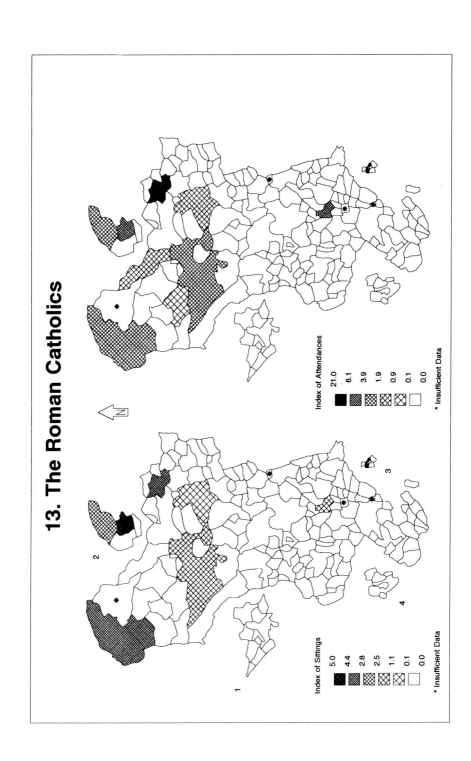

Index of Sittings

- 5.0
- 4.4
- 2.8
- 2.5
- 1.1
- 0.1
- 0.0

* Insufficient Data

Index of Attendances

- 21.0
- 6.1
- 3.9
- 1.9
- 0.9
- 0.1
- 0.0

* Insufficient Data

APPENDIX 1: STATISTICAL TABLES

Table 1: Total Sittings

Denomination	Total		Number Free	Not Free
All Denominations	186,300	(58)	104,213	82,087
Church of England	87,544	(10)	44,174	43,370
All Dissent	98,756		60,039	38,717
Independent	12,916	(1)	4,958	7,958
Unitarian	1,990	(3)	1,624	366
All Baptist	11,383		6,868	4,515
General Baptist	7,623	(2)	4,872	2,751
Particular Baptist	2,068		1,456	612
All Methodist	67,476	(34)	42,559	24,917
Wesleyan Methodist	46,281	(16)	27,865	18,416
Wesleyan Methodist Assn	1,393		716	677
Wesleyan Reformers	5,894	(4)	4,728	1,166
Primitive Methodist	19,041	(14)	13,103	5,938
Original Methodist	420		420	—
Methodist New Connexion	1,544		981	563
Roman Catholic	1,806	(3)	1,634	172
Quaker	1,147		1,147	—
C. Huntingdon's Connexion	340		100	240
Swedenborgian	340		100	240
Latter Day Saints	470	(1)	470	—

Note: 58 returns were deficient, as indicated in brackets. Not listed: one 'Methodist' and one un-denominational chapel.

Table 2: Attendance

Denomination	Total		Morning	Afternoon	Evening
All denominations	128,567		35,383	41,493	51,691
Church of England	49,502	(13)	19,795	20,790	8,917
All Dissent	79,065		15,588	20,703	42,774
Independents	8,272	(2)	2,521	1,768	3,983
Unitarians	792	(1)	169	141	482
All Baptists	9,759		2,090	2,185	5,484
General Baptists	6,291	(1)	1,092	1,564	3,635
Particular Baptists	1,834		560	450	824
All Methodists	5,4251		7,947	15,205	31,099
Wesleyan Methodist	32,761	(4)	6,092	8,766	17,903
Wes. Meth. Assn	1,119		384	190	545
Wesleyan Reformers	6,587		1,347	1,062	4,178
Primitive Methodist	19,658	(1)	1,585	6,108	11,965
Original Methodists	376		6	120	250
Meth. New Connexion	1,261		264	126	871
Roman Catholic	3,919		2,298	702	919
Quaker	184		123	61	—
C. Hunt. Connexion	364		143	88	133
Swedenborgian	234		95	0	139
Latter Day Saints	546		31	229	286

Note: No attendance figures were given on 22 returns, as indicated by the figures in brackets. In addition there are no returns for four parish churches and one Church of England chapel.

Table 3:

Median and Standard Deviation of Indices of Attendance and Sittings for Selected Denominations

Denomination	Parish Number	Median	Lower Quartile	Upper Quartile	Standard Deviation
Church of England					
Attendance	159	22.4	13.8	32.3	24.5
Sittings	158	42.9	28.4	61.3	31.9
Methodists					
Attendance	134	19.0	12.5	28.7	14.2
Sittings	130	25.0	17.8	34.9	19.3
Wesleyan Methodists					
Attendance	115	10.5	6.8	15.0	10.3
Sittings	108	18.1	12.2	25.8	13.0
Primitive Methodists					
Attendance	81	9.3	5.3	17.9	11.0
Sittings	77	9.4	6.2	18.5	13.5
Independents					
Attendance	35	4.8	3.3	8.5	4.1
Sittings	33	8.5	5.5	15.2	9.5
Baptists					
Attendance	36	6.3	3.6	13.4	9.9
Sittings	36	7.1	4.9	16.0	10.5

Table 4:

Sunday School Attendances: Selected Denominations

Total	81,049
Church of England	31,552
Wesleyam Methodist	21,653
Primitive Methodist	9,225
Baptists	6,984
Independents	7,551
Roman Catholics	1,201

Table 5:

Percentage attendances for Derbyshire parishes in Nottinghamshire registration districts

Sub-district	Tranter %	Watts %
Carburton	34	30–40
Pleasley	34	30–40
Blackwell	54	40–50
Heanor	—	30–40
Ilkeston	—	40–50
Ilkeston and Heanor	40	—

Note: Blackwell sub-district includes the parish of Blackwell with an index of attendance of 123 per cent. The extent to which the places of worship in Blackwell drew from the neighbouring parishes of Tibshelf and South Normanton, which had indices of 27 per cent and 24 per cent respectively, or from neighbouring parishes in Nottinghamshire, which would be included in Watts figure of 40–50 per cent, cannot be ascertained. Because of the division of the parishes of Heanor and Ilkeston by the sub-district boundaries they cannot be compared individually.

APPENDIX 2

DENOMINATIONAL NOTES[1]

Church of England

Donative. A benefice or living to which the patron can appoint without presentation to the bishop and without his institution.

Ecclesiastical district. A division of a parish having its own church or chapel and resident clergyman, as constituted under the Church Building Act (58 Geo. III, c. 45). Originally constituted as perpetual curacies they generally became distinct parishes for ecclesiastical purposes.

Extra-parochial. An area which is not included in any parish, as for example Sinfin Moor or Derby Hills. These were frequently either remnants of common shared by several parishes or former monastic estates.

Peculiar. A parish or church exempt from the jurisdiction of the bishop of the diocese in which it is situated. A royal peculiar is subject only to the sovereign, others may be subject to the dean and chapter of a cathedral, or the bishop of another diocese.

Perpetual curate. The incumbent of a chapel or church of an ecclesiastical district forming part of an ancient parish; frequently applied to the clergyman in charge of a chapelry. The curate was appointed by the patron and licensed by the bishop in the same way as vicars and rectors. The district is known as a perpetual curacy. In practice most perpetual curates are now known by courtesy as vicars.

---

[1] Sources for this section include: J.D. Gay, *The geography of religion in England* (1971); D.M. Grundy, 'The Original Methodists', *Proc. Wesley Hist. Soc.*, 35–36 (1966–8); R. Mansfield, 'The development of Independency in Derbyshire from the Restoration to the Methodist Revival' (Unpublished University of Manchester M.A. thesis, 1951); Idem, 'The history of Congregationalism in Derbyshire from the Methodist Revival to 1850' (Unpublished University of Manchester Ph.D. thesis, 1959); personal communication, Mrs J.M. Pearson, Salt Lake City; D.J. Steel, *National index of parish registers*, 2 (19--); J.H. Wood, *Condensed history of the General Baptists of the New Connexion* (1847).

Baptists. Although the Baptist movement was founded in the sixteenth century, it was not until the Commonwealth period that it began to flourish. There were two groupings: the General Baptists, Arminian in their theology, who believed in 'general redemption', i.e. that salvation is open to all, and the Particular Baptists, Calvinist in their theology, who believed in 'particular redemption' i.e. that salvation is only open to the elect. By 1851 most General Baptists of the old connection had become Unitarians. The New Connexion of General Baptists was founded in 1770 and it was to this that most of the Derbyshire Baptist churches belonged. Although the Particular Baptists were more numerous nationally, they had little influence in the East Midland counties of Derby, Nottingham, Leicester and Lincoln which became the heartland of the New Connexion. There were seven Particular Baptist churches in Derbyshire: Alfreton, Appleby, Charlesworth, Chesterfield Amber Row, Derby Agard St, Loscoe and Swanwick. All Baptists believed that the essential form of the church was the local congregation; their other major tenet, from which they derive their name, was their belief in adult baptism, usually by immersion. No official national membership figures are available until 1891.

Congregationalists. The original Congregationalists came from the more extreme wing of the Puritan movement in Elizabethan England. Originally hopeful of reforming the Anglican church from within, they were gradually driven out. Their leaders were quite often suspended Anglican clergy and hence some of the clergy ejected in 1662 gathered congregations of sympathisers around them. Every individual church was held to be a complete unit with a congregation of true believers bound together in a covenant relationship. All authority was vested in the congregation itself. Their freedom from outside control gave them their original name of 'Independents'. Their estimated national membership in 1851 was 165,000.

Countess of Huntingdon's Connexion. George Whitfield (1714–70) was closely associated with Wesley in the early days of the Evangelical Revival, but parted company with him on doctrinal grounds in 1751. Whitfield was a Calvinist and believed that only the elect few would be saved, while Wesley believed that salvation was open to all. Whitfield came to the attention of Selina, Countess of Huntingdon, and became her chaplain in 1748. She supported him financially, providing funds for the building of chapels and founding a college at Trevecca in North Wales. After 1751 Whitfield and Wesley followed different evangelical courses; Whitfield's followers and those of other Calvinistic preachers eventually developed into the Welsh Calvinistic Methodists and the Countess of Huntingdon's Connexion. In 1851 the form of worship used by the Connexion owed much to the liturgy of the Church of England to which was added extemporary prayer. The gradual decline of Calvinism in England (though not in Wales) in the nineteenth century led to the break-up of the Connexion. Some congregations rejoined the Methodists while others became independent Congregational churches.

Latter Day Saints (Mormons). The sect was founded by Joseph Smith in the United States in the early 1820s and despite persecution grew in numbers. In 1844 Smith was murdered in Nauvoo, Illinois, and his martyrdom gave new life to the movement. Brigham Young took on the leadership and in 1846 the Mormons moved from Nauvoo to Salt Lake City, Utah. The first missionaries to England landed at Liverpool in 1837 and a second mission arrived in 1840. The missionaries preached that the kingdom of Christ was shortly to appear at Nauvoo and it was the duty of all sincere Christians to go there. As Nauvoo was pictured in glowing colours, and as the Mormons had organised a very efficient system of emigration via Liverpool, many poor people were enticed to go. According to Mormon statistics more than 17,000 converts had emigrated by 1850. The 1851 census coincided with the period of greatest Mormon influence in England before the 1960s. In 1852 the Mormon doctrine of polygamy was officially formulated by Brigham Young and was widely publicised by the *Millenial Star*, the official organ of Mormonism in England. The ridicule thus evoked resulted in a drastic drop in membership and it was more than a hundred years before recovery took place. While there seems to be little to link the five Derbyshire congregations at Church Gresley, Heanor, Belper, Ashbourne and Chesterfield together, it would appear that conversion often spread through neighbourhood or kinship connections and occurred in industrial areas where the lower working-class had little connection with the mainstream churches.

The Wesleyan Methodist Connexion. The origins of Methodism can be traced to John Wesley's conversion experience in 1738, and in the ten years from 1740 to 1750 the main principles of the Methodist system, including itinerancy and the circuit system, were laid down. Although Wesley was a loyal Anglican and denied any intention of forming a separate denomination, his methods were so alien to the Anglican church of the time that a split was inevitable and occurred after his death. Wesley believed in 'general redemption' and disregarded the parish system. Most of the troubles which afflicted Wesleyanism subsequently arose from the dominance of the clergy and from lack of opportunity for lay participation. Almost all the breakaway movements represented a desire to return to the democratic spirit of the early Methodists. National membership in 1851 was 280,654.

Methodist New Connexion. Formed in 1797 as a result of agitation for greater lay participation in the government of the Methodist Connexion; sometimes known as Kilhamites from their leader, Alexander Kilham. National membership in 1851 was 16,962.

Primitive Methodist Connexion. This movement was started in Staffordshire by two Wesleyan local preachers, Hugh Bourne and William Clowes, who had both been expelled for taking part in 'camp meetings', the prolonged open air evangelistic gatherings. Class tickets were first issued in 1811 and the first preaching plan dates from 1812. The growth rate was phenomenal and by 1851 the national membership was 106,074.

Wesleyan Methodist Association. Formed in 1836 by an alliance between the Protestant Methodists, the Warrenites and the Arminian Methodists. The latter, who were otherwise known as the Derby Faith Methodists, seceded from the Wesleyan Methodists in the 1830s on doctrinal grounds. The WMA, which had a national membership of 20,557 in 1851, joined with the majority of the Wesleyan Reformers to form the United Methodist Free Churches in 1857.

Wesleyan Reformers. The immediate cause of the Reform agitation was the expulsion by the Wesleyan Conference of three ministers in 1849. The underlying cause was again the lack of opportunities for lay participation and the feeling that the Weslyan Connexion was led by a metropolitan clique, headed by Dr Jabez Bunting. The majority of the Reformers joined in the union which became the United Free Churches but a minority became the Wesleyan Reform Union and are still independent. National membership in 1862 was 11,355.

Original Methodists. This small sect seceded from the Primitive Methodists in 1839 after disagreement over increases in the pay of ministers. It consisted of four circuits: Selston, Brassington, Radford and Derby. One of the connexional rules stated that no 'hirelings' were to preach from their pulpits. This excluded all paid ministers, of whatever denomination, from taking part in their services.

The Moravians. The present movement dates from 1772, when refugees from Bohemia were given shelter in Saxony by Count Zinzendorf. Under his protection the religious settlement of Herrnhut was founded. The Moravians, also known as the United Brethren, first appeared in England in 1728. Like the primitive Christians they believed in living together in peace and love as a real community. To this end a number of communities were set up in

England which included Fulneck near Bradford, Fairfield near Manchester and Tytherton in Wiltshire. The settlement at Ockbrook near Derby was established in 1740 and some of the buildings date from 1750. In 1735 a large-scale mission was sent to Georgia and it was on the voyage that John Wesley met them. While the movement never grew large as they did not proselytize, its influence was particularly great in the field of education. Some Moravian ideas were incorporated into Methodism.

Quakers (Society of Friends). Founded by George Fox (1624–91), probably the most extreme form of Dissent. Quaker services were notable for their lack of formality and ritual, there were no paid clergy and the meeting houses were plain and spartan. National membership in 1847 was 15,345.

Swedenborgians (The New Church or New Jerusalemites). Emanuel Swedenborg (1688–1772), a Swedish polymath, can rank among the greatest figures of the eighteenth century and, although he did not preach or found a church, his theological writings had great influence. In 1784 his disciples founded the New Church. In England his ideas were taken up by two Anglican clergymen, Thomas Hartley, vicar of Winwick and John Clowes, vicar of Manchester. Clowes was against the formation of a new church and wished to spread Swedenborg's ideas within existing churches. The first organised congregation met in Great Eastcheap in 1788 and in 1791 the first annual conference of British Swedenborgians met there. Churches were founded in other parts of the country and by 1851 there were fifty places of worship with 11,465 sittings and 4,846 in attendance. A study of the registers tends to show that the majority of the membership belonged to the poorer classes. Members of the church played a leading part in the anti-slavery movement. There were two congregations in Derbyshire, in St Peter's parish, Derby and in Melbourne. National membership in 1851 was 2,805.

Unitarians. Although Unitarianism lacked organisation before the nineteenth century, its doctrines may be traced back to the Reformation. In seventeenth-century England a large section of the English Presbyterian church turned away from Trinitarian teaching. After the Salters' Hall conference of 1719 Unitarian beliefs spread rapidly through the old Presbyterian and Independent congregations. As the religion of only a small, often wealthy and influential group, Unitarianism played a role out of proportion to its numbers in municipal life, particularly in Birmingham, Leicester, Manchester and Liverpool. No membership figures are available for 1851.

APPENDIX 3

THE WESLEYAN REFORM MOVEMENT IN DERBYSHIRE

In August 1849 the Wesleyan Methodist Conference expelled three ministers, James Everett, William Griffith and Samuel Dunn, from the Conference and from any connection therewith for their alleged complicity in the publication of the 'Flysheets', a series of widely circulated anonymous satirical pamphlets which attacked the abuses alleged to be present in the Methodist establishment. This event, whose results profoundly affected Wesleyanism in Derbyshire, was the culmination of nearly twenty years of agitation and controversy which had severely racked the Wesleyan connexion.[1] Derbyshire Wesleyamisn was affected more acutely than any other county except Norfolk.[2] Nationally, over 100,000 members who sympathised with the 'Methodist Martyrs' were either expelled or forced into 'resignation', while in Derbyshire more than half the membership was lost in that fashion in the period 1850–55.[3] The resultant furore was widely reported in the Methodist newspapers: by the *Watchman*, which supported the conference decision, and by the more liberal and radical *Wesleyan Times* which supported the Reformers. The *Nonconformist* condemned the Conference in round terms: 'Conference, as it now exists, is perhaps the most execrable form of priestly intolerance and exclusiveness to be found in these realms. It is pharisaism rampant ...'.[4] Even the secular press took notice: *The Times* dealt with the matter at some length and concluded that 'These gentlemen are punished on mere suspicion and for refusing to criminate themselves ... Talk of the Star Chamber! A man may hold his tongue in that court, stand his trial and escape if the evidence did not support the charge'.[5]

Of the three expelled, Everett had travelled in the Cromford circuit earlier in his career; Griffith, at the time of his expulsion, was the popular superintendent of the newly-created Ripley circuit and was allied by marriage

---

[1] A full account may be found in O.A. Beckerlegge, *United Methodist Free Churches* (1957), pp. 30–9, and W.H. Jones, *History of the Wesleyan Reform Union* (1952), pp. 17ff.

[2] R. Currie, *Methodism divided: a study in the sociology of ecumenism* (1967), p. 204.

[3] Currie, *Methodism divided*, pp. 75, 204.

[4] R. Chew, *James Everett: a biography* (1875), p. 409.

[5] Chew, *James Everett* p. 408.

with the Bourne family, who were prominent Belper Wesleyans; Dunn was the superintendent of the Nottingham circuit.[1]

The organisation of giant meetings by reformers began almost at once up and down the country and from the start Derby was one of their chief centres of support. The three were expelled on 10 August and by 21 August a 'monster' meeting was held in Derby and a subscription list for the financial support of the three was opened, headed by Jedediah Strutt, grandson of the original Jedediah, founder of the mill at Belper.[2] Some weeks later Dunn was entertained to breakfast in Chesterfield with Mr Stringfellow, a local hat-manufacturer, in the chair.[3] At a tea-party held in Derby in October in aid of the three 800 were present and the chairman, Mr Holmes, a Derby silk-manufacturer, warned members of the audience not to speak, saying that if they did they were likely to be expelled.[4] At about the same time a demonstration was staged in Derby when forty local preachers, four abreast, marched through the town singing hymns and ending up in Becket Street to join a big meeting of Reformers, which was being held there.[5] The *Wesleyan Times* of the period is filled with letters of support from circuits. 'General excitement in the Ashbourne circuit' is reported on 13 August; the same issue contains a letter of support from the Chesterfield circuit and on 10 August an account of a meeting attended mainly by members of the working class which raised £20 is reported.[6] Later issues contained letters of support from Cromford, Bakewell, Ashbourne and Castle Donington circuits.[7] As Currie expresses it, 'To laymen 'agitation' was a permanent Guy Fawkes night. To ministers it provided the opportunity for a salutary bloodletting. Trouble makers of long standing could at last be expelled'.[8]

The losses to membership may be briefly summarised: the Derby circuit dropped from from 1,629 in 1849 to 912 in 1853 and lost about forty local preachers; Chesterfield circuit declined from 1,150 in 1849 to 380 in 1851; Bakewell from 484 in 1850 to 95 in 1852 (it never reached 300 again and

---

[1] D.A. Barton, 'William Griffith, 1806–83: the Hercules of the Reform Movement', *Proc. Wesley Hist. Soc.*, XLIII, 6, ii (1982), pp. 165–70.

[2] *Derby Mercury*, 29 Aug. 1849.

[3] *Wesleyan Times*, 1 Oct. 1849.

[4] *Wesleyan Times*, 22 Oct. 1849.

[5] Alger, *King St Wesleyan chapel*, p. 28.

[6] *Wesleyan Times*, 13 Aug. 1849.

[7] *Wesleyan Times*, 1849, Cromford 10 September; Bakewell 27 August; Ashbourne 27 August; Castle Donington 10 December.

[8] Currie, *Methodism divided*, p. 74.

was subsequenbtly amalgamated with Bradwell to form the North Derbyshire Mission). Similar drastic losses may be seen in the circuits at Belper, Cromford and Glossop.[1] Suffice it to say then that March 1851 found Derbyshire Wesleyanism at its most dislocated. In the Cromford circuit, to name but one example, the quarterly return for mid-summer 1850 contains a note in the superintendent's hand saying that no accurate return of members can be made, as the local societies are so broken up by agitation.[2] The circuit schedule of the Belper Wesleyan circuit for September 1849 has the following note in the minister's hand: 'the former part of this book presents a numerical view of the painful effects produced in this circuit which was originated and carried out by Messrs Everett, Dunn and Griffith (and their adherents) on account of their righteous expulsion by the Conference of 1849.'[3]

One result of the decline in membership was the resultant hardship, even near penury for some ministers, as letters from William Parker, the superintendent in the Chesterfield circuit, demonstrate.[4] Another was the bitterness caused which in some districts, as in Belper and Ripley circuits, was still too great in the twentieth century to allow Wesleyans and United Methodists to support the proposed Methodist union in 1924.[5]

For the present-day researcher looking at the Religious Census forms, there is the constant problem that some Wesleyan Reform chapels can easily be mistaken for Wesleyan chapels, and it needs local knowledge to distinguish them since many reformers, considering that they had been unjustly expelled, continued to call themselves Wesleyans. This they were particularly advised to do by the *Wesleyan Times*: 'They are so in reality; and we would not say that they should add any other distinctive appelation. In the case of Sunday schools and the temporary places where separate worship is held, the word 'Reformer' might be added in a parenthesis, thus – Wesleyan Methodist (Reformer).'[6]

By the late 1860s most of the Derbyshire Reformers had joined the United Methodist Free Churches, formed in 1857. The only circuit remaining was Bakewell, which joined the Wesleyan Reform Union on its foundation in 1859 and remains a member today.

---

[1] Figures taken from *Minutes of the Wesleyan Conference*.

[2] Derbys. RO, D1431J/MW313.

[3] Derbys RO, D544J/MM/16/1/1.

[4] Methodist Archives Centre, John Rylands Library, Manchester, MS letters from William Parker.

[5] Currie, *Methodism divided*, p. 204.

[6] *Wesleyan Times*, III, no. 125, Monday 24 March 1851.

UTTOXETER REGISTRATION DISTRICT

Uttoxeter Sub-District

NORBURY[1]

Church of England. S. Mary. *Erected:* Built before 1800. *Endowments:* 50 acres, tithe £204 p.a. *Sittings:* Free seats 280, others 64, total 344. *Attendance:* Morning: general congregation 31, besides scholars; afternoon: 86, besides scholars. *Average attendance:* Morning: 50; afternoon 150. *Signed:* Clement F. Broughton, Rector of Norbury, Norbury. [HO 129/374/2]

Primitive Methodist. *Erected:* 1847. Separate and entire, exclusively used. *Sittings:* Free all 100. *Attendance:* Morning: Sunday school 24; afternoon: general congregation 40, Sunday school 30, total 70; evening: general congregation 70. *Signed:* Joseph Walker, Stewarde, Roston, near Ashbourn. [HO 129/374/3]

Roston

Wesleyan Methodist. ['District Mr Lasseter' *entered in pencil*] *Erected:* Not known, not separate, not exclusively used. *Sittings:* 30 all free. *Attendance:* Morning: general congregation 20. *Signed:* William Orpe, society steward, Roston, near Ashbourne. [HO 129/374/4]

SUDBURY[2]

Church of England. All Saints. *Erected:* an old parish church, originating before 1800. *Endowments:* Glebe about 30 acres, tithe £600, originally rent charge, pew rents none, Easter offerings none, fees, dues small, other sources 10s. *Sittings:* Free 90; others 536, total 626. *Attendance:* Morning: general congregation 195, Sunday school 59, total 254; afternoon: general congregation 165, Sunday school 51, total 216. *Average attendance:* Morning: general congregation 200, Sunday school 57, total 257; afternoon:

[1] Population 475, including Roston.

[2] Population 570.

general congregation 170, Sunday school 36, total 206. *Signed:* Jos. Bosworth D.D., The Rectory, Sudbury, nr Uttoxeter. [HO 129/374/40]

DOVERIDGE[1]

Church of England. S. Cuthbert. *Erected:* before 1800. *Endowments:* not given. *Sittings:* Free ample, 153; others ample, 249; total 402. *Attendance:* Morning: general congregation 135, Sunday school 90, total 225; afternoon: general congregation 106, Sunday school 81, total 187. *Average attendance:* Morning: general congregation 175, Sunday school 104, total 279; afternoon: general congregation 150, Sunday school 93, total 243. *Remarks:* The Sunday was wet, which will account for the smallness of the congregation in comparison with the average attendance. The Duke of Devonshire is patron but I cannot say the exact value in consequence of the reductions I have made and the larger ones I shall have to make, owing to the depreciation of agricultural produce. 4 April 1851. *Signed:* Thomas Cavendish, minister. Doveridge, Uttoxeter. [HO 129/374/41]

Wesleyan Methodist. *Erected:* 1805. Separate and entire, exclusively used. *Sittings:* Free 50, others 50. *Attendance:* Afternoon: general congregation 51; evening: General congregation 47. *Average number:* 75. *Signed:* Thomas Deaville, farmer, society steward, Doveridge, Derbyshire. [HO 129/374/42]

Primitive Methodist. Providence Chapel. *Erected:* 1841. Separate and entire, exclusively used. *Sittings:* Free 56, others 51. *Attendance:* Morning 26; afternoon 36; evening 60; *Average attendance:* general congregation: morning: 20; afternoon: 30; evening 46. *Signed:* William Statham, chapel steward, Doveridge. [HO 129/374/43]

SOMMERSHALL HERBERT[2]

Church of England. An old parish church. *Erected:* Cons. before 1800. *Sittings:* Free 6; others 23. *Endowments:* Fees £50. *Attendance:* Morning: general congregation 31, Sunday school 15; afternoon: general congregation 16, Sunday school 15. *Average attendance:* Morning: general congregation

---

[1] Population 766, including West Broughton, Eaton and Sedsall.
[2] Population 111.

50; afternoon: general congregation 40. *Remarks:* For information with regard to land, tithe, glebe etc, I have none to give. *Signed:* Francis Mosley Spilsbury, curate, Sommershall, Uttoxeter. [HO 129/374/44]

CUBLEY

Marston Montgomery[1]

Church of England. An antient parish. Church dedicated to S. Giles. *Erected:* Before 1800. *Endowments:* Tithes commuted £140, fees £1 10s., other permanent endowment and payment from the Lord's piece 11s. *Sittings:* Free 90, others 184, total 224. *Attendance:* Morning: general congregation 31, Sunday school 54, total 85. *Remarks:* I have put down what the tithes were commuted for. The tithe tables will tell what the rent charges for the present year amount to. *Signed:* John Brownson, churchwarden. [HO 129/374/45]

Wesleyan Methodist. *Erected:* 1845. Separate and entire, exclusively used. *Sittings:* Free 80, others 40. *Attendance:* Afternoon: general congregation 50; evening 40. *Average attendance:* Afternoon: general congregation 50, Sunday school 50, total 100; evening: general congregation 40, Sunday school 0, total 40. *Signed:* Thomas Deaville, chapel steward, Rocester, nr Ashbourne. [HO 129/374/46]

Cubley[2]

Church of England. Antient parish church dedicated to S. Andrew Before 1800. *Endowments:* Tithes commuted £380, glebe, including house, garden, land £30.14s., fees £1 10s. *Sittings:* Free 87, others 162, total 249. *Attendance:* Afternoon: general congregation 56, Sunday school 20, total 76. *Average attendance:* Not given. *Remarks:* I have put down what the tithes were commuted for. Pynes tables will tell you what the Rent Charges for the year amounts to. *Signed:* William Copestake, parish clerk, Cubley. [HO 129/374/47]

[1] Population 473.

[2] Population 387.

BOYLESTON[1]

Church of England. S. John. Antient parish church. *Erected:* Before 1800. *Endowments:* Return made to the Bishop, Jan.1851. *Sittings:* Free 105, other 116, total 221. *Attendance:* No count. *Average attendance:* general congregation 70, Sunday school 30. *Signed:* Roger Bickerstaff, Rector. [HO 129/374/48]

Wesleyan Methodist. *Erected:* 1809. Separate and entire, exclusively used. *Sittings:* Free 104, others 16. *Attendance:* Morning: general congregation 62, Sunday school 10, total 72; evening: general congregation 30. *Average attendance:* General congregation 70, Sunday school 20, total 90. *Remarks:* On account of the distance of the Superentand Minesters residence, the return made to him was prespective by the previous Sabath and the 30 being stormy caused a less attendance than was estimated. *Signed:* Joseph Baker, chapel steward, Cubley, nr Sudbury. [HO 129/374/49]

Primitive Methodist. *Erected:* 1811, rebuilt 1846. Joined to house and school room; now exclusively adapted for worship. *Sittings:* Free 100, others 36, Free space 19′ x 15′ 6″. *Attendance:* Afternoon: general congregation 45, Sunday school 20; evening: general congregation 60. *Average attendance:* general congregation from 50 to 60, Sunday school 20. *Signed:* James Morley, secretary, Boylston, nr Sudbury. [HO 129/374/50]

---

[1] Population 302.

BURTON-UPON-TRENT REGISTRATION DISTRICT

Tutbury Sub-District

CHURCH BROUGHTON[1]

Church of England. S. Michael. *Erected:* Old parish church in complete repair. *Endowments:* Land £160 + tithes £24, fees £3; other permanent endowment 52 14s. 11d; Easter offerings £1 9s. 6d.; other offerings £1. *Sittings:* 300 all free. *Attendance:* Morning: general congregation 54, Sunday school 67. total 121. No service in afternoon or evening. *Average attendance:* Only one service a Sunday alternately morning and afternoon and average congregation for 3 months before March 30 1851 general congregation 80, of Sunday scholars for same time 81, total 161. *Signed:* W.S. Vawdrey, Curate, Scropton, nr Tutbury. [HO 129/375/2]

Primitive Methodist. *Erected:* 1828. Separate and entire, exclusively used. *Sittings:* Free 60. other 40, standing 30. *Attendance:* Morning: Sunday school 31; afternoon: general congregation 48, Sunday school 32, total 80; evening: general congregation 70. *Average attendance:* General congregation about 120, Sunday school 35, total 155. *Signed:* John Salesbury, Chapel steward, Church Broughton; or to Thomas Thomas, Victoria St, Burton on Trent. [HO 129/375/3]

BARTON BLOUNT[2]

Church of England. *Erected:* Before 1800. The parish church of Barton Blount is antient and a rectory. *Endowments:* Land £51 10s., rent charge £11, glebe £17 10s. *Sittings:* Free 16, others 48, total 64. *Attendance:* Morning and afternoon on alternate Sundays Morning: general congregation 26. *Average attendance:* general congregation 30. *Signed:* Alpheus Slight, curate, Alkmonton, Longford, Derby. [HO 129/375/4]

---

[1] Population 661.

[2] Population 69.

5

SUTTON ON THE HILL[1]

Thurvaston

Primitive Methodist. Lane Ends. *Erected:* 1839. Separate and entire, as a place of worship only. *Sittings:* Free 70, others 40, free standing for 30. *Attendance:* Morning: general congregation 19; afternoon: general congregation 100; evening: general congregation 136. *Average attendance:* 130. *Signed:* Thomas Thomas, minister, Victoria St, Burton on Trent, Staffs. [HO 129/375/5]

Osleston

Weslians. *Erected:* 1846. Not separate, not exclusively used. *Sittings:* no information. *Attendance:* Morning: general congregation 50. *Average attendance:* not given. *Remarks:* One Sunday morning and next evening alternately. James Woodroff. [HO 129/375/6]

Sutton on the Hill

Church of England. S. Michael. An ancient parish church. *Erected:* Cons. before 1800. *Endowments:* gross amount £314. *Sittings:* Free 72, others 173, total 245. *Attendance:* Morning: general congregation 65, Sunday school 59; afternoon 106. *Average attendance:* Morning: general congregation 75, Sunday school 69; afternoon 120. *Signed:* J. Buckston, vicar of Sutton on the Hill. [HO 129/375/7]

MARSTON ON DOVE[2]

Hilton

Wesleyan Methodist. *Erected:* 1840. Separate and entire, exclusively used. *Sittings:* Free 220, others 80. *Attendance:* Afternoon: general congregation 100, Sunday school 67, total 167; evening: general congrega-

---

[1] Population 129; the parish included the township of Osleston & Thurvaston, which had a population of 395.

[2] Population 77; the parish also included the townships of Hilton (757), Hoon (38) and Hatton (319).

tion 100. *Average attendance:* Afternoon: general congregation 150, Sunday school 70, total 220; evening: general congregation 100. *Signed:* Joseph Dawson, steward, Hilton. [HO 129/375/8]

Primitive Methodist. *Erected:* 1847. Separate and entire, exclusively used. *Sittings:* Free 90, others 8. *Attendance:* Afternoon: general congregation 60; evening: general congregation 90, total 150. *Signed:* Samuel Blood, steward, Hilton, nr Derby. [HO 129/375/9]

Hatton

Wesleyan Methodist chappele. *Erected:* 1812. Exclusively used, separate, except Sunday school on one side. *Sittings:* Free 50, others 25, standing 20. *Attendance:* Afternoon: general congregation 75, Sunday school 50, total 125; evening: general congregation 60. *Average attendance:* General congregation 60, Sunday school 50, total 110. *Remarks:* The Sabbath school opens on one side of the Chappele and will hold about 60 Scholears. *Signed:* Samuel Faulkner, attendant, Hatton. [HO 129/375/11]

Marston

Church of England. *Sittings:* Free 170, other 230, total 400. *Attendance:* Morning: general congregation 55, Sunday school 73; Afternoon: general congregation 60, Sunday school 73. *Average attendance:* not given. *Signed:* Henry Edwards, informant. [HO 129/375/10; Registrar's return]

SCROPTON[1]

Church of England. S. Paul. The church is an ancient parish one, a donative and the church of a district and separate parish. *Erected:* not known, several centuries old. *Endowments:* Land, tithe, glebe £65, other permanent endowment £700 for building a new parsonage, fees £2. *Sittings:* not given. *Attendance:* Morning: general congregation 16; afternoon no service. *Average attendance:* Only one service a day, alternate morning and afternoon. Morn. service always worst. Average $19^2/_3$ per Sunday (general congregation). *Remarks:* The church is situated in a corner of a large

---

[1] Population 375; the parish also included Foston, which had a population of 140.

agricultural parish of 3,200 acres – quite detached from $^3/_4$ of the population which is scattered. Dissent very prevalent. *Signed:* W.S. Vawdrey, curate, Scropton, Tutbury [HO 129/375/12]

Wesleyan Methodist. *Erected:* 1812. Separate building, exclusively used. *Sittings:* Free 69, other 36. *Attendance:* Morning: Sunday school 60; afternoon: general congregation 90; evening: general congregation 60. *Average attendance:* general congregation 80, Sunday school 60, total 140. *Remarks:* Sunday school adjoining chapel, opening with folding doors during service time. *Signed:* Samuel Faulkner, Sabbath school teacher. [HO 129/375/13]

EGGINTON[1]

Church of England. S. Wilfrid. *Erected:* Long before 1800. Very ancient and commonly called Egginton parish church. *Endowments:* Tithe commuted to £315, fees £3 to 5, glebe 55 acres. *Sittings:* Free 60, others 181, total 241, besides Sunday school sittings and forms. *Attendance:* Morning: general congregation and Sunday school 55; afternoon: 77. *Average attendance:* general congregation 80 to 100; Sunday school about 45. Jno. Leigh, Rector, The Rectory, Egginton. [HO 129/375/27]

Wesleyan Methodist *Erected:* Private house, not separate. Room in private house, not exclusively used. *Sittings:* Free 60. *Attendance:* general congregation: evening 35. *Signed:* William Parkinson, minister, Burton on Trent. [HO 129/375/28; *this appears to be a duplicate return for the next entry*]

Wesleyan Methodist. *Erected:* Private house licensed for preaching, a family residing in it. *Sittings:* Free 65. *Attendance:* Evening: general congregation 50. *Signed:* John Bond, steward, Egginton. [HO 129/375/29; *this appears to be a duplicate of the previous entry*]

---

[1] Population 374.

Repton Sub-District

WILLINGTON[1]

Church of England S. Michael. *Erected:* Before 1800. *Endowments:* Land £20, glebe £60, fees £1 10s. *Sittings:* Free 70, others 125, total 190. *Attendance:* Morning: general congregation 50, Sunday school 48. *Average attendance:* Morning: general congregation 60, Sunday school 48, total 108; afternoon: general congregation 80, Sunday school 48, total 128. *Signed:* James R. Holmes, curate of Willington, Barrow on Trent, nr Derby. [HO 129/375/31]

Wesleyan Methodist. *Erected:* 1835. Separate, exclusively used for divine service only. *Sittings:* Free 100, others 40. *Attendance:* Afternoon: 20; evening: 40. *Average attendance:* General congregation: 50. *Signed:* George Hinckley, steward, Willington. [HO 129/375/32]

Baptist. [*Registrar's letter dated 30 June 1852:* Will you have the goodness to furnish the following information at your earliest convenience. Gervase Smedley, registrar.] Congregation, including Sunday school scholars: Morning, afternoon: no service. Evening: 60. *Sittings:* about 70 free seats. Others all free. [HO 129/375/33]

ETWALL[2]

Wesleyan Methodist. *Erected:* 1836. Separate and entire, exclusively used. *Sittings:* Free 88, others 12. *Attendance:* Afternoon: general congregation 44; evening 86; *Average attendance:* Afternoon: general congregation 35; evening 75. *Signed:* Francis Camp, chapel steward, farmer, Etwall. [HO 129/375/34]

Burnaston

Primitive Methodist. *Erected:* 1844 or 1845. Separate and entirely used. *Sittings:* About 120. Nearly all are free. *Attendance:* Afternoon: about 40;

---

[1] Population 442.

[2] Population 579; the parish also included Burnaston, which had a population of 152.

9

evening: about 40 to 50. *Signed:* Gervase Smedley, Registrar, Repton. [HO 129/375/36]

TRUSLEY[1]

Church of England. *Erected:* Before 1800. In time of Queen Anne a good brick church the name of which is All Saints, in tolerable repair. Consecration no particulars are known from length of time. *Endowments:* Tithe £100, glebe £70, fees £5. *Sittings:* Total 120. *Attendance:* Morning: total 20; afternoon: total 20. *Average attendance:* Morning: total 25; afternoon: total 25. *Remarks:* All the seats are belonging to the different houses, except about three cottages and as the population is so small there is plenty of room for everyone. There is no Sunday school, as there are only four or five labourers' children and they have generally attended the Dalbury Sunday school which is also under my care. *Signed:* Chs. E. Cotton, Rector of Trusley. [HO 129/375/36]

DALBURY[2]

Church of England. All Saints. *Erected:* Before 1800. So old there is no date. Not known when or how the church was built but it is Norman architecture. An addition was made six years since by donations and money advanced by the Societies for Church building. *Cost:* Parochial rate £30, Diocesan society £45, Private benefactions £201 15s, total £276 15s. *Endowments:* Tithe £184, glebe £90, fees £1. *Sittings:* Free 75, others 82, total 157. *Attendance:* Afternoon: general congregation 55, Sunday school 18, total 73. *Average attendance:* General congregation 55, Sunday school 20. *Remarks:* It must be observed that two-thirds of the population live near two miles from the church and the population so small that there is duty only once a day as they could not attend more. The duty is alternate morning and evening with another church, Trusley, a mile distant. *Signed:* Charles Evelyn Cotton, rector, Dalbury Rectory. [HO 129/375/37]

---

[1] Population 90.

[2] Population 237, including Dalbury Lees, for which see p. 11.

RADBOURNE[1]

Church of England. *Erected:* Unknown from antiquity. *Endowments:* Land 130 acres, tithe £225, fees trifling, glebe the above land. *Sittings:* Free 50, sufficient, others 100, sufficient. *Attendance:* Morning: general congregation 55, Sunday school 15, total 70; afternoon: general congregation 67, Sunday school 15, total 82. *Average attendance:* The same. Signed: Hy Chandos Pole, Rector, Radbourne. [HO 129/375/38]

DALBURY[2]

Dalbury Lees

Wesleyan Methodist. *Erected:* 1846. House, not separate, not exclusively used. *Sittings:* Free 36. *Attendance:* Afternoon: general congregation 29. *Signed:* John Holden, leader, Dalbury Lees. [HO 129/375/39]

Primitive Methodist. *Erected:* 1836. A separate building, a place of worship and a Sunday school. *Sittings:* Free 50, others 30. Standing room for 30. *Attendance:* No services on 30 March. *Average attendance:* Afternoon: general congregation 20, evening: general congregation 40. *Signed:* Abimelech Hainsworth Coulson, Superintendant minister, 45 Copeland St, Derby. [HO 129/375/40]

MICKLEOVER[3]

Church of England. All Saints. *Erected:* Before 1800. Ancient parish church. *Endowments:* Land £340, fees £5. *Sittings:* Free none, others 200, total 200. *Attendance:* Morning: general congregation 117, Sunday school 85, total 202; afternoon: general congregation 50, Sunday school 85, total 135. *Average attendance:* Morning: general congregation 120, Sunday school 85, total 205; afternoon: general congregation 60, Sunday school 85, total 145. *Signed:* Frederic Curzon, vicar of Mickleover. [HO 129/375/41]

---

[1] Population 230.

[2] See also p. 10.

[3] Population 791; the parish also included Findern (467) and Littleover (551).

Wesleyan Methodist. *Erected:* 1820. Separate and entire, exclusively used. *Sittings:* Free 90, others 36, standing none. *Attendance:* Afternoon: general congregation 50 Sunday school 56, total 106; evening: general congregation 46. *Signed:* Christopher Wright, steward, joiner, Mickleover. [HO 129/375/42]

Primitive Methodist. *Erected:* Not separate, not exclusively used. *Sittings:* Free 50. *Attendance:* Evening: general congregation 40. *Signed:* Thomas Radford, leadear, Steakerfeald, Mickleovr, Dearbysh. [HO 129/375/43]

Findern

Church of England. All Saints – church of an ancient chapelry attached to the Mother Church of Mickleover. *Endowments:* Land £88, fees £1 10s. *Sittings:* Free 20, others 80. *Attendance:* Afternoon: general congregation 60, Sunday school 33. *Remarks:* The number of sittings here and at Littleover I have fixed as near as I can guess. The congregations vary with the season of the year. *Signed:* Joseph Sowter, curate, Findern. [HO 129/375/44]

Unitarian. *Erected:* Before 1800. Old meeting house; separate and entire, exclusively used. *Sittings:* Free 74, others none. *Attendance:* March 23: afternoon: general congregation 10. *Average attendance:* Under 20. *Remarks:* There was no service on the 31st as it is only once a fortnight. *Signed:* Mark Whitehouse, minister, No 10 Agard St, Derby. [HO 129/375/45]

Wesleyan Methodist. *Erected:* 1833. Separate and entire, exclusively used. *Sittings:* Free 70, others 30. *Attendance:* Afternoon: general congregation 50, Sunday school 34, total 84; evening: general congregation 70. *Signed:* Samuel Johnson, steward, Findern, Derby. [HO 129/375/46]

BARROW ON TRENT[1]

Twyford

Church of England. *Erected:* Before 1800. Twyford is an ancient parish church of a distinct and seperate parish. *Endowments:* Land £6, tithe commuted £27 10s. *Sittings:* Free 20, others 200, total 220. *Attendance:* Morning: general congregation 60, Sunday school 30, total 90; afternoon: general congregation 70, Sunday school 30, total 100. *Average attendance:* Morning: general congregation 60, Sunday school 30, total 90; afternoon: general congregation 70, Sunday school 30, total 100. *Signed:* William Heacock, vicar, Etwall, Derby. [HO 129/375/47]

Twyford and Stenson

Wesleyan Methodist. *Erected:* 1845. Seperate building, exclusively used. *Sittings:* Free 70, others 42. *Attendance:* Afternoon: general congregation 40; evening: general congregation 55. *Average attendance:* Morning: general congregation 35, afternoon: general congregation 45; evening: general congregation 60. *Signed:* Richard Forman, steward, Stenson, nr Derby. [HO 129/375/48]

REPTON

Foremark[2]

Church of England. *Erected:* An ancient parish church of a distinct and separate parish. Consecrated before 1800. *Endowments:* a donative £30 a year paid by Sir Robert Burdett, Bart. *Sittings:* Free 30, others 150, total 180. *Attendance:* Morning: general congregation 60, Sunday school 20; afternoon: general congregation 70, Sunday school 25. *Average attendance:* Morning: general congregation 60, Sunday school 20, total 90; afternoon: general congregation 80, Sunday school 25, total 105. *Signed:* William Heacock, perpetual curate, Etwall, nr Derby. [HO 129/375/49]

---

[1] Population 286; the parish also included Sinfin & Arleston (69) and Twyford & Stenson (222).

[2] Population 89; the parish also included Ingleby (149).

Ingleby

Wesleyan Methodist. *Erected:* Wesleyan preaching room occupied since 1816. Not separate, not exclusively used. *Sittings:* Free 45. *Attendance:* Evening: general congregation 45. *Average attendance:* During previous twelve months: Evening: general congregation 40. *Signed:* John Parkes, Wesleyan minister, Castle Donington, Leics. [HO 129/375/50]

Repton[1]

Church of England. S. Wystan. *Erected:* an ancient parish church. *Endowments:* Land £125, fees £6, other permanent endowments £25. *Sittings:* Free 150, others 620, total 770. *Attendance:* Morning: general congregation 264, Sunday school 97, total 361; afternoon: general congregation 184, Sunday school 96, total 280; evening: general congregation 97. *Average attendance:* Morning: general congregation 260, Sunday school 100, total 360; afternoon: general congregation 175, Sunday school 100, total 275; evening: general congregation 95. *Remarks:* The evening service is held in the schoolroom, especially for the convenience of the poor.[2] *Signed:* J. Welch, curate of Repton, Repton. [HO 129/375/51]

Wesleyan Methodist. *Erected:* 1815. Separate and entire, exclusively used. *Sittings:* Free 150, others 54. *Attendance:* Afternoon: general congregation 37; evening: general congregation 40. *Average attendance:* (during twelve months) afternoon: general congregation 80. *Signed:* Samuel Sheavyn, steward, Repton. [HO 129/375/52]

Congregational or Independent chapel. *Erected:* 1837. Separate building, exclusively used. *Sittings:* Free 90, others 260. *Attendance:* Morning: general congregation 54, Sunday school 90, total 144; afternoon: general congregation 89, Sunday school 84, total 173. *Average attendance:* evenings 120. *Remarks:* Divine service every Sunday morning and alternate afternoons and evenings; for March 30th 1851 afternoon. *Signed:* Horatio Ault, minister, Repton. [HO 129/375/53]

Primitive Methodist. *Erected:* abought the year 1833. Separate and entire, exclusively used. *Sittings:* Free 65. *Attendance:* Afternoon: general

---

[1] Population, including the hamlet of Milton, 1,863.

[2] This may imply that the majority of the evening congregation was working-class.

congregation 28, total 28; evening: general congregation 49, total 49. *Average attendance:* Morning: general congregation 35; evening: general congregation 49; total 84. *Average attendance:* 42. *Signed:* John Meakin, chapel steward, basket maker, Repton. [HO 129/375/54]

Bretby[1]

Church of England. *Erected:* Chapel of ease & donative. *Endowments:* not given. *Sittings:* Free 50, others 100, total 150. *Attendance:* Afternoon: general congregation 60, Sunday school 54, total 114. *Remarks:* The full service is alternate but the full service each Sunday. *Signed:* John Tetley Smith, incumbent, Repton. [HO 129/375/55]

Wesleyan Methodist preaching house. *Erected:* no date, dwelling house. *Sittings:* about 40, all free. *Attendance:* Afternoon: 15 to 20. *Signed:* Gervase Smedley, Registrar. [HO 129/375/56; Registrar's return]

Newton Solney[2]

Church of England. S. Mary. *Erected:* Consecrated before 1800. *Endowments:* not given. *Sittings:* Free 10, others 28, total 38. *Attendance:* General congregation 70, Sunday school included. *Average attendance:* not given. *Remarks:* Newton is exempt jurisdiction. Income is £30 per p.a. paid by Sir Henry Every, patron. *Signed:* John Hare, minister. [HO 129/375/57]

Wesleyan Methodist. *Erected:* before 1800. Preaching house. *Sittings:* Free 80. *Attendance:* Evening: general congregation 50. *Average attendance:* Morning: Sunday school 52, afternoon 260, evening 50. Average total 52)2600(50 200.[3] *Remarks:* No minister here to preach this evening. *Signed:* Thomas Stokes, occupier of the house, builder, Newton Solney. [HO 129/375/58]

---

[1] Population 369.

[2] Population 366.

[3] As on the return. This is one example of a confused interpretation of the requirements of the form.

Gresley Sub-District

CHURCH GRESLEY[1]

Church Gresley

Church of England. S. Mary and S. George. *Erected:* Before 1800. *Endowments:* Land £84, glebe £8, other permanent endowments £5 13s., fees £4, Easter offering £3. *Sittings:* Free 152, others 130, total 282 see letter. *Attendance:* Afternoon: general congregation 80, Sunday school 80. *Average attendance:* Morning: general congregation 30, Sunday school 80; afternoon: general congregation 100, Sunday school 80. *Signed:* G. Lloyd, curate, Gresley parsonage, Ashby de la Zouch. [HO 129/375/60]

Primitive Methodist. *Erected:* 1831, rebuilt 1850. Separate and entire, exclusively used. *Sittings:* Free 309, other 57. *Attendance:* Afternoon: general congregation 256; evening: 222. *Average attendance:* not given. *Signed:* Thomas Mansfield, chapel steward, Church Gresley. [HO 129/375/61]

Latter Day Saints. *Erected:* 1833. Separate and entire. Used as day school. *Sittings:* Free 80, standing space 8 sq. yards. *Attendance:* Morning: Sunday school 20, total 20; afternoon: general congregation 52; evening: general congregation 54. *Average attendance:* Morning: Sunday school 25; afternoon: general congregation 50; evening: general congregation 50. *Remarks:* Whole space of chapel 48 sq. yards inside. The chapel was erected for the Arminian Methodists. Latter Day saints have had the chapel 7 years. *Signed:* Thomas Eyley, junr, deacon, Church Gresley. [HO 129/375/62]

Swadlincote

Church of England. *Erected:* About 1845. *Sittings:* Free 200, all free. *Attendance:* Morning: Usual number – general congregation 50, Sunday school 30; afternoon: general congregation 50, Sunday school 30. *Average attendance:* Not given. *Signed:* William Wright. [HO 129/375/63; Registrar's return]

---

[1] Population 1,257. The parish also included Castle Gresley (population 190), Donisthorpe & Oakthorpe (591), Swadlincote (1,007), Drakelow (86) and Linton (279).

16

Wesleyan Methodist. *Erected:* 1816. Separate and entire, exclusively used. *Sittings:* Free 420, others 122. *Attendance:* Afternoon: general congregation 94, Sunday school 159, total 253; evening: general congregation 121. *Remarks:* This Chapel was erected in lieu of a chapel on another site built about the year 1806. *Signed:* John Fletcher Rowley, chapel steward, Swadlincote. [HO 129/375/64]

Gresley: Linton

Wesleyan Methodist. *Erected:* 1799. Separate. Place of worship and Sunday school. *Sittings:* Free 100, others 20. *Attendance:* Morning: Sunday school 36; afternoon: general congregation 42, Sunday school 37, total 79; evening: general congregation 38. *Signed:* William Burton, trustee, Linton. [HO 129/375/65]

Primitive Methodist. *Erected:* 1847. Separate building, exclusively used. *Sittings:* Free 100, standing ten or twelve. *Attendance:* Afternoon: general congregation 50; evening: general congregation 40. *Average attendance:* not given. *Signed:* George Broadhurst, Primitive Methodist, Linton. [HO 129/375/66]

LULLINGTON[1]

Church of England. All Saints. *Erected:* Before 1800. *Endowments:* Glebe 60 acres, fees about £2, other sources £5. *Sittings:* Free 100, others 100, total 200. *Attendance:* Afternoon: general congregation 90, Sunday school 57, total 147. *Average attendance:* Morning: general congregation 50, Sunday school 60, total 110; afternoon: general congregation 100, Sunday school 60, total 160. *Remarks:* The living was originally endowed with tithe – the claim to which has not been prosecuted during the present incumbency, altho' the late vicar obtained two decisions in his favour. There is morning and afternoon service alternately with Coton, which is a chapel of ease. *Signed:* Theodore Echalaz, vicar, Lullington. [HO 129/375/67]

---

[1] Population 303; the parish also included Coton-in-the-Elms (population 376).

Coton in the Elms

Church of England. S. Mary. Chapel of ease. *Erected:* October 1846. Additional as a chapel of ease to Lullington. Cost £1100. *Endowments:* Dues £18. *Sittings:* Free 250, others 25, total 275. *Attendance:* Morning: general congregation 58, Sunday school 42, total 100. *Average attendance:* Morning: general congregation 60, school 50, total 110; afternoon: general congregation 150, Sunday school 50, total 200. *Remarks:* There is one full service every Sunday, alternately with Lullington, morning and afternoon. *Signed:* Theodore Echalaz M.A., vicar of Lullington. [HO 129/375/68]

Lullington

Primitive Methodist. *Erected:* Dwelling house. Not separate, not exclusively used. *Sittings:* Free 100. *Attendance:* Evening: general congregation 60. *Average attendance:* 60. *Signed:* Wm Blunt, manager, Lullington. [HO 129/375/69]

Wesleyan Methodist. Dwelling house. Not separate, not exclusively used. *Sittings:* Free 45, others 11. *Attendance:* Afternoon: general congregation 29. *Average attendance:* 30. *Signed:* John Lee, manager, Lullington. [HO 129/375/70]

WALTON ON TRENT

Rosliston[1]

Church of England. S. Mary. *Erected:* An ancient parish church. Before 1800. *Endowments:* not given. *Sittings:* Free 200, others 60, total 260. *Attendance:* Afternoon: general congregation 90, Sunday school 54, total 144. *Average attendance:* not given. *Signed:* Isaac Hensley Bray, minister, Rosliston. [HO 129/375/71]

---

[1] Population 379.

Walton on Trent[1]

Church of England. *Endowments:* not given. *Sittings:* Free 80, children's seats 80, others 160, total 320. *Attendance:* Morning: general congregation 140, Sunday school 80, total 220; evening: general congregation 140, Sunday school 30, total 170. *Average attendance:* Morning: general congregation 140, Sunday school 80, total 220; evening: general congregation 140, Sunday school 30, total 170. *Signed:* Thomas Perrott, vicar, Walton on Trent. [HO 129/375/72]

General Baptist meeting house. *Erected:* Date uncertain. Not separate, not exclusively used. *Sittings:* Free 40. *Attendance:* Afternoon: general congregation 27. *Average attendance:* Afternoon: general congregation 30. *Signed:* James Pulsford, minister, New St, Burton on Trent. [HO 129/375/73]

STAPENHILL[2]

Church of England. S. Peter. *Erected:* Before 1800. Ancient parish church. *Endowments:* Land, glebe £175. *Sittings:* Free about 180, others 220, total 400. *Attendance:* not given. *Average attendance:* Morning: general congregation 140, Sunday school 80, total 220; evening: 180. *Remarks:* To the vicarage of Stapenhill the ancient chapelry of Caldwell is annexed, see return for Caldwell. *Signed:* W.M. Hind, licensed curate, Stapenhill. [HO 129/375/74]

Wesleyan Methodist. *Erected:* 1834. Separate building, exclusively used. *Sittings:* Free 60, other 16. *Attendance:* Afternoon: general congregation 17; evening: general congregation 10. *Average attendance:* Not given. *Signed:* Francis Wood, local preacher, Stapenhill, nr Burton on Trent. [HO 129/375/75]

Caldwell

Church of England. S. Giles. *Erected:* Before 1800. Church of the ancient chapelry of Caldwell. *Endowments:* Tithe: gross commutation £143. *Sittings:* Free about 50, others 65, total 115. *Attendance:* not given. *Average*

---

[1] Population 445.

[2] Population 635; the parish also included Caldwell (157) and Stanton & Newhall (182).

attendance: Afternoon: general congregation 45, Sunday school 8, total 53. *Remarks:* The chapelry of Caldwell is not a distinct and separate benefice in itself, but forms part of the vicarage of Stapenhill. *Signed:* W.M. Hind, curate, Stapenhill. [HO 129/375/76]

General Baptist. *Erected:* 1778. Separate and entire, exclusively used. *Sittings:* Free 160. *Attendance:* Morning: general congregation 60; afternoon: 80. *Average attendance:* Not given. *Signed:* William Norton, minnister. [HO 129/375/77]

Newhall

Church of England. S. John. A district church under 1&2 Wm IV c. 38. *Erected:* Consecrated 9 July, 1834 as an additional church. Erected jointly by the Rev. Joseph Clay, Rev. John Clay and Miss Sarah Clay. Private benefaction £2640. *Endowments:* Land £10, other permanent endowments £76, fees £4. *Sittings:* Free 250, others 190, total 440. *Attendance:* Morning: general congregation 52, Sunday school 125; afternoon: general congregation 151, Sunday school 131, total 282; evening: general congregation 71. *Remarks:* 1. The pew rents have raised from £2 10s to £6. The permanent endowment is about £76, being £79 3s. 2d. minus income tax. 2. The church will not *conveniently* hold 440. *Signed:* R.T. Burton, incumbent, Newhall. [HO 129/375/78]

Wesleyan Methodist. *Erected:* 1816. Separate and entire, exclusively used. *Sittings:* Free 260, others 50. *Attendance:* Afternoon: general congregation 52, Sunday school 125, total 177; evening: general congregation 142, Sunday school 69, total 211. *Average attendance:* Afternoon: general congregation 70, Sunday school 137, total 207; evening: general congregation 156, Sunday school 64, total 220. *Remarks:* The Sunday Scholars are not bound by the rules of the school to attend divine service in the evening. *Signed:* William Hymersley, trustee, Newhall. [HO 129/375/79]

Burton-upon-Trent Sub-District

WINSHILL[1]

District parish of Holy Trinity

Church of England. Licensed school room. *Erected:* Licensed, I think in 1847, as an existent place of worship for the parish in the hamlet. Erected by voluntary contributions, about £280. *Endowments:* not given. *Sittings:* Free: about 120. *Attendance:* Afternoon: general congregation 90, Sunday school 12, total 102. *Average attendance:* Not given. *Remarks:* The minister is assisted by a grant from the Females Aid Society. *Signed:* Peter French, minister, Burton on Trent. [HO 129/375/81]

Wesleyan Methodist. *Erected:* 1845. Separate and entire, exclusively used. *Sittings:* Free 100. *Attendance:* Afternoon: general congregation 13, Sunday school 13, total 26. *Average attendance:* Not given. *Signed:* William Parkinson, minister, Burton on Trent. [HO 129/375/82]

---

[1] Population 405.

TAMWORTH REGISTRATION DISTRICT

Tamworth Sub-District

CROXALL[1]

Church of England. S. John Baptist. *Erected:* Before 1800. *Endowments:* Land 7 acres, tithe £489, fees abt £2. *Sittings:* Free 45, other 150, children 35, total 230. *Attendance:* Morning: general congregation 72, Sunday school 26, total 98. *Average attendance:* Morning: general congregation 55, Sunday school 25, total 80. *Signed:* Theodore Echalaz, Officiating minister, Croxall. [HO 129/376/1]

EDINGALE[2]

Church of England. Holy Trinity. *Erected:* Cons. before 1800. *Endowments:* Land and rent charge about £60. *Sittings:* Free 30, other 77, total 107. *Attendance:* Morning: general congregation 17 [*Replacing* 13, *crossed through*]; afternoon: general congregation 25. *Average attendance:* Morning: general congregation about 20; afternoon general congregation about 30. *Remarks:* The Morning and Afternoon congregations are distinct with the exception of 1 or 2 Individuals. The attendance is so uncertain that the precise number of persons cannot be stated. The Church is large enough to contain the whole population. *Signed:* John Evans, minister, Edengale, Tamworth. [HO 129/376/2]

Primitive Methodist. *Erected:* Not known. Not separate, not exclusively used. *Sittings:* Free 50. *Attendance:* Afternoon: general congregation 30. *Average attendance:* general congregation 40. *Remarks:* The above named place of worship is a dwelling House at which the Meetings are held, and the Congregation varies, sometimes it is crowded and at other times the congregation is smaller. *Signed:* for James Smith, Local Preacher, Edengale, Tamworth. [HO 129/376/3]

---

[1] Population 137; the parish also included Catton (77) and Oakley (20).

[2] This parish (population 107) was divided between Derbyshire and Staffordshire; the church was in Staffordshire.

ASHBY DE LA ZOUCH
REGISTRATION DISTRICT

Hartshorn Sub-District

MEASHAM[1]

Church of England. S. Lawrence. *Erected:* Part built before the Conquest; restored 1841, 1842. *Endowments:* not given. *Sittings:* Free 312, other 300, total 612. *Attendance:* not given. *Average attendance:* Morning: general congregation 100, Sunday school 160; evening: general congregation 250, Sunday school 50. *Signed:* Jonathan K. Stubbs, incumbent. [HO 129/414/4]

APPLEBY[2]

Church of England. *Erected:* Before 1800. *Endowments:* Land X; tithe see note. *Sittings:* Free 130, others 422, total 552. *Attendance:* Morning: general congregation about 230, Sunday school 122, total 352; afternoon: general congregation about 270, Sunday school 116, total 386. *Average attendance:* general congregation from 250 300, Sunday school about 120 to 130, total from 370 to 430. *Remarks:* The rectory *is* endowed with an allotment of glebe land in lieu of tithes for value see Ecclesiastical Report but it should be stated that in consequence of agricultural distress, a large portion of the glebe (and the value of the living) is reduced by about £200 a year. *Signed:* John M. Echalaz, rector, Appleby Rectory, Atherstone. [HO 129/414/13]

General Baptist. *Erected:* 1820. Separate and entire, exclusively used. *Sittings:* Free 20, free standing 30. *Attendance:* Evening: general congregation 80. *Average attendance:* Morning: general congregation 80. *Signed:* John Barnes, minister or pastor, Austrey, nr Atherstone. [HO 129/414/14]

---

[1] Population 1,607.

[2] Appleby (population 1,181) was divided between Derbyshire and Leicestershire; the parish church was in Leicestershire and in the diocese of Peterborough, the Wesleyan chapel in Derbyshire and the Baptist chapels in Leicestershire. The Derbyshire portions were transferred to Leicestershire in 1897.

Baptist Hope Chapel. *Erected:* 1825. Separate and entire, exclusively used. *Sittings:* Free 22. *Attendance:* Morning: general congregation 18; evening: general congregation 40. *Signed:* William Orchard, deacon, Newton Regis, Tamworth. [HO 129/414/15]

Wesleyan Methodist. *Erected:* 1840. Separate and entire, exclusively used. *Sittings:* Free 60, others 8. *Attendance:* Evening: general congregation 52. [HO 129/414/16; unsigned]

MEASHAM

General Baptist. *Erected:* 1841. *Sittings:* Free 200, others 400. *Attendance:* Morning: general congregation 210, Sunday school 137, total 347; evening: general congregation 380. *Average attendance:* Not given. *Signed:* George Staples, Baptist minister, Measham. [HO 129/414/17]

Wesleyan Methodist. *Erected:* Before 1800, Separate and entire, exclusively used. *Sittings:* Free 170, others 130. *Attendance:* Afternoon: general congregation 96, Sunday school 46, total 142; evening: general congregation 72. *Average attendance:* Not given. *Signed:* John Ironmonger, chapel steward, Measham. [HO 129/414/18]

STRETTON-EN-LE-FIELD[1]

Church of England. No Man's Heath Chapel. *Erected:* Liceated *(sic)* by the Bishop of Lichfield in 1843. Built in 1843, chiefly by Sir John Cave, Bart., patron of the rectory of Stretton en le Field. Erected by Sir John Cave, Bart., and with some small contributions from the neighbourhood. No parliamentary grant, no parochial rate. Private benefaction. No endowments. *Sittings:* 120. *Attendance:* not given. *Average attendance:* Evening 90. *Signed:* William Asteley Cave Browne Cave, M.A., Minister of the above named licensed chapel, Stretton le Field rectory, nr Atherstone. [HO 129/414/20]

Church of England. S. Michael. *Erected:* Before 1800. Very ancient parish church. *Endowments:* Land £25, tithe £280, glebe £98. *Sittings:* Free 75, others 130, total 203. [*Superimposed on foregoing:* a large church].

---

[1] Population of the Derbyshire portion of the parish 105.

Attendance: Estimate morning: general congregation 40, Sunday school 6, total 46; afternoon: general congregation 60, Sunday school X, total 66. Average during 3 months: morning: general congregation 40, Sunday school 6, total 46; afternoon: general congregation 60, total 60. *Signed:* William Asteley Cave Browne Cave, M.A., Rector, Stretton le Fields Rectory, via Atherstone 20 March. [HO 129/414/21]

SEAL[1]

Netherseal

Church of England. S. Peter. *Sittings:* total 300. *Average attendance:* Morning: General congregation 60, Sunday school 60 to 70; afternoon: general congregation 60, Sunday school 60 to 70. *Signed:* Benton Dawes, Registrar, From Inquiry. [HO 129/414/24]

General Baptist. *Erected:* 1840. Separate and entire, exclusively used. *Sittings:* Free 250, others 0, free standing for 30. *Attendance:* Afternoon: general congregation 61; evening 34. *Average attendance:* general congregation 100. No general Sunday school. *Signed:* George Staples, Baptist minister, Measham. [HO 129/414/25]

Overseal

General Baptist. *Erected:* 1840. Separate and entire, exclusively used. *Sittings:* Free 244, others 3. *Attendance:* Morning: general congregation 20 to 24, Sunday school 24, total 44; evening: general congregation 75. *Average attendance:* Morning: general congregation 20, Sunday school 24; evening: general congregation 40. *Signed:* William Norton, minister, Cauldwell. [HO 129/414/26]

---

[1] The parish of Seal (population 1,085) included part of the Derbyshire township of Donisthorpe & Oakthorpe, the rest of which was in Measham and Church Gresley.

Donisthorpe[1]

An ecclesiastical district in the hamlet of Church Gresley.

Church of England. S. John. *Erected:* A church for the consolidated district of Donisthorpe, Oakthorpe and Moira. Consecrated 25 August 1838. Consecrated by the bishop as an Additional Church. By private benefaction and by grant of £400 from the Church Building Society (I believe this was the amount). Cost: Private benefaction £1600, other sources £400, total £2000. *Endowments:* Land 50, glebe X other 30, pew rents 14, fees 5 other sources 45 (Ecclesiastical Commission) Total, say £145. *Sittings:* Free 300, others 200, total 500. *Attendance: Estimate* Morning: general congregation 100, Sunday school 179, total 179; afternoon: general congregation 115, Sunday school 60, total 175. *Average attendance:* Morning: general congregation: 180, Sunday school 180, total 360; afternoon: general congregation 200, Sunday school 60, total 260. *Remarks:* Oakthorpe and Moira are each about a mile from the church. The population consists almost entirely of colliers and agricultural labourers. The diminished number of the congregation yesterday was owing to particular local causes. The average *number* given in this return is, if anything, *below the mark.* About $^2/_3$ of the afternoon congregation consists of persons not present at the morning service. Owing to the distance from the church only one school attends in the afternoon. *Signed:* Francis Jickling, incumbent of the above-named district church, Donisthorpe, Ashby de la Zouche. [HO 129/414/28]

Primitive Methodist.[2] *Erected:* Not known. Separate and entire, exclusively used. *Sittings:* Free 60, others none, no free standing. *Attendance:* Evening: general congregation 55. *Average attendance:* Evening: about 50. *Signed:* Charles Hy Boden, minister, Ashby de la Zouche, Leics. [HO 129/414/29]

---

[1] Donisthorpe (population 392) was divided between the parishes of Seal, Leics. (population 211) and Church Gresley (125) and Measham (56), Derbys.

[2] This chapel was in the parish of Seal, Leics.

Oakthorpe[1]

Wesleyan Methodist. *Erected:* About 1807. Separate and entire, exclusively used. *Sittings:* Free 150, others 67, free standing 30. *Attendance:* Morning: general congregation 50, Sunday school 42, total 92; afternoon: general congregation nil, Sunday school 43, total 43; evening: general congregation 60, total 60. *Average attendance:* general congregation 60, Sunday school 50, total 120. *Signed:* Richard Collyer, steward, Oakthorpe. [HO 129/414/30]

Primitive Methodist.[2] *Erected:* 1834. Separate and entire, exclusively used. *Sittings:* Free 120, others 10. *Attendance:* Afternoon: general congregation/Sunday school 120; evening: general congregation/Sunday school 130. *Signed:* Timothy Smith, class leader, Oakthorpe, Derbyshire. [HO 129/414/31]

SMISBY[3]

Church of England. S. James. *Erected:* not known. *Endowments:* not given. *Sittings:* Free 20, others 160, total 180. *Attendance:* Usual numbers: morning: general congregation 60 to 80, Sunday school 40; afternoon: general congregation 60 to 100, Sunday school 40. *Remarks:* Service once a day alternately. *Signed:* Benton Dawes, Registrar, From my own knowledge. [HO 129/414/32]

SEAL

Overseal

Church of England. S. Mathew. *Sittings:* Free 119, other 80, total 207. *Attendance:* Morning: general congregation 100, Sunday school 70 to 80; afternoon: general congregation ditto, Sunday school ditto. *Signed:* Benton Dawes, Registrar, From Inquiry. [HO 129/414/33]

---

[1] Oakthorpe (population 591) was divided between the parishes of Church Gresley (356), Measham and Stretton (235) in Derbyshire.

[2] This chapel was in Gresley parish.

[3] Population 293. See also p. 28.

WILLESLEY[1]

Church of England. *Erected:* Before 1800. *Endowments:* Land £32, other permanent endowments £22 10s. *Sittings:* Free 18, others 33, total 51. *Attendance:* general congregation 20. *Signed:* Wm Knight, church warden, Willesley, nr Ashby de la Zouche. [HO 129/414/34]

SMISBY[2]

Wesleyan Methodist. *Erected:* 1845. Separate and entire, exclusively used. *Sittings:* Free 80. *Attendance:* Evening: general congregation 50. *Signed:* John Hague, minister, Ashby de la Zouche. [HO 129/414/35]

HARTSHORNE[3]

Church of England. S. Peter. *Erected:* Before 1800. *Endowments:* Land £520, fees £2, total £22. *Sittings:* Free 339, others 111, total 450. *Attendance:* Morning: general congregation 97; afternoon: general congregation 107. *Average attendance:* Not given. *Signed:* Henry W. Buckley, Rector of Hartshorne, Hartshorne Rectory, nr Burton on Trent. [HO 129/414/36]

General Baptist. *Erected:* 1845. Separate and entire, exclusively used. *Sittings:* Free 84, others 16. *Attendance:* Afternoon: general congregation 45, Sunday school 19, total 64; evening: general congregation 45. *Remarks:* The society at Hartshorne is a branch of the General Baptist church at Melbourne. The informant signs as deacon of the church & is officiating at Hartshorne on this day. *Signed:* John Henry Wood, deacon, Melbourne. [HO 129/414/37]

Wesleyan Methodist. *Erected:* 1794. Separate and entire, exclusively used. *Sittings:* Free 115, others 35. *Attendance:* Afternoon: general congregation 40, total 40; evening: general congregation 100, total 100. *Signed:* John Hague, minister, Ashby de la Zouche. [HO 129/414/38; *this appears to be a duplicate of the next form*]

---

[1] Population 48. Parish transferred to Leicestershire in 1897 and to the diocese of Leicester in 1927.

[2] Population 293; see also previous page.

[3] Population 1,350.

Wesleyan Methodist.[1] *Erected:* Before 1800. Separate and entire, exclusively used. *Sittings:* Free 102, others 42. *Attendance:* Afternoon: general congregation 16; evening: general congregation 74. *Signed:* Abraham Young, chapel steward, Hartshorne. [HO 129/414/39; *this appears to be a dupliicate of the preceding form*]

REPTON

Ticknall[2]

Church of England. S. George. *Erected:* Cons. October 1842, in lieu of the old parish church, which was then taken down. Erected chiefly by the liberality of the late Sir George Crewe, Bart., of Calke Abbey, aided by private contributions and grants from the diocesan and national church building societies. Cost about £4800. *Endowments:* Land 70 acres at 2 guineas = £147, tithe £50, other permanent endowments £50, fees £5. Rates are due out of this income. *Sittings:* Free about 400, others about 300, total 700. *Attendance:* Morning: general congregation 169, Sunday school 201; afternoon: general congregation 197, Sunday school 198. *Average attendance:* Morning: general congregation not ascertainable, Sunday school 200, total 200; afternoon: general congregation not ascertainable, Sunday school 200, total 200. *Remarks:* The church accomodation is large in proportion to the population. *Signed:* Richardson Cox, Vicar, Tickenhall, Derby. [HO 129/414/40]

General Baptist. *Erected:* 1795, enlarged and rebuilt 1817. Separate and entire, exclusively used. *Sittings:* Free 240, others 14. *Attendance:* Morning: general congregation nil, Sunday school 49; afternoon: general congregation 117; evening: general congregation 250. *Remarks:* This chapel is occupied once in a fortnight by the Wesleyan Reformers, there being present last evening about 250 persons. *Signed:* John Brooks, deacon, tailor, Ticknall. [HO 129/414/41]

Wesleyan Methodist. *Erected:* 1815 Separate and entire, exclusively used. *Sittings:* Free 158, others 138. *Attendance:* Afternoon: general congregation 53; evening: general congregation 101. *Signed:* Charles Wood, society steward. [HO 129/414/42]

---

[1] This appears to be a duplicate of the preceding form.

[2] Population 1,241.

HARTSHORNE

Woodville

Church of England. S. Stephen. *Erected:* 1846 Consecrated Dec 8th 1846. *Sittings:* Free 282, others 72, total 354. *Attendance:* Morning: general congregation 70 to 90, Sunday school 95; afternoon: general congregation 85 to 110, Sunday school 97; evening: Wednesday evening & Wednesday & Friday morning under 30. *Remarks: Usual* number of *attendants* on the Sabbath 180 to 200. *Signed:* J.B. Sweet, perpetual curate. [HO 129/414/44; Registrar's form]

Ashby-de-la-Zouch Sub-District

CALKE[1]

Church of England. S. Giles. *Erected:* Supposed to be a parish church. Not known when consecrated; under what circumstances consecrated or licensed not ascertainable, supposed to be consecrated. *Endowments:* None. Clergyman's stipend a gift from Sir John Harpur Crewe, Bart. *Sittings:* Free 46, others 84, total 130. *Attendance:* Afternoon: general congregation 91, Sunday school 33, total 124. *Average attendance:* Not given. *Remarks:* Calke is a donative. *Signed:* Richardson Cox, chaplain, Tickenhall, Derby. [HO 129/414/47]

PACKINGTON[2]

Church of England. Holy Rood. *Erected:* Cons. before 1800. *Endowments:* Tithe £47 10s. (Lately commuted for a rent charge of £50), glebe £185. *Sittings:* Free 100, other 170, total 270 (exclusive of sittings for Sunday scholars). *Attendance:* Morning: general congregation 160, Sunday

---

[1] Population 79.

[2] The parish was divided between Leicestershire and Derbyshire. The parish church and the General Baptist chapel were in Leicestershire but the Wesleyan Methodist chapel was in Derbyshire. Population 1,294, of whom 277 lived in Derbyshire.

school 80, total 240; evening: general congregation 230. *Average attendance:* not given. *Signed:* Charles Pratt, curate, Packington. [HO 129/414/69]

Wesleyan Methodist. *Erected:* 1837. Separate and entire, exclusively used. *Sittings:* Free 100. *Attendance:* Afternoon: general congregation 49. *Average attendance:* not given. *Signed:* John Hague, Wesleyan minister. Ashby de la Zouch. [HO 129/414/70]

RAVENSTONE[1]

Church of England. A stone edifice dedicated to St. Michael, a Steeple and 3 bells. *Erected:* At north end of the village. Cons. before 1st Jan. 1800. *Endowments:* Land 160 acres, tithe composition £3 3s., glebe £290. *Sittings:* Free all 178. *Attendance:* Morning: general congregation 80, Sunday school 50; afternoon: general congregation 90, Sunday school 50. *Average attendance:* Morning: general congregation 80, Sunday school 50; afternoon: general congregation 90, Sunday school 50. *Remarks:* none. *Signed:* Giles Prickett, Rector, Ravenstone. [HO 129/414/73]

---

[1] Ravenstone parish was partly in Leicestershire and partly in Derbyshire: the total population was 396, of whom 188 lived in Derbyshire. The parish church was in Derbyshire and in the diocese of Lichfield but the chapelry of Snibston was in Leicestershire and the diocese of Peterborough. The Wesleyan chapel was in Leicestershire. The Derbyshire portion was transferred to Leicestershire in 1884.

WORKSOP REGISTRATION DISTRICT

Carburton Sub-District

WHITWELL[1]

Church of England. S. Laurence. *Erected:* Before 1800. *Endowments:* Tithe £642, glebe £128 1s. *Sittings:* Free 250, other 250, total 500. *Attendance:* Morning: general congregation 83, Sunday school 89, total 172; afternoon: general congregation 60, Sunday school 63, total 123. *Average attendance:* Morning: general congregation 77, Sunday school 110, total 187; afternoon: general congregation 55, Sunday school 80, total 135. *Remarks:* The number of sittings is not according to measurement but by computation of the Minister and one Churchwarden. The general average of Attendances for 12 months preceding March 30, 1851, is taken from Four Successive Sundays. *Signed:* John Ralph Dobson, minister, Whitwell. [HO 129/436/45]

ELMTON[2]

Church of England. S. Peter. *Erected:* 1771. *Endowments:* not given. *Sittings:* Free 18, other 130,total 148. *Attendance:* Morning: general congregation 30 to 40, Sunday school 0; afternoon: general congregation 20 to 30, Sunday school 0. *Average attendance:* 30 to 40. *Remarks:* Services: Morning at 11, afternoon at 3. *Signed:* Edwd Fowler, informant. [HO 129/436/46; Registrar's request form]

CLOWNE[3]

Church of England. S. John Baptist. *Sittings:* Free 10, others 100, total 110. *Attendance:* Morning: general congregation 70, Sunday school 40; afternoon: general congregation 100, Sunday school 40. *Remarks:* The Sunday school sittings are not included in the above. *Signed:* John W. Azby.[4] [HO 129/436/47; Registrar's request form]

---

[1] Population 1,355; see also p. 33.

[2] Population, including Cresswell, 435. See also p. 34.

[3] Population 660; see also p. 34.

[4] The middle initial and surname are unclear in the MS.

Wesleyan Methodist. Ebenezer chapel. *Erected:* 1845. Separate and entire, exclusively used. *Sittings:* Free 60, other 60. *Attendance:* Morning: Sunday school 40, total 40; afternoon: Sunday school 40; evening: general congregation 45. *Signed:* George Hickling, Clowne, Worksop. [HO 129/436/49]

Primitive Methodist New Connection. *Erected:* 1834. Separate and entire, exclusively used. *Sittings:* Free 30, other 32. *Attendance:* Evening 40. *Signed:* George Pepper, Clowne. [HO 129/436/50]

WHITWELL[1]

Wesleyan Methodist. *Erected:* 1821. Separate and entire, exclusively used. *Sittings:* Free 40, other 60. *Attendance:* Morning: Sunday school 20; afternoon: general congregation 50, Sunday school 20, total 70; evening: general congregation 50, total 50. *Signed:* Joseph Slaynay, Whitwell. [HO 129/436/51]

Wesleyan Methodist Association. *Erected:* August 1848. Separate and entire, exclusively used. *Sittings:* Free 30, others 90, standing 25. *Attendance:* Morning: general congregation 60, Sunday school 45, total 105; afternoon: Sunday school 45, total 45; evening: general congregation 120. *Average attendance:* Morning: general congregation 100 regularly, Sunday school 45; afternoon: Sunday school 45; evening: general congregation 120. *Signed:* Frederick Alletson, steward, Whitwell. [HO 129/436/52]

BARLBOROUGH[2]

Church of England. Parish church. *Erected:* Consecrated before 1800. *Endowments:* not given. *Sittings:* 391. See letter. *Attendance:* Morning: general congregation 102, Sunday school 50, total 152; afternoon: general congregation 87, Sunday school 34, total 121. *Average attendance:* not given. John Hawksley, curate, Barlborough. [HO 129/436/53]

Wesleyan Methodist. *Erected:* no date, not separate building, not exclusively used. *Sittings:* Free 40. See letter. *Attendance:* Evening: general

---

[1] Population 1,355; see also p. 32.
[2] Population 933.

congregation 55. *Signed:* Joseph Hopkinson, class leader, Barlborough. [HO 129/436/54]

CLOWNE[1]

Wesleyan Methodist Association. *Erected:* 1845. Separate, exclusively used. *Sittings:* Free 60, other 60. *Average attendance:* Morning: general congregation 20, Sunday school 7; afternoon: general congregation 40. *Signed:* Thomas W. Pearson, minister, Worksop. [HO 129/436/55]

ELMTON[2]

Creswell

Wesleyan Methodist Association. *Erected:* About 1835. Separate and entire, exclusively used. *Sittings:* Free 40, other 45. *Average attendance:* Morning: general congregation 40, Sunday school 30, total 70; evening: general congregation 40. *Remarks:* A day school has occasionally been taught in this chapel. *Signed:* Thomas W. Pearson, minister, Worksop, Notts. [HO 129/436/56]

---

[1] Population 660; see also p. 32.
[2] Population, including Cresswell, 435. See also p. 32.

MANSFIELD REGISTRATION DISTRICT

Pleasley Sub-District

PLEASLEY[1]

Shirebrook

Church of England. Shirebrook chapel, dedicated to the Holy Trinity, formerly was a chapel of ease to the Mother chapel of Pleasley but in 1849, Shirebrook was made a District and the Chapel a *District Chapel. Erected:* Consecrated 9 October, 1844 in lieu of an old chapel which was pulled down. Erected by Rev. J.R. Holden, Rector of Pleasley. Private benefaction £600. *Endowments:* £45. This endowment is £20 a charge on the living of Pleasley and £25 from the Ecclesiastical Commissioners. *Sittings:* Free 200. *Attendance:* Morning: general congregation 38, Sunday school 61, total 99; afternoon: general congregation 71, Sunday school 61, total 132. *Average attendance:* not given. *Signed:* Richard Lowndes, Perpetual curate, Shirebrook. [HO 129/437/13]

Pleasley

Church of England. *Erected:* Before 1800. *Endowments:* Land £50, tithe £650, glebe house, total £700. *Sittings:* Free 200. *Attendance:* Morning: general congregation 60, Sunday school 76, total 136. *Remarks:* Income £700, less rate etc £125, salary to curate of Shirebrook chapel £75, total £200; net income £500. *Signed:* Rev. James Holden, Pleasley, Mansfield. [HO 129/437/14]

Houghton

Primitive Methodist. Sunday school *Erected:* 1823. Separate and entire, exclusively used. *Sittings:* Free 80, Free standing 50. *Attendance:* Afternoon: general congregation 54, Sunday school 22. *Average attendance:* Not given. *Signed:* Francis Handley, steward, Houghton. [HO 129/437/15]

---

[1] Population 654.

Shirebrook

Primitive Methodist. *Erected:* 1849. Separate building, exclusively used. *Sittings:* Free 62, other 30, standing room 14. *Attendance:* Morning: Sunday school 12; afternoon: general congregation 30, Sunday school 12, total 42; evening: general congregation 64. *Average attendance:* Morning: Sunday school 15; afternoon: general congregation 45, Sunday school 15, total 60; evening: general congregation 75. *Signed:* William Thompson, steward, Shirebrook. [HO 129/437/16]

LANGWITH[1]

Church of England. S. Helen. Ancient parish church. *Erected:* Before 1800. *Endowments:* not given. *Sittings:* Free 77, other 83, total 160. *Attendance:* Morning: general congregation 16, Sunday school 12. *Average attendance:* not given. *Remarks:* Fees about 7s. a year. The services are a.m. and p.m. alternately. The p.m. attendance is more than treble the a.m. *Signed:* John Revill, enumerator and schoolmaster, Langwith, nr Mansfield. [HO 129/437/17]

Upper Langwith

Primitive Methodist. *Erected:* about 1814. Not separate, not exclusively used. *Sittings:* Free 60. *Attendance:* Evening: general congregation 50. *Average attendance:* not given. *Remarks:* John Charlesworth is the occupant of this dwelling house and the leader of the society meeting in the house. *Signed:* John Charlesworth, leader of the society, Upper Langwith. [HO 129/437/18]

SCARCLIFFE[2]

Church of England. S. Leonard. *Erected:* Consecrated in the 12th century. *Endowments:* Tithe £50, glebe £12, other permanent endowments £39. Income of vicar about £100 p.a. *Sittings:* 300. *Attendance:* Average for six months: Morning: general congregation from 50 to 65 or 70; afternoon:

---

[1] Population 198.
[2] Population 572.

general congregation from 100–110; Sunday scholars from 25 to 30; total 55; morning from 75 or 80 to 90 or 100; afternoon: from 125 to 135. *Signed:* Rev John Hamilton Gray, vicar of Bolsover and rural dean of Chesterfield. [HO 129/437/19]

HAULT HUCKNALL[1]

Church of England. *Erected:* Before 1800. Ancient parish church. *Endowments:* Land £18 12s. 6d., tithe £111 3s. 0d., glebe £31 10s., total £161 5s. 6d. *Sittings:* Free 18, other 282, total 300. *Attendance:* Afternoon: general congregation 150, Sunday scholars 20, total 170. *Signed:* Godfrey Arkwright, officiating minister, Hault Hucknall. [HO 129/437/20]

Hardstoft

Wesleyan Methodist New Connexion. *Erected:* 1835. Seperate and entire, exclusively used. *Sittings:* Free 12, other 39, standing for 60. *Attendance:* Morning: Sunday school 51; afternoon: general congregation 40, Sunday school 50, total 90; evening: Sunday school 68. *Average attendance:* not given. *Signed:* Robert Hickton, steward, Hardstoft. [HO 129/437/21]

Blackwell Sub-District

TIBSHELF[2]

Church of England. S. John Baptist. *Erected:* Before 1800. *Endowments:* Tithe rent charge £185 18s. 4d.; glebe 37ac. 3r. 3p., dues say £2 0s. 0d. *Sittings:* Free 100, other 200, total 300. *Attendance:* Morning: general congregation 75, Sunday school 79, total 154; afternoon: general congregation 70. *Average attendance:* Not given. *Remarks:* The Rev. F.W. Sharpe (the vicar) is at present from home tho' he has himself filled the endowment space. *Signed:* Jno. Wm. Cubbin, curate of Tibshelf, Tibshelf Vicarage, Alfreton. [HO 129/437/26]

---

[1] Population 690.

[2] Population 806; see also p. 38.

PINXTON[1]

Church of England. *Erected:* Part rebuilt about 100 years ago. Name of church forgotten. *Endowments:* not given. *Sittings:* Free nearly all, other 36. *Attendance:* Morning: general congregation 50, Sunday school 50 or 60; afternoon: general congregation 70, Sunday school 50 or 60. *Signed:* W. Mountany. [HO 129/437/27; Registrar's return]

Primitive Methodist. *Erected:* 1849. Part of a dwelling house. *Sittings:* not given. *Attendance:* Afternoon: general congregation 12; evening: general congregation 20. *Remarks:* Mary Silkstone is the wife of Thos. Silkstone the occupier. *Signed:* Mary Silkstone, Pinxton, Alfreton. [HO 129/437/28]

SOUTH NORMANTON[2]

Primitive Methodist. *Erected:* 1827. Separate and entire, exclusively used. *Sittings:* Free 44. *Attendance:* Afternoon: general congregation 20, Sunday school 100; evening: general congregation 40. *Average attendance:* not given. *Signed:* Wm Marriott's Mark, South Normanton, Alfreton. [HO 129/437/29A]

TIBSHELF[3]

Wesleyan Methodist. *Erected:* Before 1810. Separate and entire, exclusively used. *Sittings:* Free 150. *Attendance:* Afternoon: general congregation 20; evening: general congregation 20. *Average attendance:* Afternoon: general congregation 20. Sunday school 40, total 60; evening: general congregation 40, Sunday school 10, total 50. *Signed:* John Godber, steward and leader. [HO 129/437/29]

Primitive Methodist. *Erected:* Private house used for 1 year as a place of worship, not separate, not exclusively used. *Sittings:* Free 20, 81 sq. ft. will accomodate 40 persons. *Attendance:* Afternoon: general congregation 13. *Average attendance:* Afternoon general congregation 20; evening: general

---

[1] Population 943; see also p. 40.

[2] Population 1,340; see also p. 39.

[3] Population 806; see also p. 37.

congregation 20. *Signed:* Jabez Lowe, manager, Tibshelf, nr Alfreton. [HO 129/437/30]

BLACKWELL[1]

Church of England. *Erected:* not known, rebuilt 1825. *Endowments:* Land £3, tithe £80 subject to averages and other deductions; fees say £1. *Sittings:* Free 40, other 160, total 200. *Attendance:* On an average morning: general congregation 70, total 100; afternoon: general congregation 200, including 30 Sunday scholars; evening: general congregation 100. *Average attendance:* not given. *Signed:* Thos Leeson Cursham DCL, Vicar. [HO 129/437/31]

Primitive Methodist. *Erected:* Before 1800. Separate and entire, exclusively used. *Sittings:* Free 125, other 25, free standing only the isle. *Attendance:* Afternoon: general congregation 110, total 110; evening: general congregation 125, total 125. *Average attendance:* Afternoon: general congregation 60, Sunday school 30, total 90; evening: general congregation 110, Sunday school 15, total 125. *Signed:* Samuel Wilson, chapel steward, Newton, Derbyshire. [HO 129/437/32]

SOUTH NORMANTON[2]

Church of England. S. Michael. Ancient parish church. *Erected:* Before 1800. *Endowments:* Land £60, tithe £280, glebe £30, fees £4. *Sittings:* Free 50, other 300, total 350. *Attendance:* Afternoon: general congregation 90, Sunday school 55, total 145. *Average attendance:* Morning: general congregation 45, Sunday school 55, total 100; afternoon: general congregation 90, Sunday school 55, total 145; evening: general congregation 87. *Remarks:* The services are alternately morning and afternoon, with a regular evening service. *Signed:* Rd Howard Frizell, curate, South Normanton. [HO 129/437/33]

Wesleyan Methodist. *Erected:* 1846. Entire, Sunday school. *Sittings:* Free 100, others 40. *Attendance:* Afternoon: general congregation 50; evening:

[1] Population 467.
[2] Population 1,340; see also p. 38.

general congregation 60. *Signed:* Samuel Gill, steward, South Normanton. [HO 129/437/34]

Original Methodists. *Erected:* 1800. Separate and entire, exclusively used. *Sittings:* 50 yards space, Free 110. *Attendance:* Afternoon: general congregation 20, Sunday school 32, total 52; evening: general congregation 54. *Average attendance:* Afternoon: general congregation 20, Sunday school 30, total 50; evening: general congregation 50. *Remarks:* The ministers who preach at this Chapel are all unpaid Ministers. Both the school and the congregation are gradually increasing but the whole of the scholars do not allways attend the afternoon service and none in the evening, not in the capasity of Scholars. *Signed:* John Tomlinson, chapel steward, South Normanton. [HO 129/437/35]

PINXTON[1]

Wesleyan Methodist. Pinxton Wharf chapel. *Erected:* Built before 1830. Separate and entire, exclusively used. *Sittings:* Free 33, other 0. *Attendance:* Morning: Sunday school 97; afternoon: general congregation 65, Sunday school 76, total 141; evening: general congregation 72, Sunday school 37, total 109. *Signed:* Thomas Reynolds, manager, Pinxton Wharf. [HO 129/437/36]

Primitive Methodist. *Attendance:* evening: general congregation 30. *Signed:* Francis Mycroft, leader, farmer, Pinxton. [HO 129/437/37]

Wesleyan Methodist. *Erected:* 1842. Separate and entire, exclusively used. *Sittings:* Free X, other 20, standing 120. *Attendance:* Afternoon: general congregation 25, Sunday school 60, total 85; evening: general congregation 56, Sunday school 25, total 81. *Average attendance:* Afternoon: general congregation 25, Sunday school 60, total 85; evening: general congregation 56, Sunday school 25, total 81. *Signed:* Jas Evans, Wesleyan, Pinxton. [HO 129/437/38]

---

[1] Population 943; see also p. 38.

BASFORD REGISTRATION DISTRICT

Greasley Sub-district

HEANOR

Codnor[1]

Church of England. *Erected:* New parish church of Codnor and Loscoe. Built under the provisions of 6 & 7 Victoria c. 37. Consecrated 10 October 1845. Cost: Diocesan Society £350, Incorporated Society £250, private benefaction £1,100, total £1,700. *Endowments:* Ecclesiastical Commissioners £150. *Sittings:* Total 400. *Attendance:* Morning: general congregation 60, Sunday school 60, total 120; afternoon: general congregation 150, Sunday school 70, total 220. *Signed:* Henry Middleton, minister, Ripley, Alfreton. [HO 129/438/30]

Wesleyan Methodist. *Erected:* 1827. Separate and entire, exclusively used. *Sittings:* Free 180, other 105. *Attendance:* Morning: Sunday school 174; afternoon: general congregation 50, Sunday school 174, total 224; evening: general congregation 160. *Signed:* John Peake, trustee. Codnor, Derby. [HO 129/438/31]

Loscoe

Particular Baptist. *Erected:* Before 1810. Separate and entire, exclusively used. *Sittings:* Free 400. *Attendance:* Afternoon: general congregation 200; evening 250. *Remarks:* No regular minister; having supplies. *Signed:* Thomas Hickling, deacon, Loscoe. [HO 129/438/32]

---

[1] Population 1,439, including Loscoe (population 451); the parish adjoined the extra-parochial district of Codnor Park (735).

Ilkeston Sub-District

Heanor[1]

Church of England. S. Mary. *Erected:* Before 1800. *Endowments:* Land £60, glebe £33, other permanent endowments £47, fees £10. *Sittings:* Free 50, other 600, total 650. *Attendance:* Morning: general congregation 200, Sunday school 100, total 300; afternoon: general congregation 200, Sunday school 100, total 300; evening: general congregation 50, Sunday school 20, total 70. *Signed:* Blain Mandale, curate. [HO 129/438/34]

Millhay

Primitive Methodist. *Erected:* 1836. Separate and entire, Preaching, Sunday school, day school, night school. *Sittings:* Free 60, other 50. *Attendance:* Afternoon: general congregation 79; evening: general congregation 82. *Average attendance:* Morning: Sunday school 90; afternoon: general congregation 40, Sunday school 90, total 130; evening: general congregation 50. *Signed:* Joseph Watson, trustee, Langley Mill. [HO 129/438/35]

Langley Mill

General Baptist New Connexion. *Erected:* October 1839. Separate and entire, exclusively used. *Sittings:* Free 129, other 21. *Attendance:* Afternoon: general congregation 54, Sunday school 89, total 143; evening: general congregation 75. *Remarks:* This place of worship and the school connected with it are out of debt and are in the hands of trustees appointed by the society. There is no gallery in it but it is in contemplation to erect one. *Signed:* Wm. Stanhope, deacon, Langley, near Heanor, Derby. [HO 129/438/37]

Heanor

Wesleyan Methodist. *Erected:* 1839. Separate and entire, exclusively used. *Sittings:* Free 318, other 214. *Attendance:* Morning: general congregation 92, Sunday school 136, total 228; evening: general congregation 167.

---

[1] Population 3,427; the parish also included Shipley (665).

42

Average attendance: Morning: general congregation 137, Sunday school 141, total 278; evening: general congregation 244. *Signed:* John Horridge, chapel steward, Heanor. [HO 129/438/37]

Quakers. Friends Meeting House. *Erected:* 1834. *Sittings:* Measurement in superficial feet: floor 757, gallery 273, total 1030. Approximately 300. *Attendance:* Morning 13. No meeting in afternoon or evening. *Remarks:* The Bible Meetings are held occasionally also lectures on Philanthropic subjects. *Signed:* Francis T. Howitt, Heanor. Signed by special appointment of the Chesterfield monthly meeting. [HO 129/438/38]

Latter Day Saints. *Erected:* Separate and entire, exclusively used. *Sittings:* Free 70, standing 30. *Attendance:* Morning: general congregation and Sunday school 15; afternoon: 50; evening: 70. *Signed:* Samuel Gamble, secretary, Heanor, nr Belper, Derbys. [HO 129/438/39]

General Baptist. *Erected:* 1849. *Sittings:* Free 200, other 35. *Attendance:* Afternoon: general congregation 51, Sunday school 53; evening: general congregation 67; total 171. *Signed:* Thomas Cresswell, local preacher, Shipley, Derbyshire. [HO 129/438/40]

Primitive Methodist. Hope Chapel. *Erected:* 1849. Separate and entire, exclusively used. *Sittings:* Others 42. *Attendance:* Afternoon: general congregation 80, Sunday school 81; evening: general congregation 100. *Average attendance:* The same. *Signed:* George Birley, Suprintendent & Society steward, Traviler, Heanor. [HO 129/438/41]

Congregational Independent. Mount Zion chapel. *Erected:* 1821. Separate and entire, exclusively used. *Sittings:* Free 265, other 215. *Attendance:* Morning: general congregation 150, Sunday school 218, total 368; afternoon: Sunday school 332; evening: general congregation 230. *Average attendance:* Morning: general congregation 150, Sunday school 210, total 360; afternoon: Sunday school 300; evening: general congregation 300. *Remarks:* For 30th March the total number is correct but for the morning service the division into general congregation and Sunday Scholars is supposed, a very large number of Sunday Scholars being adult, married and able to read and write well. *Signed:* Henry Brentnall, deacon, Shipley, Derbys. [HO 129/438/42]

Cotmanhay[1]

Church of England. Christ church. Church of a new parish. *Erected:* Consecrated 26 April 1848 as an additional church. By subscription, private benefaction, total cost £2650. *Endowments:* Other permanent endowment £150. *Sittings:* Free 600. *Attendance:* Morning: general congregation 130, Sunday school 73, total 203; afternoon: general congregation 150, Sunday school 75, total 225. *Signed:* E.W. Symons, incumbent, Cotmanhay, Nottingham. [HO 129/438/43]

ILKESTON[2]

Church of England commonly called S. Mary. An ancient parish church. *Erected:* Consecrated before 1800. *Endowments:* Land £10, glebe £100, other permanent endowment annual benefaction of the Duke of Rutland £100, fees £22, Ecclesiastical Commissioner £34; total gross £266, net £238. *Sittings:* Free 512. *Attendance:* Morning: general congregation 105, Sunday scholars 196, total 301; afternoon: general congregation 170, Sunday scholars 212, total 382. *Average attendance:* Morning: general congregation 150, Sunday school 250, total 400; afternoon: general congregation 250, Sunday school 250, total 500. *Signed:* Octavius Claydon, curate, Ilkeston. [HO 129/438/44]

Cotmanhay

Primitive Methodist. Cotmanhay Room. *Erected:* N.K. Not separate, not exclusively used. *Attendance:* Evening: general congregation 35. *Average attendance:* Evening: 40. *Signed:* Saml Sisson, leader, Cotmanhay. [HO 129/438/45]

Ilkeston

Primitive Methodist. Slade Chapel. *Erected:* 1823 and 1824, separate and entire, exclusively used. *Sittings:* Free 170, other 160, standing none. *Attendance:* Morning: general congregation 60, Sunday school 105; afternoon: Sunday school 190; evening: general congregation 300. *Average*

---

[1] Population 2,129; see also p. 46.

[2] Populatiom 6,122.

attendance: during 6 months. Morning: general congregation 50, Sunday school 165, total 215; afternoon: Sunday school 190; evening: general congregation 300. *Remarks:* Filled in to the best of our knowledge. *Signed:* John Robinson, chapel steward, Bath St, Ilkeston. [HO 129/438/46]

Wesleyan Methodist Reformers. *Erected:* Before 1800. *Sittings:* Free 180, other 160, standing 30. *Attendance:* Morning: general congregation 100, Sunday school 170; afternoon: Sunday school 250; evening: general congregation 350. *Average attendance:* not given. *Signed:* Samuel Carrier, steward, Ilkeston. [HO 129/438/47]

General Baptist. South St. *Erected:* Before 1800. Separate and entire, exclusively used. *Sittings:* Free 104, other 196. *Attendance:* Morning: general congregation 91, Sunday school 107, total 198; afternoon: Sunday school 122; evening: general congregation 204. *Average attendance:* not given. *Signed:* Caleb Springthorpe, minister, Lawn Cottage, Ilkeston. [HO 129/438/48]

Unitarian Old Meeting House. Anchor Row. *Erected:* Before 1800. *Sittings:* Free 100. See letter. *Attendance:* Afternoon: general congregation: 10 to 12. *Average attendance:* Afternoon: from ten to twelve. *Signed:* Mark Whitehouse, minister, 10 Agard St Derby. [HO 129/438/49]

Wesleyan Methodist. *Erected:* 1845 in lieu of one erected before 1800. Separate and entire, exclusively used. *Sittings:* Free 250, other 280. *Attendance:* Morning: general congregation 35, Sunday school 30; evening: general congregation 50. *Average attendance:* Morning: general congregation 120, Sunday school 170; evening: general congregation 150. *Remarks:* The usual Average attendance has been lately affected by certain temporary local circumstances.[1] *Signed:* Alexr Hume, minister. [HO 129/438/50]

---

[1] In a letter to John Beecham, then President of the Methodist Conference, dated 5 November 1850, Alexander Hume outlines these 'temporary local circumstances': 'such is the state of anarchy and disruption in which we found the circuit, we have not been able to take any account of who are members and who are not, so that for the last quarter the Schedule Book is a *blank*. With the exception of *one* or *two* only of the congregations, all the congregations in the circuit are the most disorderly riotous assemblies of wild beasts: and the *pulpits* regularly the spit of contention between the *authorised* local preachers and those patronised by the mob. I have instructed the Brethren on the Plan [i.e. the local preachers] to retire quietly from the ungodly contest when they have claimed their places. ... I do not think it right to be any further a party to the desecration of all that is sacred on God's day, by contending with infuriated men, some of whom have again and again, squared their fists in my face in regular pugilistic style and all but struck me ...' (Quoted by W.R. Ward, *Religion and society in England, 1790–1850* (1972), p. 269).

Independent. *Erected:* Before 1800. Separate and entire, exclusively used. *Sittings:* Free none, other 320. *Attendance:* Morning: general congregation 103, Sunday school 75, total 178; evening: general congregation 143, Sunday school 22, total 165. *Average attendance:* Morning: general congregation 130, Sunday school 70, total 200; evening: general congregation 200, Sunday school 30, total 230. *Remarks:* Although there are no 'Free sittings' in the Independent Chapel, Ilkeston that is, *professedly so and marked out as such,* yet there are poor people amongst us who regularly occupy sittings without any charge – thus enjoying the advantage of a free sitting, without having the badge of poverty affixed to it. *Signed:* Charles Hargreaves, minister. Ilkeston. [HO 129/438/51]

Cotmanhay[1]

Wesleyan Methodist Reformers. *Erected:* 1806. Separate and entire, exclusively used. *Sittings:* Free 140, other 75, standing 60, space 10 yards x 8. *Attendance:* Morning: Sunday school 129, teachers 10, total 139; afternoon: general congregation 40, Sunday school 135, total 175; evening: general congregation 109. *Average attendance:* Afternoon: general congregation 30, Sunday school 130, total 160; evening: general congregation 70. *Remarks:* Owing to the proceedings of the Wesleyan Conference which hath caused the very extencive agatation in the conexion and the arbatrary conduct of the preachers in the Ilkeston circuit in expelling a number of righteous men without charge or trial the number of worshippers has greatly decreased the last twelve months to what there formerly were.[2] *Signed:* Matthew Strangeways, chapel steward, Cotmanhay. [HO 129/438/54]

---

[1] See also p. 44.

[2] Many members of the Ilkeston Wesleyan Circuit were expelled because they contributed to the fund for the relief of the three expelled ministers (William Smith, *A history of Methodism in the Ilkeston Circuit, 1809–1909* (n.d.), pp. 38ff.).

SHARDLOW REGISTRATION DISTRICT

PART 1

Melbourne Sub-District

MELBOURNE[1]

Church of England. S. Michael. *Erected:* Before 1800. *Endowments:* Land £165, glebe £5, other £35, total £208; deduct payments to Queen Annes's Bounty money £35 = £173. *Sittings:* Free 70, other 240, total 310, beside children of schools. *Attendance:* Morning: general congregation 89, Sunday school 59, total 148; afternoon: general congregation 99, Sunday school 74, total 173; evening: general congregation 86. *Remarks:* There is a licensed room for Public worship at King's Newton in this parish for which a return is sent. *Signed:* Joseph Deans, vicar of Melbourne, Melbourne. [HO 129/444/24]

King's Newton

Church of England. Licensed room. *Erected:* Jan.1851 for additional accomodation. *Sittings:* Free 120. *Attendance:* Afternoon: 100. *Signed:* Joseph Deans, vicar of Melbourne. [HO 129/444/25]

Wesleyan Methodist. Preaching room. *Erected:* Occupied since 1849, not separate, not exclusively used. *Sittings:* Free 30. *Attendance:* Afternoon: general congregation 10. *Average attendance:* Afternoon: general congregation 20. *Signed:* John Parks, Wesleyan minister, Castle Donington. [HO 129/444/26]

---

[1] Population 2,680.

Melbourne

General Baptist. *Erected:* 1750. Rebuilt and enlarged 1832, separate and entire, exclusively used. *Sittings:* Free 150, other 420, total adults 570, standing none except the aisles. *Attendance:* Morning: general congregation 200, Sunday school 250 [*Note added:* The congregations below average on Mar. 30 for a special occasion.], total 450; evening: general congregation 350 *Average attendance:* Morning: general congregation 250, Sunday school 290, total 540; evening: general congregation 480. *Remarks:* From 60 to 100 of the smaller S.S. children attend a separate service in the school room on Sabbath mornings instead of coming into chapel. These are included in the morning total. *Signed:* Thomas Gill, Regular minister, Melbourne. [HO 129/444/27]

Wesleyan Methodist. *Erected:* Before 1800, separate and entire, exclusively used. *Sittings:* Free 130, other 170. *Attendance:* Morning: general congregation 75, Sunday school 90, total 165; evening: general congregation 180. *Average attendance:* Morning: general congregation 90, Sunday school 90, total 180; evening: general congregation 180. *Signed:* John Parks, Wesleyan minister, Castle Donington. [HO 129/444/28]

New Jerusalem Chapel. Penn Lane. *Erected:* 1825. Separate, adjoining to dwelling house, exclusively used. *Sittings:* All free. There may be standing room for perhaps 30 persons. *Attendance:* Morning: general congregation 30, Sunday school 26, total 56; evening: general congregation 54. *Average attendance:* See above. *Remarks:* Out of the 56 attending in the morning there were 26 Sunday school children. These, it will be seen I have deducted leaving 30 Adults as the morning congregation and 54 as the evening. This I am told has been about the average attendance for the last 6 months. I have only acted as Minister during the last 2 months. *Signed:* David Geo. Goyder, minister, Melbourne. [HO 129/444/29]

Independent alias **Congregationalists.** *Erected:* 1779 Separate and entire, exclusively used. *Sittings:* Free 50, other 190. *Attendance:* Morning: general congregation 32, Sunday school 45, total 77; afternoon: Sunday school 51; evening: general congregation 55. *Average attendance:* Morning: general congregation 30, Sunday school 50, total 80; afternoon: Sunday school 60; evening: general congregation 50. *Remarks:* Remark 1. Total and immediate abolition of *all* Church Rates. 2. The immediate and complete separation of the church from the state 3. The National Universities to be open to *all* classes of Her Majestie's subjects. *Signed:* Joseph Watts Lethbridge, minister, Melbourne. [HO 129/444/30]

STANTON BY BRIDGE[1]

Church of England. S. Michael. *Erected:* Ancient. *Endowments:* Land £348 10s.; fees £1. *Sittings:* Free 97, other 90, total 187. *Attendance:* Morning: general congregation 44, Sunday school 21, total 65; afternoon: general congregation 60, Sunday school 19, total 79. *Average attendance:* Morning: general congregation 40, Sunday school 20, total 60; afternoon: general congregation 65, Sunday school 22, total 87. *Signed:* Thos W. Whitaker, Rectory, Swarkestone. [HO 129/444/3]

BARROW ON TRENT[2]

Church of England. S. Luke.[3] *Endowments:* The living is a vicarage valued in the King's Books £5 18s. 5d. now £115. *Sittings:* Free 70, other 250, total 320. *Attendance:* Morning: no service; afternoon: general congregation 70, Sunday school 22, total 92; evening: no service. *Average attendance:* Morning: general congregation 50, Sunday school 22, total 72; afternoon: general congregation 70, Sunday school 22, total 92. *Signed:* James R. Holmes, curate of Barrow. [HO 129/444/32]

Congregational or Independent Bethel. *Erected:* 1839. Separate and exclusively used. *Sittings:* Free 80, other 96. *Attendance:* Morning: Sunday school 41; afternoon: Sunday school 41; evening: general congregation 60. *Average attendance:* Morning: general congregation 38, Sunday school 37, total 75; afternoon: general congregation 60, Sunday school 37, total 97, evening: general congregation 65. *Remarks:* Divine Service in this chapel alternate being one Sunday in the Morning and Afternoon, the other in the evening. On March 30 1851 the Public Worship was in the evening. The Sunday School Meeting in the morning and afternoon. *Signed:* Horatio Ault, minister, Repton, Burton on Trent. [HO 129/444/33]

Wesleyan Methodist. *Erected:* 1839. Not separate and entire, exclusively used. *Sittings:* Free 48, other 22, standing none. *Attendance:* Afternoon: general congregation 30; evening: general congregation 70; no school. *Average attendance:* Afternoon: general congregation 35; evening: general

---

[1] Population 215.

[2] Population 577.

[3] The present dedication is to St Wilfrid.

congregation 60. *Signed:* James Bentley, steward, Barrow, nr Derby. [HO 129/444/34]

SWARKESTON[1]

Church of England. S. James. *Erected:* Before 1800. *Endowments:* £170. Fees 15s. other sources £11 17s. *Sittings:* Free 100, other 100, total 200. *Attendance:* Morning: general congregation 45, Sunday school 25, total 70; afternoon: general congregation 86, Sunday school 25, total 111. *Average attendance:* Morning: general congregation 40, Sunday school 35, total 75; afternoon: general congregation 80, Sunday school 35, total 115. *Signed:* John Moss Webb, curate, Swarkestone nr Derby. [HO 129/444/35]

Wesleyan Methodist. *Erected:* School room, not separate, not exclusively used. *Sittings:* Free 70. *Attendance:* Evening: general congregation 50. *Signed:* Sampson Massey, steward, Swarkestone, nr Derby. [HO 129/444/36]

WESTON ON TRENT[2]

Church of England. S. Mary. *Erected:* not given. *Endowments:* Tithe scarcely any. Glebe chiefly £594, fees about 10s. *Sittings:* Free about 90, other probably 60, total 150. *Attendance:* no returns given. *Average attendance:* morning: general congregation varies, Sunday school 65; afternoon general congregation: varies, Sunday school 65. *Signed:* William Dewe, curate, Weston on Trent, Derby. [HO 129/444/37]

Wesleyan Methodist. *Erected:* 1846. Separate and entire, exclusively used. *Sittings:* Free 70, other 30, standing none. *Attendance:* Afternoon: general congregation 22, Sunday school 15, total 37; evening: general congregation 33, Sunday school 2, total 35. *Signed:* William Henshaw, steward, Weston on Trent, nr Chellaston. [HO 129/444/38]

General Baptist. *Erected:* 1845. Separate and entire, exclusively used. *Sittings:* Free 90, other 16, standing none. *Attendance:* Afternoon: general congregation 20; evening: general congregation 50. *Signed:* Matthew Newbold, Manager, Weston on Trent.[HO 129/444/39]

---

[1] Population 289.

[2] Population 399.

Shardlow Sub-District

ASTON ON TRENT[1]

Church of England. *Erected:* Before 1800. *Endowments:* not given. *Sittings:* Free 400. *Attendance:* Morning: general congregation about 200, Sunday school 100, total 300; afternoon: general congregation about 250, Sunday school 100, total 350; evening: no service. *Average attendance:* not given. *Remarks:* Having only very recently been presented to the living I am unable accurately to reply to the other questions. *Signed:* F.A. Weekes, Rector, Aston on Trent. [HO 129/444/40]

Shardlow[2]

Church of England. S. James. *Erected:* 1839. Cons. as an additional church. Erected by private benefaction, cost £4,285 19s. 11d. *Endowments:* Tithe £65. *Sittings:* Free 69 pews = 414, total 414. *Attendance:* Morning: general congregation 106, Sunday school 124, total 230; afternoon: general congregation 138, Sunday school 118, total 256. *Remarks:* The amount of living is about £350. Some children who attend school were absent from church. *Signed:* John Eaton, minister, Cavendish Bridge, nr Derby. [HO 129/444/41]

Church of England. Large room in which Divine Service is regularly performed by the Chaplain according to the rites of the Church of England. *Erected:* By the guardians of the Shardlow Poor Law Union as a part of the Union Workhouse. *Endowments:* Other sources £50. *Sittings:* Free 160. *Attendance:* Afternoon: general congregation 100. *Average attendance:* general congregation 100. *Remarks:* Not being confident that this form applies to places of worship in Union workhouses, I shall (if the return be incorrect) be happy to supply any information which may be desired on receiving an application. *Signed:* John Bamford, Master of the Union House, Shardlow. [HO 129/444/42]

---

[1] Population 693.

[2] Population, including Great Wilne, 1,121.

Aston on Trent

Wesleyan Methodist. *Erected:* 1830. Seperate and entire, exclusively used. *Sittings:* Free 100, other 24, standing room 15. *Attendance:* Evening: general congregation 120. *Average attendance:* Morning: Sunday school 60; afternoon: Sunday school 60; evening: general congregation 80, Sunday school 60, total 140. *Signed:* Thomas Cook, deacon, Aston on Trent. [HO 129/444/43]

Shardlow

Primitive Methodist. *Erected:* Used as a dwelling house as well. *Sittings:* about 30. *Attendance:* No services. *Average attendance:* Afternoon: general congregation 15; evening: general congregation 20. *Signed:* Abimelech Hainsworth Coulson, Superintendant Minister, 45 Copeland St, Derby. [HO 129/444/44]

Wilne

Methodist New Connexion. *Erected:* 1816. Separate and entire, only used as a place of worship and Sunday school. *Sittings:* Free 170, other 31. *Attendance:* Morning: general congregation 24, Sunday school 30, total 54; afternoon: general congregation 40; evening: general congregation 50, Sunday school 31, total 81. *Remarks:* We have a Debt of £200 on the Chapel. *Signed:* W.H. Chambers, steward, Wilne, nr Shardlow. [HO 129/444/45]

General Baptist. *Erected:* 1830. Separate and entire, exclusively used. *Sittings:* Free 80, other 70. *Attendance:* Evening: general congregation 70. *Remarks:* The service is held in this Chapel every Sabath Evening and every Tuesday Evening. *Signed:* Thomas Gilbert, Manager, Shardlow. [HO 129/444/46]

CHELLASTON[1]

Church of England. S. Peter. *Erected:* Before 1800. *Endowments:* Land £80. *Sittings:* Free 145, other 76, total 321. *Attendance:* Morning: general congregation 38, Sunday school 45, total 83; afternoon: general congregation 50, Sunday school 45, total 95. *Average attendance:* Morning: general congregation 35, Sunday school 40, total 75; afternoon: general congregation 45, Sunday school 40, total 85. *Remarks:* The Revd F.F. O'Donaghue with whom the form was left has neglected to enter the number of persons attending Divine Service Sunday March 30 1851. They were correctly taken by the enumerator. *Signed:* Charles Forman.[2] Fredc F. O'Donoghue, curate, Chellaston. [HO 129/444/47]

Wesleyan Methodist. *Erected:* 1816. Separate and entire, exclusively used. *Sittings:* Free 97, other 24. *Attendance:* Afternoon: general congregation 36, Sunday school 42, total 78; evening: general congregation 118. *Signed:* Henry Forman, chapel steward, farmer, Chellaston. [HO 129/444/48]

General Baptist. *Erected:* 1832. Separate and entire, exclusively used. *Sittings:* Free 70. *Attendance:* Afternoon: general congregation 16; evening: general congregation 30. *Average attendance:* general congregation 20; evening: general congregation 35. *Signed:* John Stevens, chapel steward, farmer, Chellaston. [HO 129/444/49]

NORMANTON[3]

Church of England. S. Giles. Church of an ancient chapelry of S.Peter Derby. *Erected:* Before 1800. *Endowments:* Land £46, tithe £13 14s., fees £5, Easter offering £1 5s. *Sittings:* Free 40, other 70, total 150. *Attendance:* Morning: general congregation 54, Sunday school 43, total 97; afternoon: general congregation 50, Sunday school 43, total 93. *Average attendance:* Morning: general congregation 20, Sunday school 60, total 80; afternoon: general congregation 40, Sunday school 60, total 100. *Signed:* William Hope, M.A. Vicar. The Vicarage, S. Peter's Derby. [HO 129/444/50]

---

[1] Population 499.

[2] This was entered in the enumerator's hand.

[3] Population 385.

Independent. *Erected:* 1844. *Sittings:* Free 120 see letter. *Attendance:* Afternoon: general congregation 22; evening 18. *Signed:* James Gawthorn, minister, Becket Well Lane, Derby. [HO 129/444/51]

Primitive Methodist. *Erected:* 1820. Not separate, exclusively used. *Sittings:* not given. *Attendance:* Afternoon: general congregation 15; evening: general congregation 30. *Signed:* Thos Roe, Assistant Leader, Normanton, nr Derby. [HO 129/444/52]

MICKLEOVER

Littleover[1]

Church of England. S. Peter. The church of an ancient chapelry attached to the mother church of Mickleover. *Erected:* Before 1800. *Endowments:* Land £105, tithe £22, fees £2. *Sittings:* Other 80. *Attendance:* Morning: general congregation 48, Sunday school 20. *Signed:* Joseph Sowter, curate, Findern, nr Derby. [HO 129/444/53]

General Baptist. *Erected:* 1820. Separate and entire, exclusively used. *Sittings:* Free 100. *Attendance:* Afternoon: general congregation 33, Sunday school 56, total 89; evening: general congregation 43. *Average attendance:* Morning: general congregation: 40, Sunday school 53, total 93. *Signed:* Jos. Hadfield, Local Preacher, 94 Park St. Derby. [HO 129/444/54]

Primitive Methodist. *Erected:* cannot tell. Separate and entire, exclusively used. *Sittings:* Free 80, standing 20. *Attendance:* none. *Average attendance:* In the previous 3 months. Afternoon: general congregation 30; evening: general congregation 80. *Remarks:* Rented by the Primitive Methodists three months ago. Formerly occupied by the Wesleyan Methodists. *Signed:* Abimelech Hainsworth Coulson, Superintendant minister, 45 Copeland St, Derby. [HO 129/444/55]

---

[1] Population 551.

OSMASTON[1]

Church of England. *Erected:* not given. *Endowments:* not given. *Sittings:* not given. *Attendance:* Afternoon: general congregation 50, Sunday school 3, total 53. *Average attendance:* not given. *Signed:* John Gilman, Churchwarden, Osmaston. [HO 129/444/56]

BOULTON[2]

Church of England. Ancient church or chapel formerly belonging to S. Peter Derby. *Erected:* before 1800. *Endowments:* Glebe or land £115, other permanent endowments £5, fees 15s. *Sittings:* Free 180, others 12, total 192. *Attendance:* Morning service in Alvaston; afternoon: general congregation 120, Sunday school 70, total 190. *Average attendance:* Morning: general congregation 95, Sunday school 65, total 160; afternoon: general congregation 135, Sunday school 65, total 200. *Remarks:* The service is alternately morning and afternoon at Alvaston and Boulton the churches being within half a mile of each other. *Signed:* Edward Poole, Incumbent, Alvaston, nr Derby. [HO 129/444/57]

ALVASTON[3]

Church of England. *Erected:* before 1800. An ancient church or chapel formerly belonging to S. Michael, Derby. *Endowments:* Glebe or land £150, fees £1 5s., other sources £1 10s. 10d. *Sittings:* total 180. *Attendance:* Morning: general congregation 87, Sunday school 69, total 156; afternoon service this day at Boulton. *Average attendance:* Morning: general congregation 100, Sunday school 65, total 165; afternoon: general congregation 125, Sunday school 65, total 190. *Remarks:* The service is alternately morning and afternoon at Alvaston and Boulton, the churches being within half a mile of each other. *Signed:* Edward Poole, Vicar [HO 129/444/][4]

---

[1] Population 125.

[2] Population 206.

[3] Population, including the extra-parochial liberty of Sinfin Mor, 504.

[4] This form has no official number and written in pencil at the head is 'not in list'.

ELVASTON[1]

Church of England. S. Bartholomew. *Erected:* an ancient parish church. Consecrated before 1800. *Endowments:* not given. *Sittings:* Free 46, other 180, total 226. *Attendance:* Morning: general congregation 127, Sunday school 44, total 171; evening: general congregation 72, Sunday school 20, total 92. *Average attendance:* Morning: general congregation 150, Sunday school 50, total 200; evening: general congregation 160, Sunday school 30, total 190. *Remarks:* The incumbent is absent on licence in consequence of illness and the churchwarden does not know the particulars of the endowment. *Signed:* Eggleston Thacker, churchwarden, Ambaston Grange, Shardlow. [HO 129/444/58]

Wesleyan Methodist. *Erected:* Part of a house, not separate, not exclusively used. *Sittings:* not given. *Attendance:* Afternoon: general congregation 27. *Average attendance:* Afternoon: general congregation 27. *Signed:* Samuel Woodward, occupier, Thulston. [HO 129/444/59]

Ambaston

Wesleyan Methodist. *Erected:* 1832. Seperate and entire, exclusively used. *Sittings:* Free 64, other 16, standing 20. *Attendance:* Morning: no service; afternoon: general congregation 28, Sunday school 15, total 43; evening: general congregation 42, Sunday school 7, total 49. *Average attendance:* general congregation 42, Sunday school 16, total 58. *Signed:* Thomas Smith, Manager and Steward, Ambaston. [HO 129/444/60]

---

[1] Population 498.

PART 2

Stapleford Sub-District

CHURCH WILNE[1]

Risley[2]

Church of England. *Erected:* Church or chapel in the parish or soke of Sawley. Consecrated before 1800. *Endowments:* not given. *Sittings:* Free 109, other 140, total 249. *Attendance:* No returns given. *Remarks:* This Benefice is the united perpetual curacy of Risley and Breaston. *Signed:* H.B. Hall, Incumbent, Risley, nr Derby. [HO 129/444/1]

SAWLEY[3]

Church of England. All Saints. *Erected:* before 1800. *Endowments:* Land £12, glebe house and garden, other permanent endowment £176, fees £5. *Sittings:* Free 250, other 250, total 500. *Attendance:* Morning: general congregation 82, Sunday school 97, total 179; afternoon: general congregation 116, Sunday school 95, total 211; evening: no service. *Average attendance:* Morning: general congregation 95, Sunday school 95, total 190; afternoon: general congregation 125, Sunday school 110, total 235. *Signed:* Samuel Hey, minister, Sawley, nr Derby. [HO 129/444/2]

Long Eaton[4]

Church of England. Chapel of S. Lawrence. *Erected:* Consecrated before 1800. *Endowments:* Fees (surplice) £3. *Sittings:* Free 190, other 60, total 250. *Attendance:* Morning: general congregation 27, Sunday school 50, total 77; afternoon: general congregation 85, Sunday school 60, total 145. *Signed:* Henry Dickenson Hubbard, curate, Long Eaton, Derby. [HO 129/444/3]

---

[1] Parish population 2,094.

[2] Population 211.

[3] Parish population, including Wilsthorpe and Long Eaton, 1,934.

[4] Population 933.

Sawley[1]

Primitive Methodist. *Erected:* 1819. Separate and entire, exclusively used. *Sittings:* Free 120, other 45, standing 25. *Attendance:* not given. *Average attendance:* Morning: general congregation 40; evening: general congregation 120. *Remarks:* We, the Primitive Methodists purchased the chapel of the Methodist New Connexion about four months ago. *Signed:* Abimelech Hainsworth Coulson, Superintendant minister, 45 Copeland St, Derby. [HO 129/444/4]

Wesleyan Methodist. *Erected:* 1823. Separate and entire, exclusively used. *Sittings:* Free 102, other 48. *Attendance:* Afternoon: general congregation 50, Sunday school 23, total 73; evening: general congregation 90. *Average attendance:* Afternoon: general congregation 70, Sunday school 23. *Signed:* Robert Tingle, steward, Sawley. [HO 129/444/5]

General Baptist. *Erected:* 1800. Separate and entire, exclusively used. *Sittings:* Free 145, other 165. *Attendance:* Afternoon: general congregation 130, Sunday school 68, total 198; evening: general congregation 120. *Average attendance:* not given. *Signed:* William Bennett, Deacon, Sawley. [HO 129/444/6]

Long Eaton

Wesleyan Reformers. *Erected:* 1830. Separate and entire, exclusively used. *Sittings:* Free 80, other 135. *Attendance:* Morning: general congregation 70, Sunday school 120, total 190; evening: general congregation 144. *Average attendance:* Morning: general congregation 110, Sunday school 130, total 240; evening: general congregation 160. *Signed:* James Purcell, local preacher, Denton St, New Radford. [HO 129/444/8]

Primitive Methodist. *Erected:* Made into chapel June 1849, separate and entire, exclusively used. *Sittings:* Free 70. *Attendance:* Afternoon: general congregation 60; evening: general congregation 60. *Average attendance:* Afternoon: general congregation 50; evening: general congregation 50. *Signed:* William Clay, Local Preacher and Steward, Long Eaton, Derby. [HO 129/444/9]

---

[1] Population, with Wilsthorpe, 1,001.

SANDIACRE[1]

Church of England S. Giles. An ancient parish church. *Erected:* not given. *Endowments:* Land £43, other permanent endowments £54, fees £5. *Sittings:* Free 130, other 80, total 210. *Attendance:* Morning: general congregation 25, Sunday school 30, total 55; afternoon: general congregation 45, Sunday school 25, total 70. *Average attendance:* not given. *Signed:* J.L. Longmill, incumbent, Sandiacre, Derby. [HO 129/444/19]

Wesleyan Methodist. *Erected:* 1827. Separate and entire, exclusively used. *Sittings:* Free 200, other 108, standing the isle. *Attendance:* Morning: general congregation 72, Sunday school 78, total 150; afternoon: general congregation 162. *Average attendance:* not given. *Signed:* John Smedley, steward and trustee, Lace Manufacturer, Sandiacre. [HO 129/444/20]

Wesleyan Reformers. *Erected:* a room not separate and entire, exclusively used. *Sittings:* 4 Free 120 see letter. standing 24 feet long 16 feet wide, 8 feet high. *Attendance:* Morning: general congregation 50; evening: general congregation 108. *Average attendance:* Morning: general congregation 60; evening: general congregation 110. *Signed:* William Barker, steward, Sandiacre. [HO 129/444/21]

Primitive Methodist. *Erected:* 1833. Separate and entire, not exclusively used. *Sittings:* Free 120, other 45. *Attendance:* Afternoon: general congregation 110, Sunday school 63, total 173; evening: general congregation 100, Sunday school 30, total 130. *Average attendance:* Afternoon: general congregation 60, Sunday school 63, total 123; evening: general congregation 60, Sunday school 30, total 90. *Signed:* Joseph Richards, steward, Sandiacre. [HO 129/444/22]

STANTON BY DALE[2]

Church of England. S. Michael. *Erected:* Before 1800. *Endowments:* Land £21, tithe award £300, glebe house £35, fees £2. *Sittings:* Free length of seating 59 feet = 64, other 267 feet = 178, gallery free 38 feet. Total length of seating = 364 feet. Total 242. *Attendance:* Morning: general congregation 57, Sunday school 17, total 74; afternoon: general congregation

---

[1] Population 1,065.
[2] Population 689.

80, Sunday school 20, total 100. *Average attendance:* not given. *Signed:* J.G. Howard, Rector, Stanton Rectory, Derby. [HO 129/444/23]

Wesleyan Methodist. Dwelling house. *Erected:* an inhabited cottage. *Sittings:* not given. *Attendance:* Evening: general congregation 45. *Average attendance:* not given. *Signed:* Thomas Morral, Leader, Stanton by Dale. [HO 129/444/24]

Methodist New Connexion. Club room. *Erected:* 1789. Separate and entire, not exclusively used. *Sittings:* Free 120. *Attendance:* Morning: Sunday school 101; evening: general congregation 80. *Average attendance:* Morning: Sunday school 101; afternoon: Sunday school 101; evening: general congregation 90. *Signed:* Thomas Mee, steward, Stanton by Dale. [HO 129/444/25]

Primitive Methodist. Dwelling house. *Erected:* 1850. Not separate, not exclusively used. *Sittings:* not given. *Attendance:* Afternoon: general congregation 30; evening: general congregation 30. *Average attendance:* not given. *Remarks:* Commenced preaching in house 1850. It is a private dweling house. *Signed:* Herbert Walker, steward, Stanton by Dale. [HO 129/444/26]

DALE ABBEY[1]

Church of England. extra-parochial chapel and a peculiar. *Erected:* Before 1800. *Endowments:* Fees £2. *Sittings:* Free 180. *Attendance:* Morning: general congregation 67, Sunday school 62; total 129. *Average attendance:* not given. *Remarks:* Held with Stanton. *Signed:* J.G. Howard, A.M., minister, Stanton Rectory, nr Derby. [HO 129/444/27]

Wesleyan Methodist. *Erected:* Before 1810. Separate and entire, exclusively used. *Sittings:* 100 all free, see letter. *Attendance:* Afternoon: general congregation 67; evening: general congregation 72, Sunday school none. *Average attendance:* Afternoon: general congregation 60, Sunday school none; evening: general congregation 80. *Signed:* James Hollingsworth, steward, Dale Abbey. [HO 129/444/28]

---

[1] Population 442.

Primitive Methodist. dwelling house. *Erected:* 1842. Dwelling house, not exclusively used. *Sittings:* Free 36, standing 12. *Attendance:* Afternoon: general congregation 31; evening: general congregation 29. *Average attendance:* afternoon: general congregation 28; evening: general congregation 30. *Signed:* John Farington Reedman, Joseph Wheatley.[1] [HO 129/444/29]

CHURCH WILNE

Breaston[2]

Church of England. Breaston church or chapel in the parish or soke of Sawley. *Erected:* Consecrated before 1800. *Endowments:* not given. *Sittings:* Free 95, other 200, total 295. No other returns given. *Remarks:* This Benefice is the united perpetual curacy of Risley and Breaston. *Signed:* H.B. Hall, Incumbent, Risley. [HO 129/444/30]

Methodist New Connexion. *Erected:* 1803. Separate and entire, exclusively used. *Sittings:* Free 178, other 92. *Attendance:* Morning: Sunday school 80; afternoon: general congregation 41, Sunday school 88, total 129; evening: general congregation 157. *Average attendance:* Morning: general congregation 100, Sunday school 90, total 190; afternoon: general congregation 120, Sunday school 99, total 219; evening: general congregation 180, total 180. *Signed:* John Plackett, steward, Breaston. [HO 129/444/31]

Primitive Methodist. preaching room. *Erected:* 1850. [*Note added:* Formerly a wheelwright's shop but converted into a place of worship in 1850.] *Sittings:* Free 100, 20 standing. *Attendance:* no returns given. [*Note added:* Several of the congregation connected with the above Place of Worship will attend the Borrowash chapel opening, so that the numbers could not fairly be represented on the above day.] *Average attendance:* Afternoon: general congregation 60, evening: general congregation 100. *Signed:* Abimelech Hainsworth Coulson, Superintendant minister, 45 Copeland St, Derby. [HO 129/444/32]

---

[1] On the side of the form is written: The proper address is John Farington Reedman, 45 Burscows's Walk, Derby. John Wheatley, manager, Dale Abbey, Derby.

[2] Population 680.

Spondon Sub-District

CHURCH WILNE[1]

Church of England. Parish church. *Erected:* Before 1800. *Endowments:* Land £12, other permanent endowments £67, fees £4. *Sittings:* Free 250, other 170, total 420. *Attendance:* Morning: general congregation 50, Sunday school 40, total 90; afternoon: general congregation 70, Sunday school 100, total 170. *Average attendance:* Morning: general congregation 40, Sunday School 40, total 80; afternoon: general congregation 120, Sunday school 100, total 220. *Signed:* William Lloyd, minister, Draycott, Shardlow. [HO 129/444/33]

Draycott[2]

Wesleyan Methodist. *Erected:* Old chapel about 1800, the new one not on the same site in the year 1830. Separate and entire, exclusively used. *Sittings:* Free 230, other 168. *Attendance:* Afternoon: general congregation 88, Sunday school 85, total 173; evening: general congregation 210. *Average attendance:* Morning: general congregation 100, Sunday school 80, total 180; evening: general congregation 190. *Remarks:* Divine Service held alternately morning and evening and afternoon and evening. Sunday scholars not compelled to come in the evening. *Signed:* Joseph Bosworth, trustee, Draycott. [HO 129/444/34]

Draycott Wilne

Primitive Methodist. *Erected:* Not separate, not exclusively used. *Sittings:* Standing space 30. *Attendance:* Afternoon: general congregation 15; evening: general congregation 20. *Average attendance:* aftenoon: general congregation 15; evening: general congregation 20. *Signed:* Sarah Simpkin, householder and inmate, Draycott. Her Mark. [HO 129/444/35]

---

[1] Parish population 2,094; Church Wilne township 174.

[2] Population 987.

OCKBROOK[1]

Church of England. All Saints. *Erected:* Before 1800. *Endowments:* Land £143, glebe house and gdn, fees £5 10s. *Sittings:* Free 338, other 139, sittings in chancel 24, total 501. *Attendance:* Morning: general congregation 200, Sunday school 128, total 328; afternoon: general congregation 300, Sunday school 126, total 426. *Average attendance:* Morning: general congregation 250, Sunday school 120, total 370; afternoon: general congregation 300, Sunday school 130, total 430. *Remarks:* A new Primitive Methodist chapel was opened this morning 30 March which somewhat diminished the morning congregation. *Signed:* Samuel Hey, minister, Ockbrook. [HO 129/444/36]

Borrowash

Wesleyan Methodist. *Erected:* 1825. Separate and entire, exclusively used. *Sittings:* Free 220, other 162. *Attendance:* Morning: general congregation 62, Sunday school 58; afternoon: Sunday school 58; evening: general congregation 78. *Average attendance:* Morning: general congregation 60, Sunday school 70, total 130; afternoon: general congregation 100, Sunday school 70, total 170; evening: general congregation 100. *Remarks:* Divine Service held alternately morning and evening and afternoon and evening. *Signed:* John Dyche, class leader, Borrowash, nr Derby. [HO 129/444/37]

Primitive Methodist. *Erected:* 1851. Separate and entire, exclusively used. *Sittings:* Free 100, other 68. *Attendance:* Afternoon: general congregation 80; evening: general congregation 120. *Remarks:* This place of worship was opened for Public Worship first time 30 March. *Signed:* Edwin Hill, trustee, Borrowash. [HO 129/444/38]

Ockbrook

Moravian settlement. Protestant church of the United Brethren or Unitas Fratrum, also Moravian Brethren. *Erected:* Before 1800. Separate and entire, exclusively used. *Sittings:* 227 all free, no standing room, seats added if required. *Attendance:* Morning: general congregation 117, Sunday school 24, total 141; afternoon: general congregation 110; evening: general congregation

---

[1] Population 1,763.

150. *Average attendance:* Morning: general congregation 120, Sunday school 20, total 140; afternoon: general congregation 100; evening: general congregation 150. *Remarks:* In the Moravian Chapels all sittings are free, the benches or forms being generally moveable, the number of sittings can be increased as occasion may require by the introduction of additional seats. *Signed:* Revd Samuel Rudolph Reichel, Warden and Manager, Ockbrook. [HO 129/444/39]

Wesleyan Methodist. *Erected:* 1808. Separate and entire, exclusively used. *Sittings:* Free 100, other 50. *Attendance:* not given. *Average attendance:* Afternoon: general congregation 30; evening: general congregation 70. *Signed:* Thomas White, steward, Ockbrook. [HO 129/444/40]

Primitive Methodist. *Erected:* 1824. Separate and entire, exclusively used. *Sittings:* Free 44, other 56. *Attendance:* no services. *Average attendance:* Afternoon: general congregation 25, evening: general congregation 45. *Remarks:* Services given up in consequence of a new chapel being opened at Borrowash one mile distant. Several will be at Borrowash in the evening. Given up both times. *Signed:* Abimelech Hainsworth Coulson, Superintendant Minister, 45 Copeland St, Derby. [HO 129/444/41]

KIRK HALLAM[1]

Church of England. *Registrar's letter:* Parish Church – Will you be so good as to supply the following information at your earliest convenience: Free seats 150, Other 0, Total 150. Also West Hallam Free seats 240, Other 0, Total 240. Date: 25 Aug. 1852. *Signed:* Thos Chas Cade. [HO 129/444/42]

SPONDON[2]

Locko Chapel. Church of England. *Erected:* Consecrated before 1800. *Sittings:* 45. See letter. *Attendance:* Morning: general congregation 19. *Remarks:* Locko Chapel strictly a private chapel attached to the house – the Chaplain appointed by the Proprietor. *Signed:* Wm Drury-Lowe, Proprietor. [HO 129/444/43]

---

[1] Parish population 473, including Mapperley (359).

[2] Parish population 2,052, including Stanley (380).

Spondon[1]

Church of England. S. Mary the Virgin.[2] *Erected:* Consecrated before 1800. *Endowments:* Glebe £146, other permanent endowment £60, fees £30. *Sittings:* Free 300 other 400, total about 700. *Attendance:* Morning: general congregation 236, Sunday school 126, total 362; evening: general congregation 275, children not taken to church. *Average attendance:* not given. *Signed:* A.S. Holden, Vicar, Spondon. [HO 129/444/44]

Wesleyan Methodist. *Erected:* Before 1800, separate and entire, exclusively as a place of worship except for Sunday school. *Sittings:* Free 144, other 88. *Attendance:* Morning: Sunday school 68; afternoon: general congregation 80, Sunday school 64; evening: general congregation 78. *Average attendance:* Morning: general congregation 100, Sunday school 70. *Signed:* Gervase Malin, Chapel steward, Spondon. [HO 129/444/45]

Primitive Methodist. *Erected:* Cannot say when it was erected but was purchased in 1840 by us, Primitive Methodists. *Sittings:* Free 32, other 40, standing 40. *Attendance:* no services held [*Remarks:* Service given up in consequence of a new chapel being opened within three miles at Borrowash.]. *Average attendance:* Afternoon: general congregation 25; evening: general congregation 35. *Signed:* Abimelech Hainsworth Coulson, Superintendant Minister, 45 Copeland St, Derby. [HO 129/444/46]

Weslean Reformed Methodists. *Erected:* Before 1800. Room exclusively used. *Sittings:* Free 50 standing 100. *Attendance:*Afternoon: general congregation 35, evening: general congregation 40. *Average attendance:* not given. *Signed:* James Hall, Local Preacher, No 45 Siddals Rd, Derby. [HO 129/444/47]

Stanley[3]

Church of England. *Erected:* unknown. *Endowments:* Land £40, other permanent endowment interest of £400 Queen Ann's Bounty. *Sittings:* Free 20, other 50, total 70. *Attendance:* Morning: general congregation 30, Sunday school 40. *Average attendance:* Morning: general congregation 35, Sunday

---

[1] Township population 1,672.

[2] The present dedication is to S. Werburgh.

[3] Population 380.

school 40; afternoon: general congregation 40, Sunday school 40. *Signed:* Edward Muckleton, officiating priest or curate, Chaddesden, Derby. [HO 129/444/48]

Wesleyan Methodist. *Erected:* 1827. Seperate and entire, exclusively used. *Sittings:* Free 10 pews = 60, other 6 = 36, standing 20. *Attendance:* Afternoon: general congregation 45; evening: general congregation 50. *Average attendance:* Afternoon: general congregation 30; evening: general congregation 35. *Signed:* Samuel Lakin, minister, Sandiacre. [HO 129/444/49]

Stanley Common

Wesleyan Methodist. *Erected:* 1835. Separate and entire, exclusively used. *Sittings:* Free 112, other 36. *Attendance:* Afternoon: general congregation 45. *Average attendance:* not given. *Signed:* Robert Bardill, leader and trustee, Stanley Common. [HO 129/444/50]

Chaddesden[1]

Church of England. *Erected:* not known. *Endowments:* Land £68, interest of £400 Queen Ann's Bounty. *Sittings:* Free 25, other 165, total 190. *Attendance:* Afternoon: general congregation 150, Sunday school 20. *Average attendance:* Morning: general congregation 100, Sunday school 40; evening: general congregation 140, Sunday school 4. *Signed:* Edward Muckleton, officiating clergyman, Chaddesden. [HO 129/444/51]

Wesleyan Methodist. *Erected:* 1828. Separate and entire, exclusively used. *Sittings:* Free 72, other 28, no standing. *Attendance:* Evening: general congregation 38. *Average attendance:* Evening: general congregation 50. *Signed:* Herbert Barber, steward, wheelwright, Spondon. [HO 129/444/52]

---

[1] Population 433.

BREADSALL[1]

Church of England. An ancient parish church. *Erected:* before 1800. *Endowments:* not given. *Sittings:* Free 153, other 212, total 365. *Attendance:* Morning: general congregation 104, Sunday school 50. total 154; afternoon: general congregation 98, Sunday school 50, total 148. *Average attendance:* Morning: general congregation 120, Sunday school 50, total 170; afternoon: general congregation 150, Sunday school 50, total 200. *Signed:* Henry R. Crewe, rector, Breadsall Rectory. [HO 129/444/53]

Wesleyan Methodist. *Erected:* 1826. Separate and entire, exclusively used. *Sittings:* Free 80, other 36. *Attendance:* Evening: general congregation 52. *Average attendance:* not given, no school. *Signed:* William Brown, society steward, 13, Mansfield Road, Derby. [HO 129/444/54]

LITTLE EATON[2]

Church of England. S. Paul. A chapelry of S. Alkmund Derby. *Erected:* Consecrated before 1800. *Endowments:* Land £22, other permanent endowment £57, fees £1 5s., other sources £35. *Sittings:* Free 117, other 137, total 254. *Attendance:* Morning: general congregation 105, Sunday school 110, total 215; afternoon: general congregation 135, Sunday school 109, total 244; evening: no service. *Average attendance:* not given. *Remarks:* As we have no means of returning a correct average for any number of months we must let the actual attendance on March 30 tho' a little under the average stand for the usual attenders. *Signed:* John Latham, minister, Little Eaton. [HO 129/444/55]

Wesleyan Methodist. *Erected:* 1829. Separate and entire, exclusively used. *Sittings:* Free 100, other 50. *Attendance:* Afternoon: general congregation 34; evening: general congregation 67, total 101. *Average attendance:* not given. no scholars. *Remarks:* length of building 35 feet, width 13 feet. *Signed:* William Barber, class leader, Little Eaton. [HO 129/444/56]

Congregational or Independent. *Erected:* 1843. Separate and entire, exclusively used. *Sittings:* Free 72, other 64, standing none. *Attendance:* Afternoon: general congregation 27, Sunday school 35, total 62; evening:

---

[1] Population 621.
[2] Population 692.

general congregation 63, total 63. *Average attendance:* not given. *Signed:* James Gawthorn, one of the ministers, Becket Well Lane, Derby. [HO 129/444/57]

DERBY REGISTRATION DISTRICT

S. Alkmund Sub-District

DERBY S. ALKMUND[1]

Chester Green[2]

Church of England. Parish church of new parish of S. Paul. *Erected:* By a committee of the friends of the late Bishop Shirley. Private benefaction £2700 about. Consecrated 22 May 1850 immediately upon its erection. *Endowments:* Eccles. Commiss. Pew rents about £12, Easter offering not yet collected. *Sittings:* Free 216, other 384, total 600. *Attendance:* Morning: general congregation 75, Sunday school 119, teachers 10, total 204; afternoon: at present not a regular and full service; evening: general congregation 107. *Average attendance:* not given. *Signed:* J.M. Pratt, perpetual curate of S. Paul's, Derby. [HO 129/445/1]

S. Alkmund

Church of England. S. Alkmund. *Erected:* On ancient site. A church rebuilded. *Endowments:* Land £137 6s., other permanent endowment £90, fees £45 7s.6d., Easter offering £9 17s. 6d., other £18 1s. 6d. *Sittings:* Free c. 500, other 560, total 1,060. [*Remarks:* The architects estimate returns accomodation for a larger number but this I believe to be very nearly accurate.] *Attendance:* Morning: general congregation 432, Sunday school 295, total 727; afternoon: general congregation 187, Sunday school 247 [*Remarks:* Many of the younger boys are allowed to go home after the afternoon school.], total 434; evening: general congregation 475. *Average attendance:* not given. About 60 went home this afternoon. *Signed:* Edward Henry Abney, vicar, The Firs, nr Derby. [HO 129/445/2]

Roman Catholic. Nottingham Road S. Joseph. *Erected:* 1847. Separate and entire, exclusively used. *Sittings:* Convent chapel. *Attendance:* Morning:

---

[1] Parish population 13,040.

[2] Population 430.

69

general congregation 44. *Average attendance:* not given. *Signed:* Joseph Daniel, Catholic Priest, S. Mary's, Derby. [HO 129/445/3]

Independent or Congregational. Chester Road. *Erected:* 1836. Separate and entire, *not* exclusively used. *Sittings:* Free 200, other 76. *Attendance:* Afternoon: general congregation 31, Sunday school 165, total 196; evening: general congregation 81. *Average attendance:* not given. *Remarks:* A part of the chapel is used as day school. *Signed:* Jonathan Merwood, minister, 19, Mansfield Rd, Derby. [HO 129/445/4]

Roman Catholic. S. Mary. *Erected:* 1836. Separate and entire, only used as a church and for a short time as a Sunday school until a school built. *Sittings:* Free 500, standing 300. *Attendance:* Morning: general congregation 400 at first Mass 800 at 2nd Mass, total 1,200; afternoon: general congregation 350; evening: general congregation 700. *Average attendance:* general congregation 2,000, Sunday school 200 boys. *Signed:* Thomas Sing, Senior Priest. [HO 129/445/5]

Quakers. St Helen's St. *Erected:* 1808. Separate and entire, exclusively used. *Sittings:* 1,400 feet, no galleries, 300 seated. *Attendance:* Morning: general congregation 42; afternoon: general congregation 30. *Average attendance:* not given. *Signed:* Robert Brigdon 3 Jun. 1851. [HO 129/445/6]

Wesleyan Methodist. King St. *Erected:* 1805, in lieu of one erected 1765. Separate and entire, exclusively used. *Sittings:* Free 350, other 1050. *Attendance:* Morning: general congregation 550, Sunday school 180, total 730; evening: general congregation 650. *Average attendance:* Morning: general congregation 650, Sunday school 180, total 830; evening: general congregation 850. *[Unsigned]* Superintendent Minister,[1] 11 North Parade, Derby. [HO 129/445/7]

Baptist. Duffield Road. *Erected:* As it was not erected for our denomination I cannot ascertain when it was built. Separate and entire, exclusively used. *Sittings:* Free 50, other 250, standing perhaps 50 or a few more. *Attendance:* Morning: general congregation 87, Sunday school 59, total 146; evening: general congregation 132, Sunday school 27, total 159. *Average attendance:* Morning: general congregation 100, Sunday school 90, total 190; evening: general congregation 150, Sunday school 50, total 200. *Remarks:*

---

[1] The superintendent minister was William Horton.

Ours is an infant cause commenced in a new part of the town. *Signed:* John James Owen, 2 North Parade, Derby. [HO 129/445/8]

General Baptist. Brook St. *Erected:* 1802. Separate and entire, exclusively used. *Sittings:* Free 581, other 119, all sitting room. *Attendance:* Morning: general congregation 94, Sunday school 60, total 154; afternoon: Sunday school 53; evening: general congregation 270. *Average attendance:* Morning: general congregation 95, Sunday school 90, total 185; afternoon: Sunday school 90; evening: general congregation 190. *Signed:* G. Needham, minister, 32, Sacheverel St, Derby. [HO 129/445/9]

Primitive Methodist. Kedleston St. *Erected:* 1850. Separate and entire, a place of worship and a Sunday school. *Sittings:* Free 360, other 260, standing 150. *Attendance:* Morning: general congregation 200, Sunday school 120; afternoon: Sunday school 139; evening: general congregation 600. *Average attendance:* Morning: general congregation 180, Sunday school 100; afternoon: Sunday school 120; evening: general congregation 560. *Signed:* Abimelech Hainsworth Coulson, Superintendant Minister, 45, Copeland St, Derby. [HO 129/445/10]

Darley Abbey[1]

Church of England. S. Matthew. *Erected:* Consecrated 24 June 1819 as an additional church to the Parish church of S. Alkmund's. *Endowments:* Land per annum £132 10s., Q. Ann Bounty £4 16s. 10d., fees 7s. 6d., other sources £2 13s. 2d., total £150 7s. 6d. *Sittings:* Free 473, other 27, total 500. *Attendance:* Morning: general congregation 103, Sunday school 212, total 315; afternoon: general congregation 196, Sunday school 205, total 300. *Average attendance:* Morning: general congregation 95, Sunday school 210, total 305; afternoon: general congregation 110, Sunday school 210, total 320. *Remarks:* The rent of land viz. of £142 10s. is subject to a payment of £5 per year to the poor of Repton. Also another payment of £5 per annum in perpetuity is due to the vicar of St Alkmund leaving £132 10s. The nos. of the average may be from 5–12 wrong. *Signed:* John Griffiths, Officiating minister, Darley. [HO 129/445/11]

Reformed Wesleyan Methodist. *Erected:* before 1800. Not separate, not exclusively used. *Sittings:* [60 *crossed through*]. Length 15 feet, width 14

---

[1] Population 925.

feet. *Attendance:* Evening: general congregation 70. *Average attendance:* not given. *Signed:* Joseph Oldknow, a class leader, Darley Abbey. [HO 129/445/12]

Wesleyan Methodist. Schoolroom. *Erected:* 1826. Not separate, not exclusively used. *Sittings:* no sittings. 30ft x 24ft. *Attendance:* Evening: general congregation 30. *Average attendance:* not given. *Signed:* Thomas Stevens, class leader, Darley Abbey. [HO 129/445/13]

All Saints Sub-District

DERBY ALL SAINTS[1]

Church of England. All Saints. *Erected:* Before 1800. *Endowments:* Land nil, tithe nil, glebe nil, other permanent endowment £30, pew rents £20, fees £28, dues nil, Easter offering £20, other sources £22. *Sittings:* Free 215, other 643, children 350, total 1208. *Attendance:* Morning: general congregation 521, Sunday school 185, total 706; afternoon: general congregation 270, Sunday school 321, total 591; evening: general congregation 536. *Average attendance:* not given. *Signed:* Charles Lee, curate, The Elms, Derby. [HO 129/445/14]

Baptist. S. Mary's Gate. *Erected:* 1750 built as a gentleman's mansion, converted into chapel 1842. Separate and entire, exclusively used. *Sittings:* Free 322, other 878, none but the aisles. *Attendance:* Morning: general congregation 308, Sunday school 116, total 424; afternoon: general congregation 157, Sunday school 58, total 215; evening: general congregation 711. *Average attendance:* not given. *Signed:* John G. Pike, Minister, Derby. [HO 129/445/15]

---

[1] Population 4,396.

S. Michael's Sub-District

DERBY S. MICHAEL[1]

Church of England S. Michael. *Erected:* Ancient parish church. Consecrated before 1800. *Endowments:* Glebe £65, other permanent endowments £49, fees £3, Easter offerings £2. *Sittings:* Free 161, other 103, total 264. *Attendance:* Morning: general congregation 112, Sunday school 97, total 209; afternoon: general congregation 132, Sunday school 97, total 229. *Average attendance:* not given. *Signed:* R.N. Hope, Vicar, S. Michael's, Derby. [HO 129/445/16]

S. Peter's Sub-District

DERBY S. PETER[2]

Church of England. Trinity. *Erected:* By private subscription, licensed 1836 under 1 & 2 Willm 4th c. 38, consecrated 1837 an additional church. Thos. West Esq. of Brighton gave £1,000 for endowment, private benef. £3,900. *Endowments:* Other permanent endowment £31 18s. 4d., pew rents £112. *Sittings:* Free 300, other 600, total 900. *Attendance:* Morning: general congregation 290, Sunday school 575, total 865; afternoon: in school 634; evening: general congregation 387. *Average attendance:* not given. *Signed:* Edward M. Wade, Incumbent, Derby. [HO 129/445/17]

DERBY S. WERBURGH

Church of England S. Werburgh.[3] *Sittings:* Free 256, other adults 431, children 254, total 941. [HO 129/445/18]

---

[1] Population 1,036.

[2] Parish population 15,628.

[3] This is a loose half-sheet inserted into the volume. See also p. 76 for S. Werburgh.

DERBY S. PETER

Church of England S. Peter. *Erected:* An ancient parish church, consecrated before 1800. *Endowments:* Tithe £111 13s. 4d., glebe £50, fees £80, Easter offering £10. *Sittings:* Free 65, other 585, total 650. *Attendance:* No services. *Average attendance:* Morning: general congregation 300, Sunday school 180, total 480; afternoon: general congregation 40, Sunday school 180, total 220; evening: general congregation 500, total 500. *Signed:* William Hope, M.A., The Vicarage, S. Peter's, Derby. [HO 129/445/19]

Particular Baptist. Agard St. *Erected:* Before 1800. Separate and entire, exclusively used. *Sittings:* 500. *Attendance:* Morning: general congregation 160, Sunday school 60, total 220; afternoon: general congregation 40 [*Remarks:* At a monthly prayer meeting for the school.], Sunday school 71, total 111; evening: general congregation 192, total 192. *Average attendance:* Morning: general congregation 160, Sunday school 60; afternoon: general congregation 80 [*Remarks:* At prayer meetings of Lord's Supper.], Sunday school 100; evening: general congregation 300. *Signed:* Abraham Perrey, M.A., Minister, 2, Kingston Terrace, Derby. [HO 129/445/20]

Congregational. Victoria St.[1] *Erected:* 1783. Separate and entire, exclusively used. *Sittings:* Free 70, other 630, standing 120. *Attendance:* Morning: general congregation 425, Sunday school 122, total 547; afternoon: general congregation 91, Sunday school 344, total 435; evening: general congregation 454, total 454. Average congregation: not given. *Remarks:* On weekdays we hold religious services in 3 dwellings in the extremities of the town at which there is an average of 80 the greater part of whom do *not* attend our chapel on the Sunday. *Signed:* James Gawthorn, John Corbin, pastors, Becket Well Lane, Friargate. [HO 129/445/21]

Wesley Methodist Reformers. Wardwick lecture hall. *Erected:* Separate and entire, not exclusively used. *Sittings:* Free 360, other 374. *Attendance:* Morning: general congregation 370, Sunday school 165, total 543; afternoon: Sunday school 186; evening: general congregation 682. *Average attendance:* not given. *Signed:* Henry Hawgood, one of the expelled, Local preacher, 25, Cornmarket, Derby. [HO 129/445/22]

Primitive Methodist. Traffic St. *Erected:* 1843. Separate building, a private chapel, exclusively used. Place of worship and Sunday school.

---

[1] Formerly Brookside Chapel.

Sittings: Free 300, other 372, standing 150. *Attendance:* Morning: general congregation 354; afternoon: Sunday school 306; evening: general congregation 710. *Average attendance:* Morning: general congregation 400, Sunday school 25; afternoon: Sunday school 300; evening: general congregation 650. *Signed:* Abimelech Hainsworth Coulson, Superintendant Minister, 45, Copeland St, Derby. [HO 129/445/23]

Wesleyan Methodist. North St. *Erected:* Not separate and entire, exclusively used. *Sittings:* Free 100, other 65. *Attendance:* Morning: general congregation 62; evening: general congregation 93. *Average attendance:* not given. *Signed:* John Relph, Wesleyan Minister, 11, Wilmot St, Derby. [HO 129/445/24]

Methodist New Connexion Temple. *Erected:* about the year 1815. Separate and entire, exclusively used. *Sittings:* Free 150, other 330. *Attendance:* Morning: general congregation 180, Sunday school 76, total 256; evening: general congregation 384. *Average attendance:* not given. *Signed:* James Maugham, minister, 5, Abbey St, Derby. [HO 129/445/25]

Independent or Congregational. London Road. *Erected:* 1843. Separate and entire, exclusively used. *Sittings:* Free 228, other 384, standing none except in the aisle. *Attendance:* Morning: general congregation 147, Sunday school 153, total 300; evening: general congregation 245. *Average attendance:* Morning: general congregation 150, Sunday school 150, total 300; evening: general congregation 260. *Remarks:* In reference to my answer 'Yes' to Division 6 it may be right to state that the schoolroom under the chapel is used for instruction during the week as well as on Sundays. *Signed:* Richard Charles Pritchett, minister, 3, Normanton Terrace, Derby. [HO 129/445/26]

General Baptist. Sacheverell St. *Erected:* 1830. Separate and entire, exclusively used. *Sittings:* Free 70, other 480, standing none. *Attendance:* Morning: general congregation 160, Sunday school 150; evening: general congregation 240. *Average attendance:* Morning: general congregation 150, Sunday school 150; evening: general congregation 240. *Signed:* John Winfield, Deacon, 47 Sacheverell St., Derby. [HO 129/445/27]

Wesleyan Methodist. Green Hill. *Erected:* 1821. Separate and entire, exclusively used. *Sittings:* Free 300, other 384. *Attendance:* Morning: general congregation 165, Sunday school 84, total 249; afternoon: general congregation 36, Sunday school 104, total 140; evening: general congregation 245.

Average attendance: not given. *Signed:* Willm Williamson, steward, No 8, Friar Gate, Derby. [HO 129/445/28]

New Jerusalem Church, commonly called Swedenborgian. Babington Lane. *Erected:* Built about 1835, purchased for this society 1846. Separate and entire, exclusively used. Sittings Free 100, other 240. *Attendance:* Morning: general congregation 65, Sunday school 86, total 151; evening: general congregation 85. *Average attendance:* Morning: general congregation 70, Sunday school 85, total 155; evening: general congregation 85. *Remarks:* There is no service in the afternoon but the Sunday scholars come to school and average 100. There is also a mutual improvement class of Teachers one evening in each week and a Library. *Signed:* William Mason, minister, 6, Wilmot St, Derby. [HO 129/445/29]

DERBY S. WERBURGH[1]

Church of England. S. John, Bridge St. *Erected:* Church of the 'consolidate chapelry of S. John, Derby' under sect. 9 of the 8th & 9th Victoria chapter 70. Consecrated Aug. 19 1828 as a chapel of ease in S. Werburgh's parish. By the Eccles. Comm. aided by voluntary subscriptions. Private benefactions £4,443 3s. Total cost £8,000 or thereabouts. *Endowments:* Pew rents £136, fees 2s. *Sittings:* Free c. 650, other c. 550, total 1,200. *Attendance:* Morning: general congregation 261, Sunday school 370, total 631; afternoon: general congregation 158, Sunday school 275, total 433; evening: general congregation 375. *Average attendance:* not given. *Remarks:* A large proportion of the persons who attend in the afternoon or evening do not attend more than once a day; The total number of *distinct persons* is probably c. 900 which is about one-fifth of the population of the district. *Signed:* Thomas Arthur Scott, M.A., incumbent. [HO 129/445/30]

Church of England. Christchurch, having a district Normanton Rd. *Erected:* Licensed 1840, consecrated 1843. By a committee and 5 trustees; cost: private benefaction £3,500. *Endowments:* Other permanent endowments £1,000, pew rents £120, fees 10s. *Sittings:* Free 350, other 450, total 800. *Attendance:* Morning: general congregation 357, Sunday school 269, total 626; evening: general congregation 320. *Average attendance:* Morning: general congregation 350, Sunday school 300, total 650; evening: general congregation 400. *Remarks:* We are now erecting a school in connexion with

---

[1] Population 10,482.

the church to accomodate 450 scholars. *Signed:* Roseingrave Macklin, Incumbent, Wardwick. [HO 129/445/31]

Church of England. S. Werburgh.[1] *Erected:* before 1800. *Endowments:* Land £86, tithe £150, other permanent endowments £102, fees £30, Easter offerings £10, other sources £10, total £386. *Sittings:* Free 510, other 451, total 941. *Attendance:* Morning: general congregation 367, Sunday school 165, total 532; afternoon: general congregation 238, Sunday school 174, total 442; evening: general congregation 390. *Average attendance:* not given. *Remarks:* At least one-third of the general congregation in the afternoon and evening had not attended in the morning. *Signed:* W.F. Wilkinson, vicar, 21, Ashbourne Rd, Derby. [HO 129/445/32]

Church of England. Chapel for the use of prisoners confined in the County Gaol erected by Magistrates for the County of Derby. *Attendance:* Morning: 200; evening: 200. *Signed:* Geo. Pickering, County Prison Chaplain. [HO 129/445/33]

Unitarian.[2] Friargate. *Erected:* Before 1800. Separate and entire, exclusively used. *Sittings:* Chapel has about 450 sittings – the no. free varies. *Attendance:* Morning: general congregation 89, Sunday school 128, total 217; evening: general congregation 107. *Average attendance:* not given. *Signed:* Henry W. Crosskey, minister, New Uttoxeter Rd. [HO 129/445/34]

---

[1] See also p. 73.
[2] 'Presbyterian Dissenters' crossed out.

BELPER REGISTRATION DISTRICT

PART 1

Duffield Sub-District

KEDLESTON[1]

Church of England.[2] *Erected:* About twelvth Century. *Endowments:* not given. *Sittings:* Free about 16, other about 64, total about 80. *Attendance:* Average congregation about 35; Sunday school none. *Signed:* John E.A. Fenwick, clerk. [HO 129/446/1]

MUGGINTON[3]

Church of England. All Saints. *Erected:* before 1800. *Endowments:* not given. *Sittings:* Free 200, other 150, total 350. *Attendance:* Morning: general congregation about 150, Sunday school 44; afternoon: general congregaton 130, Sunday school 44; evening: not any. *Signed:* John Hinds, Assistant Overseer. [HO 129/446/2]

MACKWORTH[4]

Church of England. All Saints. *Erected:* Before 1800. *Endowments:* Land 17 acres, other permanent endowment £60, fees £1, other sources, Queen Ann's Bounty, £6 10s. *Sittings:* not given. *Attendance:* no services. *Average attendance:* Morning: general congregation 150, Sunday school 50; afternoon: general congregation 160, Sunday school 50. *Remarks:* Church under repair. *Signed:* Geo. Pickering, vicar, Mackworth, nr Derby. [HO 129/446/3]

---

[1] Population 85.

[2] This entry is on an alternative form which does not ask for average attendance nor for endowments.

[3] Parish population 719, Mugginton township 262.

[4] Parish population 510, Mackworth township 306.

DUFFIELD[1]

Wesleyan Methodist. *Erected:* 1843. Separate and entire, exclusively used. *Sittings:* Free 180, other 120. *Attendance:* Afternoon: general congregation 100, Sunday school 70; evening: general congregation 120, Sunday school 30. *Average attendance:* Afternoon: general congregation 120, Sunday school 80, total 200; evening: general congregation 130, Sunday school 20, total 150. *Signed:* Gervase Cooper, Society Steward, Duffield. [HO 129/446/4]

ALLESTREE[2]

Church of England. S. Andrew, an old parish church.[3] *Erected:* Before 1800. *Endowments:* Land £44 per an., fees average of £3. *Sittings:* Free about 170, other none. *Attendance:* Morning: general congregation about 70, Sunday school 112, total 182; afternoon: general congregation about 100, Sunday school 108, total 208. *Average attendance:* not given. *Signed:* John Hullett, minister, Allestree, nr Derby. [HO 129/446/5]

Wesleyan Methodist. *Erected:* In the year 1821. Separate and entire, exclusively used. *Sittings:* Free 84, other 36, standing none. *Attendance:* Evening: general congregation 70. *Average attendance:* general congregation from 70 to 80. *Signed:* Thomas Woolley, Trustee and Leader, Allestree, nr Derby. [HO 129/446/6]

DUFFIELD

Milford

Wesleyan Methodist. *Erected:* In 1815, this taken down, the 2nd built in 1842 in lieu of the 1st. Separate and entire, exclusively used. *Sittings:* Free 220, other 200, standing none. *Attendance:* Morning: Sunday school 127; afternoon: general congregation 164, Sunday school 110, total 274; evening: general congregation 139. *Average attendance:* Morning: Sunday school 120; afternoon: general congregation 150, Sunday school 110, total 260; evening:

---

[1] Parish population 17,749, Duffield township 2,926.

[2] Population 557.

[3] The present dedication is to S. Edmund.

general congregation 110. *Remarks:* The congregation connected with this place of worship is considerably lessened owing to a secession having taken place. The party gone away forms a separate congregation in the neighbourhood calling themselves Wesleyan Reformers. *Signed:* John Holbrook, steward to the Trustees, Milford, Derbys. [HO 129/446/7]

Duffield

General Baptist. *Erected:* 1849. Separate and entire, exclusively used. *Sittings:* Free 150, other none. *Attendance:* Afternoon: general congregation 90; evening: general congregation 80. *Average attendance:* not given. *Signed:* William Parkinson, Deacon, Milford. [HO 129/446/8]

QUARNDON[1]

Church of England. All Saints, originally, I believe a chapelry to All Saints in Derby. *Erected:* Before 1800. *Endowments:* Land £44, other permanent endowment £64, fees £2, aggregate annual amount of endowment £110. *Sittings:* Free 90, other 132, total 222. *Attendance:* Morning: general congregation 85, Sunday school 46, total 131; afternoon: general congregation 83, Sunday school 45, total 128; evening: no service. *Average attendance:* Morning: general congregation 102, Sunday school 50, total 152; afternoon: general congregation 98, Sunday school 48, total 146. *Signed:* W.H. Barber, Minister, Quarndon Parsonage, near Derby. [HO 129/446/9]

DUFFIELD

General Baptist Chappil. *Erected:* 1830. Separate and entire, exclusively used. *Sittings:* Free 100, other 170. *Attendance:* Morning: general congregation 62, Sunday school 57, total 109; afternoon: Sunday school 67, total 62; *(sic)* evening: general congregation 95. *Average attendance:* Morning: general congregation 60, Sunday school 50, total 110; evening: general congregation 90. *Signed:* Samuel Jennels, Deacon, R.W. Station, Duffield. [HO 129/446/10]

---

[1] Population 529.

KIRK LANGLEY[1]

Church of England. Ancient parish church dedicated to S Michael & commonly known as the Parish Church of Kirk Langley. *Erected:* Consecrated before 1800. *Endowments:* Tithe £222, glebe £135, fees £2, Easter offering £1, total £360. *Sittings:* Free 107, other 274, total 381. *Attendance:* Morning: general congregation 126, Sunday school 84, total 210; afternoon: general congregation 82, Sunday school 95, total 177. *Average attendance:* Morning: general congregation 120, Sunday school 86, total 196; afternoon: general congregation 75, Sunday school 96, total 171. *Signed:* Heny Jas Feilden, Rector, Langley Rectory, Derby. [HO 129/446/11]

QUARNDON

Wesleyan Methodist. *Erected:* about 1800. Not separate and entire, exclusively used. *Sittings:* Free 100. *Attendance:* Evening: general congregation 45. *Average attendance:* not given. *Signed:* William Keeling, Steward, Quarndon, Derby. [HO 129/446/12]

KIRK LANGLEY

Primitive Methodist. *Erected:* 1817. Separate and entire, exclusively as a Place of Worship. *Sittings:* Free 30, other 24, standing 20. *Attendance:* no services returned. *Average attendance:* Evening: general congregation 40. *Signed:* Abimelech Hainsworth Coulson, Superintendant Minister, 45, Copeland St, Derby. [HO 129/446/13]

MUGGINTON

Weston Underwood[2]

Wesleyan Methodist. *Erected:* Not separate and entire, exclusively used. *Sittings:* not given. *Attendance:* Afternoon: general congregation 34. *Average attendance:* not given. *Signed:* George Draycott, Leader and Steward, Ivy House, Weston Underwood, Derbys. [HO 129/446/14]

---

[1] Population 657.
[2] Population 245.

DUFFIELD

Church of England. All Saints.[1] *Erected:* Consecrated before 1800. *Endowments:* Land: £19, tithe £66, glebe £27, fees £25, other sources £15. *Sittings:* Free 218, other 332, total 550. *Attendance:* Morning: general congregation 140, Sunday school 80, total 220; afternoon: general congregation 150, Sunday school 45, total 195. *Average attendance:* not given. *Signed:* Wm Barber, vicar, Duffield, Derby. [HO 129/446/15]

Milford

Church of England. Holy Trinity. New parish under the Provisions of 6th & 7 Vict. c. 37. *Erected:* Consecrated July 28 1848 as an additional church. Cost defrayed by Parliamentary and other Grants and Private Subscription and by collections in the church at the consecration and opening. Cost Parl. and other grants £1,116, Private benefactions £1,344 18s. 9d. Debt £167 7s. 7^{1}/$_{2}$d, Total £2,628 6s. 4^{1}/$_{2}$d. *Endowments:* Other permanent endowment: £150, pew rents £12, fees 10s. *Sittings:* Free 387, other 129, total 516. *Attendance:* Morning: general congregation 120, Sunday school 108, total 228; afternoon: general congregation 450. *Average attendance:* not given. *Remarks:* Cost how defrayed Lichfield Diocesan Society £616, H.M. Commissioners for Buildings £250, Incorporated Society for Buildings £230, Co-operative Society £20, Subscriptions etc. £1344 18s. 9d. Total raised £2,460 18s. 9d., deficiency £167 7s. 7^{1}/$_{2}$d. Total cost £2,628 6s. 4^{1}/$_{2}$d. *Signed:* Robert Leigh, Incumbent, Belper. [HO 129/446/16]

Windley[2]

General Baptist. *Erected:* In the year 1847. Separate and entire, exclusively used. *Sittings:* 7 yards by Ten 100 sitings free. *Attendance:* Morning: Sunday school 17; afternoon: general congregation 50; evening: general congregation 25. *Average attendance:* not given. *Signed:* George Houlgate, Manager, Hazzlewood. [HO 129/446/17]

---

[1] The present dedication is to S. Alkmund.

[2] Population 219.

Hazelwood[1]

Church of England. S. John the Evangelist. District church under the provision of 59 King George the 3rd. *Erected:* Consecrated May 14 1846 as an additional church by the munificence of Col. H. Colvile aided by public and private grants and subscriptions. Cost £2,000. *Endowments:* Other permanent endowment £50 together with house & garden, pew rents £6. *Sittings:* Free 136, other 91, children 66, total 293. *Attendance:* Morning: general congregation 60, Sunday school 50, total 110; afternoon: general congregation 100, Sunday school 50, total 150; evening: general congregation 50. *Average attendance:* Morning: general congegation 60, Sunday school 60, total 120; afternoon: general congregation 150, Sunday school 60, total 210; evening: general congregation 40. *Remarks:* The total cost of the church, school and Parsonage House was about 6000£. The congregation depends on the weather. *Signed:* John Horner Jenkins, Incumbent, Hazelwood, nr. Belper. [HO 129/446/18]

Turnditch[2]

Primitive Methodist. *Erected:* A.D. 1814. Separate and entire, used exclusively for a place of worship. *Sittings:* Free 46, other 54. *Attendance:* Afternoon: general congregation 50; evening: general congregation 100. *Average attendance:* afternoon: general congregation 40; evening: general congregation 100. Thomas Peach, Steward, Cowhouse Lane, Turnditch, nr Derby. [HO 129/446/19]

Independents. Green Bank. *Erected:* 1818. Separate and entire, exclusively used. *Sittings:* Free 100, other 50. *Attendance:* Afternoon: general congregation 50, Sunday school 30, total 80; evening: general congregation 50, Sunday school 30, total 80. *Average attendance:* not given. *Signed:* A.E. Statham, Manager, address Mrs Wm Statham, Greenbank, Derbys. [HO 129/446/20]

Church of England. All Saints Church, an ancient chapelry. *Erected:* Before 1800. *Endowments:* Land about £44. *Sittings:* Free 167. *Attendance:* Morning: general congregation 54, Sunday school 56, total 110. *Average*

---

[1] Population 416.

[2] Population 380.

attendance: not given. *Signed:* James P. Deacon, Clergyman, Turnditch, nr Derby. [HO 129/446/21]

Hazelwood

Wesleyan Methodist. *Erected:* 1813. Separate and entire, exclusively used. *Sittings:* Free 80, other none. *Attendance:* Afternoon: 16; evening: 15. *Average attendance:* Morning: general congregation 25. *Signed:* John Goodwin, John Holbrook, Local Preacher, address John Goodwin, Hazlewood, Derbys. [HO 129/446/22]

Holbrooke[1]

Church of England. Church of an ancient chapelry. *Erected:* Licensed before 1800, but only consecrated September 28 1835. The church when consecrated had been built (as an additional church) about 74 years. *Endowments:* Rent charge on land £50, other permanent endowment £6 10s., fees £1 10s. *Sittings:* Free 250 including those for children, other 158, total 408. *Attendance:* Morning: general congregation 78, Sunday school 95, total 173; afternoon: general congregation 114, Sunday school 96, total 210; evening: 56, 64, total 120. *Remarks:* This evening service is held in the Infant School Room. *Average attendance:* not given. *Signed:* Wm Leeke, Incumbent, Holbrook, Derby. [HO 129/446/23]

Horsley Sub-District

MORLEY[2]

Smalley[3]

Church of England. S. John Baptist chapel room. *Endowments:* not given. *Sittings:* not given. *Erected:* Before 1800, an ancient chapelry.

---

[1] Population 981.

[2] Parish population 1090. Morley included the chapelry of Smalley until 1877.

[3] Population 804.

Attendance: Morning: general congregation 60; afternoon: general congregation 90. *Remarks:* The minister declined to give me any information on the subject in this return. Have returned the above from information otherwise obtained. [*Unsigned, no address*] [HO 129/446/24]

HORSLEY[1]

Kilbourn[2]

Wesleyan Methodist. *Erected:* 1836. Separate and entire, used exclusively as a place of worship and a Sunday school. *Sittings:* Free 13 feet by 9 feet or 117 feet, other 80. *Attendance:* not given. *Average attendance:* Morning: general congregation 50, Sunday school 160, total 210; afternoon: general congregation 60, Sunday school 160, total 220; evening: general congregation 70. *Signed:* William Crofts, Member, Horsley Woodhouse. [HO 129/446/25]

DUFFIELD

Coxbench

Independent or **Congregationalist.** *Erected:* 1827. Separate and entire, exclusively used. *Sittings:* Free 80, other 60, standing 20. *Attendance:* Evening: general congregation 40. *Average attendance:* Evening: general congregation 50. *Signed:* George Bowmer, Mr Williams. [HO 129/446/26]

Holbrook Moor

Wesleyan Reform. *Erected:* Built in the year 1827. By Subscription. Debt 30£. Seperate Building Standing Alone. Only Place of Worship Except Sunday School and Monday night meeting. *Sittings:* One half free. [Free 100 other 40 see letter *superimposed*]. *Attendance:* Morning: Sunday school 107; afternoon: general congregation 50, Sunday school 100. *Average attendance:* Morning: general congregation 100, Sunday school 114, total 214. *Remarks:* This chappel was built for the Old Methodists but they having no legal claim

---

[1] Parish population 2,161, Horsley township 507.

[2] Population 814.

to it Reformers claim it through certain documents in their hands. *Signed:* Robert Sheldon, trustee, Charles Sims, steward, Holbrook, nr Derby. [HO 129/446/27]

HORSLEY

Church of England. S. Clement. Ancient parish church old as King John's time. *Erected:* Consecrated and licensed before 1800. *Endowments:* Land £10, tithe commuted £170, other permanent endowment £30, fees (surplice) about £10. *Sittings:* Free 120, other 180, children 130, total 430. *Attendance:* Morning: general congregation 53, Sunday school 42, total 95; afternoon: general congregation 100, Sunday school 53, total 153. *Average attendance:* Morning: general congregation 50, Sunday school 50, total 100; afternoon: general congregation 130, Sunday school 60, total 190; evening: no service. *Remarks:* the £30 is put down as arising from a Parliamentary Grant of £995 15s. 1d. now in the three per cent Reduced Bank Annuities. The 10£ as arising from rent of four acres of land purchased some years ago in the parish of Heanor. The entire income is considered to be £210. *Signed:* Henry Moore, Minister (curate), Horsley, nr Derby. [HO 129/446/28]

Wesleyan Methodist. *Erected:* 1845. Separate and entire, exclusively used. *Sittings:* Free 80, other 20. *Attendance:* Evening: general congregation 7, Sunday school 18, total 25. *Average attendance:* general congregation 6, Sunday school 18, total 24. *Remarks:* Congregation is much injured by the despotic acts of the Wesleyan Conference. *Signed:* Geo. Parker, steward, Horsley, nr Derby. [HO 129/446/29]

Wesleyan Reformers. *Erected:* Used as a place of worship since September last, not separate, not exclusively used. *Sittings:* Free space/standing 70 to 80. *Attendance:* Afternoon: general congregation 30; evening: general congregation 65. *Average attendance:* afternoon: general congregation 30; evening: general congregation 65. *Remarks:* It being a dwelling house used on Sundays for Public Worship till other arrangements are made. *Signed:* Samuel Parker, Manager, Horsley. [HO 129/446/30]

Horsley Woodhouse[1]

Wesleyan Methodist. *Erected:* 1799. Separate and entire, exclusively used. *Sittings:* Free 254, other 118. *Attendance:* Afternoon: general congregation 78, Sunday school 132, total 210; evening: general congregation 102. *Average attendance:* not given. Isaac Woodhouse, steward, Horsley Woodhouse, Derbys. [HO 129/446/31]

Wesleyan Methodist Reformers. *Erected:* Service commenced 1850, not separate and entire, not exclusively used. *Sittings:* Free 300, other none. *Attendance:* Afternoon: general congregation 65; evening: general congregation 40. *Average attendance:* Afternoon: general congregation 70; evening: general congregation 40. *Signed:* Thomas Jordan, steward, Horsley Woodhouse. [HO 129/446/32]

Primitive Methodist. Club room. *Erected:* Not separate, not exclusively used. *Sittings:* Free all, standing 200. *Attendance:* Morning: general congregation 40; evening: general congregation 100. *Average attendance:* General congregation 150, Sunday school none. *Signed:* Thomas Oldknow, Lay Preacher, Horsley Woodhouse. [HO 129/446/33]

Kilburn

General Babtist. *Erected:* 1832. Separate and entire, exclusively used. *Sittings:* Free 65, other 36. *Attendance:* Morning: general congregation 43; evening: general congregation 60. *Average attendance:* General congregation 40 to 50. *Remarks:* No regular minister. *Signed:* Thomas Bennett, Deacon, Kilburne, Derbys. [HO 129/446/34]

Wesleyan Reformers. *Erected:* Before 1800. Not separate and entire, not exclusively used. *Sittings:* Free all, other none. *Attendance:* Evening: general congregation 45. *Average attendance:* not given. *Signed:* John Brown, junr, Manager, Kilburne. [HO 129/446/35]

---

[1] Population 840.

MORLEY

Church of England. S. Matthew. *Erected:* Before 1800. *Endowments:* not given. *Sittings:* Free 50, other 94, total 144. *Attendance:* not given. *Average attendance:* Morning: general congregation 100, Sunday school 38, total 138; afternoon: general congregation 120, Sunday school 38, total 158. *Remarks:* Sunday March 30th was a very wet day & the village being scattered the attendance was less than the average. *Signed:* Saml Fox, Rector, Morley. [HO 129/446/36]

Morley Moor

Wesleyan Methodist. *Erected:* 1845. Separate and entire, exclusively used. *Sittings:* Free whole, other 16.[1] *Attendance:* Afternoon: general congregation 23; evening: general congregation 34. *Average attendance:* Afternoon: general congregation 20; evening: general congregation 50. *Signed:* Jane Boden, leader, Morley Hays, Derby. [HO 129/446/37]

Smalley

General Baptist. *Erected:* 1788. Separate and entire, exclusively used. *Sittings:* Free 168, let 132, standing 50. *Attendance:* Morning: general congregation 80, Sunday school 51, total 131; evening: general congregation 160. *Average attendance:* Morning: general congregation 80, Sunday school 50, total 130; afternoon: general congregation 150, Sunday school 50, total 200; evening: general congregation 200. *Remarks:* The service changes every Sunday. Morning one Sunday, Afternoon the next and so on, but every evening. On special occasions have seen from 400 to 450. *Signed:* Edward Roe, Deacon, Smalley, Derby. [HO 129/446/38]

[1] 80. 'See letter' is superimposed.

KIRK HALLAM

Mapperley[1]

Wesleyan Methodist. *Erected:* 1830. uper room built for the purpose of religious worship exclusively except for Sabboth school. *Sittings:* Free all. *Attendance:* Afternoon: Sunday school 20; evening: general congregation 95, Sunday school 90, total 185. *Average attendance:* Evening: general congregation 90, Sunday school 90, total 180. *Remarks:* Divine Service is conducted every Sabboth evening when from 90 to 100 and sometimes more attend and in addition there is service in an afternoon every other Sabboth when the congregation would be 100 and on some occasions 120 including the school. *Signed:* John Green, Local preacher, Farmer, Mapperley, nr Shipley. [HO 129/446/39]

HORSLEY

Denby[2]

Church of England. S. Mary. The church of an ancient chapelry. *Erected:* Consecrated before 1800. *Endowments:* Land £55, tithe £12, other permanent endowment £40, fees £5, other sources £3, total £115. *Sittings:* Free 230, other 170, total 400. *Attendance:* Morning: no service; afternoon: general congregation 85, Sunday school 83, total 168. *Average attendance:* Morning: general congregation 50, Sunday school 86, total 136; afternoon: general congregation 100, Sunday school 86, total 186. *Signed:* Jas. Mockler, Clerk, Minister, Denby, nr Belper. [HO 129/446/40]

Wesleyan Methodist. *Erected:* Oct. 1841. Separate and entire, only used as a place of worship except for a Sunday school exclusively used. *Sittings:* Free 190, other 130. *Attendance:* No service. *Average attendance:* Morning: Sunday school 80[3]; afternoon: general congregation 180 70; evening: general congregation 150. *Signed:* Arthur Smith, chapel steward, Denby, Derbys. [HO 129/446/41]

---

[1] Population 359.

[2] Population 1,208.

[3] Both Sunday School figures are crossed out.

Wesleyan Methodist. *Erected:* Before 1800 occupied dwelling, not separate and entire, not exclusively used. *Sittings:* standing 19 feet by 18. *Attendance:* Afternoon: general congregation 75; evening: general congregation 57. *Average attendance:* Afternoon: general congregation 66; evening: general congregation 66. *Signed:* Arthur Smith, Society Steward, Denby. [HO 129/446/42]

Belper Sub-District

DUFFIELD

Belper[1]

Church of England. Christchurch new parish of Bridge Hill 6 & 7 Vict. Cap. 37.[2] There being no consecrated place of worship in the then district. *Erected:* Consecrated July 30 1850. Erected by a local & general subscription aided by grants from H.M. Commissioners, the diocesan and incorporated society. Cost £2859 0s. 8^1/$_2$d. *Endowments:* Other permanent endowments £150, pew rents about £18, fees uncertain. *Sittings:* Free 448, other 152, total 600. *Attendance:* Morning: general congregation 70, Sunday school 101, total 171; evening: general congregation 140. *Average attendance:* Morning: general congregation 70, Sunday school 110, total 180; evening: general congregation 200. *Remarks:* The Cost (IV) is given as nearly as possible inclusive of fitting, purchase of site, architects' Commission etc. A few small bills for extras are unpaid and a few subscriptions have not yet been paid to the Treasurer. *Signed:* John Bannister, B.A., Perpetual Curate, Field House. [HO 129/446/43]

Church of England. S. Peter, an ancient chapelry. *Erected:* Consecrated Sept. 6 1824 This church was built and consecrated in the place of the old chapel of S. John's Belper; by Parliamentary Grant & private subscription. Parl. grant about £9,000, private about £2,000, total about £11,000. *Endowments:* Land £42 5s., other permanent endowment £47 8s. 4d., pew rents about £55, fees about £18, total £162 13s. 4d. *Sittings:* Free 1,200, other 600, total 1,800. *Attendance:* Morning: general congregation 160, Sunday school 140, total 300; afternoon: general congregation 130, Sunday school

---

[1] Population 10,082.

[2] The parish was formed in 1845 from the chapelry of S. Peter.

270, total 400; evening: general congregation 237. *Average attendance:* Morning: general congregation 200, Sunday school 160, total 360; afternoon: general congregation 150, Sunday school 350, total 500; evening: general congregation 500. *Signed:* Robert Hey, minister, Belper. [HO 129/446/44]

CHRISTCHURCH PARSONAGE AND SCHOOLS[1]

NEW PARISH OF BRIDGE HILL, BELPER

Belper, situated on the Midland Railway, eight miles north of Derby, is a long scattered, irregularly built town which, to a stranger passing through the place has the appearance of a long straggling village; – the population, however is upwards of 10,000. A very small proportion of the inhabitants are of the middle class of society. – By far the greater part are operatives, engaged in Cotton-spinning, Nail-making or the Stocking-frame. Like many of our large manufacturing towns, it has attained its present extent in the last few years. A local historian, (Davies) thus speaks of it 'Prior to the year 1776, Belper though now holding second rank in point of population among the towns in Derbyshire, was as low in population, as it was backward in civility, and considered as the insignificant residence of a few uncivilized nailers'.

Until 1824 the only provision made by the Church for the spiritual instruction of the inhabitants was a chapel said to have been built by John of Gaunt, dependent on the Parish Church at Duffield, four miles distant. In the year 1824 by public subscription, aided by a large parliamentary grant, a church was erected to seat 1800 adults and children.

During the last six years, great efforts have been made for the moral culture and spiritual improvement of the town and parish at large, with its population of about 21,000 souls scattered over a space of 17,390 acres. The beautiful and ancient Parish Church at Duffield has been restored. A Church, Parsonage, Schools and School-Houses have been erected in the wild and hilly township of Hazlewood. A church has been built at, and a new parish formed of, the compact and populous hamlet of Milford. National Schools with school-houses have been erected in the scattered townships of Heage and Turnditch, and also at Belper, where till their erection a Sunday School was the only means of training up the children of the poor in the principles of the Established Church. There were, however, two Day Schools in the

---

[1] This consists of a single sheet printed both sides, published by the incumbent of Christchurch.

town, one attached to one of the Methodist Chapels, and the other belonging to the Mills, where on Sunday morning writing, etc., is taught, and the scholars taken in the afternoon to the Unitarian Chapel.

By an order in Council bearing date August 1845, the lower part of Belper with a population of 3,000 was formed into a separate district. In April 1846, a clubroom was licensed for Divine Worship, and a congregation collected. On July 30th 1850, after many difficulties and much labour to procure funds (the more difficult in consequence of the great works that had been accomplished) a neat, though plain and unassuming church was consecrated, and the district became a new parish for ecclesiastical purposes.

It is the Minister's constant endeavour to teach and to preach plainly and faithfully, not only in the church, but also from house to house, the glorious truths of the life-giving Gospel of Jesus Christ, in all their fullness and freeness, and he has reason to hope that his labours have not been in vain in the Lord. Exclusive of teachers and scholars belonging to the Sunday school, he has but a small congregation on Sunday morning, but the evening attendance is very good, and the cottage lectures twice in the week in various parts of his parish are usually very crowded.

In order to secure a regular system of visitation, which is so important in all cases, and more especially in a new parish where the ground is new and requires breaking up to prepare it for the reception of the seed to be sown, a residence for the Minister within the limits of his charge, and near the church is unquestionably most desirable. In this instance the Minister has to lodge out of his Parish. One object therefore proposed by this appeal is to *raise Funds for the erection of a Parsonage.*

But there is a want more felt than this; – There is no School building in connection with the church. The Minister almost at the commencement of his labours opened a Sunday school, which has been going on gradually increasing, so that it now numbers about 150 children and young persons, who have to be taught in the church, no other building can be obtained. This use of a place of worship, must ever be found objectionable, as it diminishes the respect of the children for the house of God, and rendering them insensible to the difference between church and school, makes it more troublesome for the teachers to keep them peaceable and quiet, not to say reverent and devout during the service. – It is therefore proposed as soon as sufficient funds have been raised, to justify the commencement of the undertaking, *to erect a School-Room, etc.,* near to the church to accommodate 300 children.

In consequence of the great efforts that have been made for Educational and Religious purposes, as has already been stated, all available local resources have been exhausted. The Incumbent of the Parish is therefore obliged to appeal to the sympathizing benevolence of the Christian Public.

Deeply grateful for the assistance already afforded in his work of faith and labour of love, he sends forth this appeal, in the prayerful hope, that the God of all grace, whose is the silver and the gold will incline the hearts of those, to whom he has entrusted this world's wealth, to lend that assistance which is needed.

Contributions however small are earnestly solicited of those who have a stake in the peace and stability of the country, who need not be reminded that the removal of ignorance and vice is 'the cheapest defence of nations;' – of those who are anxious that our reformed protestant faith should be handed down to our children and children's children, pure and intact; – in fine of all who feel an interest in the welfare of immortal souls, and who are wishful that the operative classes, while labouring in the concerns of time should also be making provision for a happy and glorious eternity.

BALANCE AS FAR AS HAS BEEN ASCERTAINED
(Fuller particulars will be forwarded to each Subscriber)

Purchase of site for Church, Cost of erection, Fencing, Lighting, Heating, Furniture, Repair Fund, Architects Commission, Salary of Clerk of Works and Incidental expenses, £2,946 19s. 8$\frac{1}{2}$d.

Amount of Subscriptions and Collections for the erection of the Church formerly advertised and interest allowed on the deposits by the Derby and Derbyshire Banking Company, £1,738 9s. 8$\frac{1}{2}$d.

Grants from H.M. Church Building Commissioners, the Incorporated and Diocesan Church extension Society, £1,050 0s 0d

Total Net Receipts £2,788 9s. 8$\frac{1}{2}$d.
Deficiency about £160.

The following additional Contributions towards making up the deficiency and erecting the Parsonage and Schools are thankfully acknowledged.

The Right Rev. the Lord Bishop of Lichfield.	£10.0.0.
The Right Hon. Earl Manvers	5.0.0.
The Venerable Archdeacon Hill,	
(a second donation)	2.0.0.
Henry Blackden, Esq.	
(a second donation)	10.0.0.
Miss Wakefield, Sedgwick Hall Westmoreland	10.0.0.

T. Dickinson, Esq., Upper Holloway	10.0.0.
S. Oliver, Esq., per Messrs Williams	10.0.0.
Anonymous, (a second donation)	10.0.0.
Lieut.Col. Wigram	5.0.0.
Rev. C.J. Vaughan, Harrow School	5.0.0.
Robert Daw, Esq., Cardiff	5.0.0.
C. Dixon, Esq., Stanstead, Herts.	5.0.0.
Miss Phillips, Cheltenham	5.0.0.
Mrs Touchet, Exton, Hants.	5.0.0.
G.S. Richmond, Surrey.	5.0.0.
Two Ladies	5.0.0.
Miss Gabriel, Rowde, Wilts.	5.0.0.
Mrs Rush, Elsenham Hall	5.0.0.
Miss Skurray, Norwood, Surrey	5.0.0.
John Ollivant, Manchester	5.0.0.
James Haig, Esq., Bois House, Bucks	5.0.0.
Mrs Hill, Peplow Hall (Paintings)	5.0.0.
John Rogers, Seven Oaks	5.0.0.
John Silvester, Esq., Atherton	5.0.0.
H.S. Montagu, Esq., (a second donation)	3.10.0.
Rev. R. Gell, Kirk Ireton	3.3.0.
Hon. John Dutton, Sherborne	3.0.0.
Charles Holt Bracebridge, Esq.	2.0.0.
Henry Eyre, Esq., Shaw House	1.0.0.

In Postage Stamps, Zech. IV.10

Miss Sophia Childers	7.0.
Lady Ford, Hon Mrs Childers; Mrs Col. Abbott;	
Mrs Alston, F.W. Brock, Collins, George, Giles,	
Jones, King, Lax, Myers, Sanderson, Scott, Tatton,	
Windus; Miss Acton, Bancks, Banks, Cheney, Frere,	
Honey, Jacomb Hood, Lavender, Lemoyne, Palfreeman,	
Rumney, Stewart, Yonge, Young; Rev. O. Brock, M.H.G.	
Buckle, John Graham, George Greaves, P. Johnson,	
P.H. Jennings, George Hunt, C.W. Lander, H. Price;	
Messrs Hesketh, H.H. Hulbert, Ilott, Michell,	
J. Ferrar Ransom; G. Redmayne, W. Sims, J.E. Turner.	each 5s. 0d.
Rev. T.O. Routh	4s. 6d.
Mrs Cranston, Mrs F. Curteis, Miss Harmer,	
Rev. W.B. Jacob	each 4s. 0d.
Lady Selsey, Mrs Cope, Cox, Dickinson, Gregg,	

Moore, Pascoe, Pitman; – Miss S. Day, Harding, Hunter, Stretton; Rev. Percy Smith, Harvey Vachell; Messrs Mayhew and West.	each 3s. 0d.

Lady Newborough, Mrs Blagg, W. Carey, C. Cooper
Morris, Oates, Roby, Sparkes, Tarrant,
Whittingham; Miss Duffield, Halcombe, Monteith,
Pell, Reade, Rohde, Antonina Rotten, Rickerby,
Rushton, Schneider, Sharpe, Wilkinson, Yeoman,
Rev. D. Davies, Reginald Smith, G. Spooner, Richard
Withington, Messrs Edward Chapman, F. Davies,
J.E. Fraser, Hunt, H.Langley, Newcomb, George
Reeves, Hugh Spencer, Stanhope, R.R. Whitehead.   each 2s. 6d.
Mrs Bunce, Miss Creser, Dirom, Gilmour,
Wallesby, Messrs J. Boldero, Dunning,
F.S. Einley, Holt, H. Puckle.   each 2s. 0d.
Rev. E. Falle   1s.6d.
Lady H. St Maure, Mrs Eardley, Meadows, Mickley,
Pampluton, Ricketts, Sawyer; Miss Butts, Farncombe,
Guillemard, Price, Strong; Rev. W. Allen, W. Green;
Messrs Blackburn, Braithwaite, Ellerton, George,
Tandy.   each 1s. 0d.

Subscriptions will be kindly received by the Right Reverend the Lord Bishop of Lichfield; the Venerable Thos. Hill, Archdeacon of Derby; the Rev. Robert Hey, A.M., Incumbent of Belper; the Derby and Derbyshire Banking Company at Belper and Derby; Messrs Williams, Deacon, Labouchere, and Co. Birchin Lane, London, and also by the Incumbent who will thankfully acknowledge the same, and on completion of the work forward to each subscriber full particulars.

J. BANNISTER, B.A. INCUMBENT. [HO 129/446/45]

[HO 129/446/46 is a duplicate of HO 129/446/43 for Christchurch, Belper. Both are signed and dated March 31st.]

Belper Lane End

Wesleyan Methodist. *Erected:* 1849. Separate and entire, exclusively used. *Sittings:* Free 360, other 440 see letter. *Attendance:* None. *Average attendance:* Morning: general congregation 60, Sunday school none. *Signed:*

George Birley, minister of Belper Circuit, Chapel St, Belper, Derbys. [HO 129/446/47]

Wesleyan Reform. *Erected:* Not separate, not exclusively used. *Sittings:* Free 80, standing 80. *Attendance:* Morning: general congregation 18, Sunday school 35; evening: general congregation 56. *Average attendance:* General congregation 200, Sunday school 130. *Signed:* James Clark, Manager, Belper Lane End, Derbys. [HO 129/446/48]

Bridge Street

General Babtist.[1] *Erected:* cannot tell, seperate for public worship and Sunday school only. *Sittings:* Free 250, other 100. *Attendance:* Afternoon: general congregation 50; evening: general congregation 60. *Average attendance:* 60 each Sunday. *Remarks:* No regular minister at this place. *Signed:* Abraham Booth, Member, Crown Court, Bridge St, Belper. [HO 129/446/49]

The Separation Church of Jesus Christ of the Latter-day Saints. *Erected:* The Lepard Inn Club Room, cannot tell, not separate, not exclusively used. *Sittings:* Free all 200. *Attendance:* Afternoon: general congregation 35; evening: general congregation 46. *Average attendance:* Morning: general congregation 50, Sunday school 18. *Remarks:* We have 100 members in this town but they range rather wide and do not all attend the Room having a meeting in a house. We have 2 Elders, 1 priest, 2 teachers, 1 deacon and a superintendent to the school besides. *Signed:* William Smith a Priest, New Street, Canweady,[2] Belper. [HO 129/446/50]

Wesleyan Methodist. *Erected:* Before 1800 enlarged since. Separate and entire, exclusively used. *Sittings:* Free 450, other 550. *Attendance:* no entries. *Signed:* George Birley, Chapel St, Belper. [HO 129/446/51]

King St 'Christians'.[3] *Erected:* not known, not separate, not exclusively used. It is a club room. *Sittings:* Free about 150, other none, standing 30.

---

[1] Actual spelling. This entry is not on a printed form but is handwritten following the style of the official form exactly.

[2] Or Canmady.

[3] It seems probable that this congregation is the group that broke away from the Congregational chapel following the resignation of the co-pastor, F.R. Broadbent in 1845.

Attendance: Afternoon: general congregation 36; evening: general congregation 42. *Average attendance:* not given. Henry Lomas, surgeon, Belper. 'not any official status, only an ordinary member'.[1] [HO 129/446/52]

Unitarian. *Erected:* Before 1800 (in 1788). Separate and entire, exclusively used. *Sittings:* Free 310, other 166. *Attendance:* Afternoon: general congregation 80; evening: general congregation 260. *Average attendance:* Afternoon: general congregation 90; evening: general congregation 200 (in winter only). *Remarks:* There is no Sunday school *connected with the chapel* but 180 to 200 scholars from Messrs Strutt's private Sunday school occupy the free sittings *in the afternoon.* Evening lectures *during winter months only* with an average of 200 attendants. *Signed:* Rees S. Heyes, Minister, King St, Belper. [HO 129/446/53][2]

Congregational or **Independent.** *Erected:* 1798. Separate and entire, exclusively used. *Sittings:* Free 320, other 380. *Attendance:* Morning: general congregation 170, Sunday school 136, total 306; afternoon: general congregation 148; evening: general congregation 193. *Average attendance:* not given. *Signed:* Robert Wolstenholme, minister, Belper. [HO 129/446/54]

Methodist New Conection. Ebenezer. *Erected:* In the year 1838. Separate building, exclusively except for Sunday school. *Sittings:* Standing 10 yds by 12, no pews all free. 100 see letter. *Attendance:* Morning: Sunday school 35; afternoon: Sunday school 35; evening: general congregation 70. *Average attendance:* not given. *Remarks:* This chapel was nearly consumed by fire in 1843, rebuilt 1849. *Signed:* Alexr Sanders, Superintendent and steward, Chapel Hollow, Belper. [HO 129/446/55]

Wesleyan Reformers. Court House, Market Place. *Erected:* 1850. Although let with a large inn yet the Room is a separate building, not exclusively used. *Sittings:* Free say 400, other 200, standing 100. *Attendance:* Morning: general congregation 200, Sunday school 100, total 300; evening: general congregation 400. *Average attendance:* Morning: general congregation 3200, Sunday school 1600, total 4800; evening: general congregation 6400. *Remarks:* The Sunday school is taught in another part of the Town and has been established 2 months. The Children attend morning service. The

---

[1] This comment is added in a different hand.

[2] The handwriting on this form is unusually fine; decorative pointing hands emphasize specific points.

Preachers who perform Divine Worship preach gratuitously. *Signed:* Joseph Palmer, one of the local preachers, Bridge St, Belper. [HO 129/446/56]

Congregational or Independent. Cow Hill. *Erected:* 1842. Separate and entire, used also for DAY School. *Sittings:* Free 200. *Attendance:* Evening: general congregation 46. *Average attendance:* not given. *Remarks:* The building was erected for a Day School, Sunday school and Place of Worship and is used for these exclusively. *Signed:* Robert Wolstenholme, minister properly of another with the controul, Belper. [HO 129/446/57]

Wesleyan Methodist. Belper Pottery chapel. *Erected:* 1816. Separate and entire, exclusively used. *Sittings:* Free 160, other 114. *Attendance:* Afternoon: general congregation 63, Sunday school 205; evening: general congregation 20. *Average attendance:* not given. *Signed:* John Longden Sunday school superintendent, Market Place, Belper, Grocer. [HO 129/446/58]

Primitive Methodist. Field Head. *Erected:* 1817. Separate and entire, exclusively used. *Sittings:* Free 270, other 230, standing 160. *Attendance:* Afternoon: general congregation 243, Sunday school 195, total 438; evening: general congregation 425. *Average attendance:* afternoon: general congregation 250, Sunday school 220; evening: general congregation 430. *Signed:* George Edwards, Steward, No 64 Long Row, Belper, Derbys. [HO 129/446/59]

Primitive Methodist. *Erected:* 1823. Separate and entire, exclusively used. *Sittings:* Free 130, other 200, standing none. *Attendance:* Morning: general congregation 100, Sunday school 60; afternoon: Sunday school 60; evening: general congregation 150. *Average attendance:* not given. *Signed:* Samuel Yates, Steward, Milford, near Derby. 20 April. [HO 129/446/60]

PART 2

Ripley Sub-District

DUFFIELD

Heage[1]

Church of England. It is believed that the name of S. Luke was given it on its consecration. Ancient chapelry being in fact a chapel of ease to Duffield, its mother church. *Erected:* Consecrated before 1800. The Date 'A.D. 1752' is cut in stone on the porch of the church but it is well known that this is the date of the porch only, the church itself being built long before. *Endowments:* Land £61 9s. 10d., glebe £6, other £83 17s. 8d., fees £5 9s. 2d. *Sittings:* Free 384, other in pews 149, total 533. *Attendance:* Morning: general congregation 68, Sunday school 94, total 162; afternoon: general congregation 114, Sunday school 82, total 196. *Average attendance:* Morning: general congregation 47, Sunday school 103, total 150; afternoon: general congregation 83, Sunday school 88, total 171. *Remarks:* The attendance at the church will appear small when compared with the population of the place and the number of sittings in the church but it should be stated that the population is scattered over 2330 acres, that there are seven dissenting places of worship and only during the last few years a resident Church minister. *Signed:* Richard Barber, Minister or Perpetual Curate, Heage Parsonage, nr Belper. [HO 129/446/1]

Ambergate

Wesleyan Methodist. *Erected:* May 16 [18]37. Separate and entire, exclusively used with Sunday school. *Sittings:* 9 yds x 10, sitting seat 42, 100, standing 50. *Attendance:* Afternoon: general congregation 11, Sunday school 10, total 21. *Average attendance:* not given. *Signed:* Henry Adams, Steward, Ambergate, nr. Belper. [HO 129/446/2]

---

[1] Population 2,278.

Heage

Wesleyan Reformers. *Erected:* Separate and entire, exclusively used. *Sittings:* Free Yes, other none, 100 see letter. *Attendance:* Afternoon: general congregation 60; evening: general congregation 68. *Average attendance:* not given. *Signed:* Job Thompson, chapel steward, [Frame work Knitter *crossed through*], Heage, Derbys. [HO 129/446/3]

Origional Methodist. Nether End chapel. *Erected:* 1837. Separate and entire, exclusively used. *Sittings:* Free 140. *Attendance:* Afternoon: general congregation 40, Sunday school 38, total 78; evening: general congregation 73. *Average attendance:* Afternoon: general congregation 50, Sunday school 40, total 90; evening: general congregation 75. *Signed:* Thomas Share, chapel steward, Heage, Nr Belper. [HO 129/446/4]

Ridgeway

Wesleyan Reformers. *Erected:* Separate and entire, exclusively used. *Sittings:* 300 all free, all free for Poor as well as Rich. *Attendance:* Afternoon: general congregation 200, 50 children additional; evening: general congregation 200; *Average attendance:* not given. *Remarks:* The children are not taught in this chapel but are brought to it from another Chapel for Divine Worship. *Signed:* Thomas Summerside, Unpaid minister or Local preacher, occasionally preaching in the above chapel and responsible for that partly. [HO 129/446/5]

Buckland Hollow

Wesleyan Methodist. *Erected:* 1839. Separate and entire, exclusively used. *Sittings:* Free 128, other 30. *Attendance:* Morning: general congregation 40, Sunday school 50, total 90; evening: general congregation 75. *Average attendance:* Morning: general congregation 45, Sunday school 50, total 95; evening: general congregation 90.[1] *Remarks:* In consequence of the Reform party separating the general congregation has fallen off by about 73. *Signed:* John Hanshaw, chapel steward, Marble and Stone Works, near Belper, Derbys. [HO 129/446/6]

---

[1]　2260, 2100, 4680 crossed out.

Heage

Wesleyan Methodist Chappel. *Erected:* 1828. Separate and entire, exclusively used. *Sittings:* Free 100, other 108. *Attendance:* Morning: Sunday school 99; afternoon: general congregation 27, Sunday school 99, total 126; evening: general congregation 21. *Average attendance:* Afternoon: general congregation 150; evening: general congregation 150. *Signed:* Robert Weston, local preacher, Horsley Woodhouse. [HO 129/446/7]

Primitive Methodist. *Erected:* 1828. Not separate, exclusively used. *Sittings:* Free 84, other 84. *Attendance:* Afternoon: general congregation 50, Sunday school 102, total 152. *Average attendance:* Afternoon: general congregation 60, Sunday school 102; evening: general congregation 110, Sunday school 30, total 140. *Signed:* Richd Breithwaite, Lay Man, Upper Heage, Derbys. [HO 129/446/8]

PENTRICH[1]

Independent let to **Reform Methodists** for a time. *Erected:* 60 years ago or more. Seperate and entire building place of worship only. *Sittings:* Free 40, other 80, standing 30 or upwards. *Attendance:* Evening: general congregation 42. *Average attendance:* evening: 45 persons. *Signed:* W.H. Fletcher Senr, Deacon of the Independent Church, occasionally worshiping at the above chapel. Hartshay, near Belper. [HO 129/446/9]

Ripley[2]

Church of England. Ripley chapel of All Saints in aid of the antient parish church of Pentrich. *Erected:* Consecrated in the year 1821. Built and consecrated on account of the distance from the parish church and the great mass of the population residing in Ripley. Built by private subscriptions, site given by the Revd J. Wood aided by a grant from the Society for building Churches and Chapels. Cost £1,600. *Endowments:* Land in Alfreton parish £80, in Ripley £18, other permanent £2 per ann. out of land at Heanor the property of John Ray, Esq., fees due to the vicar of Pentrich. *Sittings:* Built

---

[1] Parish population 3,557, Pentrich township 486.

[2] Population 3,071.

for 600, two-thirds free. *Attendance:* Morning: general congregation 112, Sunday school 97, total 209; evening: general congregation 115. *Average attendance:* Morning: general congregation 110, Sunday school 90, total 200; afternoon: general congregation 200, Sunday school 90, total 290; evening: general congregation 130. *Signed:* John Wood, Incumbent, Swanwick, Alfreton, Derbys. [HO 129/446/10]

Wesleyan Methodist. Worshiping apart from the Conference party.[1] *Erected:* Before 1800. Not separate, not exclusively used; *Sittings:* Free 150, other none, standing none. *Attendance:* Afternoon: general congregation 90; evening: general congregation 116, Sunday school none. *Average attendance:* Afternoon: general congregation 100; evening: general congregation 150, Sunday school none. *Remarks:* Our chief difficulty is want of room but we are building a large Room capable of holding from 500 to 600 which we hope to enter upon the 1st of June 1851. *Signed:* George Rowland, Manager, Market Place, Ripley, nr Alfreton. [HO 129/446/11]

General Baptist of New Connexion. *Erected:* 1846. Separate and entire, school rooms adjoining, exclusively used for place of worship. *Sittings:* Free 100, other 120. *Attendance:* Afternoon: general congregation 248, Sunday school 170, total 418; evening: general congregation 300, Sunday school 150, total 450. *Average attendance:* Morning: general congregation 90, Sunday school 150, total 240; evening: general congregation 180. *Remarks:* This day was our Sabbath School Anniversary consequently more than an average attendance. *Signed:* William Gray, minister, Ripley, nr Alfreton, Derbys. [HO 129/446/11A]

Primitive Methodist. *Erected:* 1850. Separate and entire, exclusively used. *Sittings:* Free 220, other 80, we have no standing room. *Attendance:* Morning: Sunday school 50; afternoon: general congregation 100, Sunday school 50, total 150; evening: general congregation 200. *Average attendance:* Morning: Sunday school 40; afternoon: general congregation 100, Sunday school 40; evening: general congregation 200. *Signed:* James Norton, Minister, Butterley Hill, Ripley. [HO 129/446/12]

---

[1] William Griffith, one of the three ministers expelled by the 1849 Wesleyan Conference, was before his expulsion the superintendant of the Ripley Wesleyan Circuit. A man with radical views, he had strong local support, particularly amongst working people. For the views of his opponents see comments on HO 129/446/14 (p. 103).

Presbyterian. *Erected:* 1817 and 1818. One entire building, exclusively used. *Sittings:* for about 300 persons. *Attendance:* From 12 to 24. *Average attendance:* From 12 to 24. *Remarks:* They attend other places also. *Signed:* Evan O. Jones, Minister, Duffield. [HO 129/446/13]

Wesleyan Methodist. *Erected:* 1847 in lieu of a chapel erected about 1810. Separate and entire, exclusively used. *Sittings:* Free 310, other 246. *Attendance:* Morning: general congregation 121, Sunday school 173, total 294; evening: general congregation 119. *Average attendance:* not given. *Remarks:* General congregation is reduced about two-thirds of its number since 1849. This loss is chiefly from the free sittings. The seceders mistaking the noble stand made by the Conference of that year to maintain the purity of the ministry for arbitrary exercise of power to deprive the members of perfectly voluntary society of Liberty. *Signed:* Daniel Norman, steward, Ripley, nr Alfreton. [HO 129/446/14]

Pentrich

Church of England. Antient parish church. The Duke of Devonshire patron. *Erected:* A vicarage formerly belonging to Abbey of Darley. V. antient, the date of consecration unknown. *Endowments:* Land p.a. £40, tithes commuted at 80£, glebe 6 acres, fees (surplice) 10£ about. *Sittings:* Free about 40, other 350, total 390. *Attendance:* Afternoon: general congregation 100, Sunday school 78, total 178. *Average attendance:* Morning: general congregation 50, Sunday school 90, total 140; afternoon: general congregation 140, Sunday school 90, total 230. *Signed:* John Wood, Vicar, Swanwick, Alfreton. [HO 129/446/15]

CRICH[1]

Church of England. The church of Crich in the county of Derby is an ancient parish church placed in an elevated and commanding position; patron saint S. Michael.[2] *Erected:* an ancient parish church before 1800. *Endowments:* Tithe £40, glebe £47 4s., other permanent endowment Q. Ann's Bounty £39 11s., fees £13. *Sittings:* 600 all free. *Attendance:* Morning: general congregation 20, Sunday school 50, total 70; afternoon: general

---

[1] Parish population 3,670, Crich township 2,562.

[2] The present dedication is to S. Mary.

congregation 90, Sunday school 50, total 140. *Average attendance:* Morning: general congregation 12, Sunday school 40, total 52; afternoon: general congregation 80, Sunday school 40, total 120. *Remarks:* In past years a much neglected parish now progressively improving. *Signed:* C.B. Dunn, Curate, Crich, Alfreton. [HO 129/446/16]

TANSLEY[1]

Wesleyan Methodist.[2] *Erected:* A.D. 1829. Separate and entire, exclusively used; *Sittings:* Free 140, other 100. *Attendance:* Afternoon: general congregation 40, Sunday school 60, total 100; evening: general congregation 30, Sunday school 12, total 42. *Average attendance:* Afternoon: general congregation 40, Sunday school 60, total 100; evening: general congregation 30, Sunday school 12, total 42. *Signed:* Jno. F. England, Minister, Wirksworth. [HO 129/446/17]

CRICH

Wesleyan Methodist.[3] *Erected:* A.D. 1770. Separate and entire, exclusively used. *Sittings:* Free 120, other 180. *Attendance:* Morning: general congregation 86, Sunday school 153, total 239; afternoon: Sunday school 160; evening: general congregation 60, Sunday school 26, total 86. *Average attendance:* Morning: general congregation 80, Sunday school 160, total 240; afternoon: Sunday school 160; evening: general congregation 65, Sunday school 30, total 95. *Signed:* Jno. F. England, minister, Wirksworth. [HO 129/446/18]

Fritchley

Congregational or **Independent.** *Erected:* 1841. Separate and entire, exclusively used. *Sittings:* Free 50, other 200, standing none. *Attendance:* Morning: Sunday school 30; afternoon: Sunday school 32; evening: general

---

[1] Population 593. The township was in Crich parish, which accounts for its position here in the Census returns, but (unlike the rest of the parish) in Bakewell Registration District, for the remainder of which see pp. 171ff.

[2] Compare this entry with HO 129/449/76 (p. 191).

[3] Compare this entry with HO 129/446/20 (p. 105).

congregation 58; *Average attendance:* Morning: Sunday school 28; afternoon: Sunday school 30; evening: general congregation 50. *Signed:* Thomas Bowmer, Deacon, Fritchley Green, nr Alfreton. [HO 129/446/19]

Crich

Wesleyan Methodist.[1] *Erected:* 1770. Separate and entire, exclusively used. *Sittings:* Free 225, other 175. *Attendance:* Morning: general congregation 30; evening: general congregation 32. *Average attendance:* not given. *Signed:* Saml Barker, Society steward, Cliff Wood, Crich. [HO 129/446/20]

Primitive Methodist. *Erected:* Not separate, not exclusively used. *Sittings:* 160. See letter. *Attendance:* Afternoon: general congregation 50, Sunday school 30, total 80; evening: general congregation 98. *Average attendance:* not given. *Remarks:* This place belongs to a sick society and has been used by us as a place of worship 7 years. *Signed:* Benjamin Walker, Society Steward, Crich, near Alfreton. [HO 129/446/21]

Fritchley

Primitive Methodist. *Erected:* 1829. Separate, as both a Place of Worship and a Sunday school. *Sittings:* Free 100, standing none. *Attendance:* Morning: Sunday school 78; afternoon: general congregation 110, Sunday school 78, total 188; evening: general congregation 110. *Average attendance:* Morning: Sunday school 60; afternoon: general congregation 100, Sunday school 60; evening: general congregation 100. Humy. Cokayne [*inserted in pencil, replacing* Thomas Amott *crossed through*], class leader, Fritchley, nr Alfreton. [HO 129/446/22]

Crich Carr

Primitive Methodist. *Erected:* 1843. Separate, exclusively used except for a Sabbath school. *Sittings:* Free 60, other 42. *Attendance:* Morning: Sunday school 62; afternoon: general congregation 80; evening: general congregation 105. *Average attendance:* Morning: general congregation 40,

---

[1] Compare this entry with HO 129/446/18 (p. 104).

Sunday school 60, total 100; evening: general congregation 60. *Signed:* F.C. Turton, Chapel Steward, Ambergate. [HO 129/446/23]

Crich

General Baptist. Ebenezer chapel. *Erected:* 1839. Separate, private, exclusively used. *Sittings:* Free 152, other 48. *Attendance:* Morning: Sunday school 90; afternoon: general congregation 50, Sunday school 84, total 134; evening: general congregation 130. *Average attendance:* not given. *Signed:* Thomas Mills, Elder, Crich, near Alfreton. [HO 129/446/24]

Wheatcroft

Wesleyns Reformers. *Erected:* 1818. Separate and entire, exclusively used. *Sittings:* Standing 16' x 14'. *Attendance:* Morning: Sunday school 44; afternoon: general congregation 44. *Average attendance:* Afternoon: general congregation 44, Sunday school 44; evening: general congregation 50. *Remarks:* Average number of persons the last six months would be 50 each service. *Signed:* John Hopkinson, Manager, Wheatcroft. [HO 129/446/25]

Washington

Wesleyan Methodist. *Erected:* A.D. 1847. Separate and entire, exclusively used. *Sittings:* Free 150. *Attendance:* Morning: Sunday school 40, afternoon: Sunday school 40; evening: general congregation 60, Sunday school 13, total 72. *Average attendance:* Morning: Sunday school 40; afternoon: Sunday school 40; evening: general congregation 60, Sunday school 12, total 72. *Signed:* Jno. F. England, minister, Wirksworth. [HO 129/446/26]

SOUTH WINGFIELD[1]

Oakerthorpe

Church of England. All Saints an ancient parish church. *Erected:* Consecrated before 1800 A.D. *Endowments:* Land £69, Rent Charge £195 4s. 6d., glebe £22, fees £2. *Sittings:* Free none, other 300. *Attendance:* Morning: general congregation 15; afternoon: general congregation 50, Sunday school 50, total 100. *Average attendance:* Morning: general congregation 20, Sunday school 50, total 70; afternoon: general congregation 100, Sunday school 50, total 150. *Remarks:* A reduction of rent charge, a reduction of rent for glebe, a reduction of rent for other lands must inevitably take place; The above calculations are up to Michaelmas last. *Signed:* J. Halton, minister, vicar, South Winfield, Alfreton. [HO 129/446/27]

South Wingfield

Reformed Methodist. *Erected:* Opened March 1851. Not separate. *Sittings:* Free 100 see letter. *Attendance:* Evening: general congregation 62. *Average attendance:* not given. *Signed:* Thos Bramley, South Winfield. [HO 129/446/28]

Wesleyan Methodist. *Erected:* 1811. Separate and entire, exclusively used. *Sittings:* Free 80, other 47, standing 20. *Attendance:* Afternoon: general congregation 40. *Average attendance:* not given. *Signed:* Thos Smith, steward, South Wingfield. [HO 129/446/29][2]

Wesleyan Methodist. *Erected:* A.D. 1810. Separate and entire, exclusively used. *Sittings:* Free 80, other 70. *Attendance:* Afternoon: general congregation 70, evening: general congregation 50. *Average attendance:* Afternoon: general congregation 75; evening: general congregation 60. *Signed:* Jno. F. England, minister, Wirksworth. [HO 129/446/30][3]

[1] Population 1,092.
[2] Compare with entry with the next.
[3] Compare this entry with the previous one.

Alfreton Sub-District

ALFRETON[1]

Riddings

Church of England. S. James, church of the district parish of Riddings. *Erected:* Consecrated June 28 1834. Riddings was formerly an ancient chapelry to the old parish of Alfreton but the chapel having been for many years in ruins and a large population having risen at the place it was made an ecclesiastical division and a church built. Afterwards it became a district parish. £1,000 was raised by local subscription & £1,000 received from Gov't. Jno Oakes, Esq. of Riddings House exerted himself much in the erection. Cost: Parl. Grt £1,000, Private £1,000, total £2,000. *Endowments:* Other permanent endowment £125, pew rents £25, fees £7. *Sittings:* Free 630, other 306, total 936. *Attendance:* Morning: general congregation 103, Sunday school 243, total 346; afternoon: general congregation 178, Sunday school 251, total 429. *Average attendance:* Morning: general congregation 110, Sunday school 240, total 350; afternoon: general congregation 200, Sunday school 250, total 450. *Remarks:* There is a parsonage house in addition to the returns made under the head 'How Endowed'. *Signed:* John Mee, Perpetual Curate, Riddings, Alfreton. [HO 129/446/31]

Birchwood

Church of England. Episcopal chapel. *Erected:* a small room fitted up as a chapel for evening service licensed about 1843, the hamlet of Birchwood being 2 miles from the main part of the parish this place was licenced for an evening service. Cost: by private subscription for an Independent Chapel. Endowment: none. *Sittings:* Free 80, other 30, total 110. *Attendance:* No service. *Average attendance:* general congregation 40. *Remarks:* There is only an Evening Service in this place. *Signed:* John Mee, Incumbent, Riddings in which district Birchwood is situated. [HO 129/446/32]

[1] Population 8,326.

Alfreton

Church of England. S. Mary.[1] *Erected:* Before 1800. *Endowments:* Land 63 acres let for £80, tithe £15, glebe £22, other permanent endowment £12, fees £15, Easter offering £10, total £154 p.a. *Sittings:* Free 50, other 366, children 66, total 482. *Attendance:* Morning: general congregation 300, Sunday school 40, total 340; afternoon: general congregation 360, Sunday school 60, total 420. *Average attendance:* not given. *Remarks:* The church is ill arranged & sadly inadequate to the accomodation of the Parishioners. A Gov't Grant towards enlarging it would be of immense advantage & would be duly appreciated. *Signed:* R.J. Baines,[2] Vicar, Alfreton. [HO 129/446/33]

Ironville

Church of England. Generally called Ironville Chapel – a Schoolroom licensed by the Bishop for Divine Worship and intended shortly to be made into a church and consecrated. *Erected:* Licensed 13 Oct. 1841 as additional church to the district church of Riddings in which district it then was by the Butterley Company. Cost £3,000, private benefaction Butterley Co. *Endowments:* Other permanent endowments Ecclesiastical Commissioners £130. *Sittings:* Free 600. *Attendance:* Morning: general congregation 103, Sunday school 289, total 392; afternoon: Sunday school 324; evening: general congregation 200. *Average attendance:* not given. *Remarks:* The no. of the general congregation in the evening about forty less than the usual attendance in consequence of a funeral sermon being preached in a neighbouring place as well as also a Sunday school sermon in another place. *Signed:* John Casson, minister, Ironville, Alfreton. [HO 129/446/34]

Summercotes

Primitive Methodist. *Erected:* In the year 1839. Separate and entire, used as place of worship & for a Sunday school. *Sittings:* Free 80, other 200 see letter. *Attendance:* Morning: Sunday school 130; aftenoon: general congregation 30, Sunday school 130, total 160; evening: general congregation 50.

---

[1] The present dedication is to S. Martin.
[2] The signature is unclear in the MS.

Average attendance: not given. *Signed:* William Batison, Greenhill Lane, Alfreton. [HO 129/446/35]

Alfreton

Congregational Independents. Church St. *Erected:* 1850 in lieu of one before 1700. Separate and entire, exclusively used. *Sittings:* Free 130, other 180. *Attendance:* Morning: general congregation 50, Sunday school 72; evening: general congregation 320. *Average attendance:* not given. *Remarks:* A funeral sermon which caused an increase on that day. *Signed:* Joshua Roberts, Church St, Alfreton. [HO 129/446/36]

Wesleyan Methodists. Chapel St. *Erected:* Separate and entire, exclusively used. *Sittings:* Free 254, other 186. *Attendance:* Afternoon: general congregation 35, Sunday school 38, total 73; evening: general congregation 60. *Average attendance:* Afternoon: general congregation 50, Sunday school 95, total 245; evening: general congregation 150. *Remarks:* The decrease of attendance owing to the mischievous efforts of a party of Radicals calling themselves Reformers who have seceded from our Society. *Signed:* William Wray, Steward, Tailor and Draper, Alfreton. [HO 129/446/37]

Wesleyan Reformers. *Erected:* A lecture room Red Lion Yard, Feb. 1851, separate and entire, exclusively used. *Sittings:* Free 240, other 60, total 300, standing none. *Attendance:* Afternoon: general congregation 100, Sunday school 59, total 159; evening: general congregation 158. *Average attendance:* General congregation 800, Sunday school 290, total 1090. Joshua Birley, steward, gardener, Alfreton. [HO 129/446/38]

Swanwick[1]

Particular Baptist. *Erected:* Before 1800. Separate and entire, exclusively used. *Sittings:* Free 200, other 300, standing Strangers, Poor etc. *Attendance:* not taken. *Average attendance:* Morning: general congregation 150, Sunday school 180; evening: general congregation 300, Sunday school 220. *Remarks:* Service for the Sunday school at Ripley lessened the

---

[1] 'Hamlet in Alfreton parish' added.

attendance at our chapel yesterday. *Signed:* Richard Miller, minister, Swanwick, nr Alfreton. [HO 129/446/39]

Wesleyan Methodist. *Erected:* 1845. Separate and entire, exclusively used. *Sittings:* Free body of the chapel, other 40, standing none. *Attendance:* Afternoon: general congregation 30, Sunday school 52; evening: general congregation 40. *Average attendance:* Afternoon: general congregation 40, Sunday school 60. *Signed:* George Kerry, Jun., steward, Swanwick, nr Alfreton. [HO 129/446/40]

Primitive Methodist. *Erected:* 1849. Domestic chapel, exclusively used. *Sittings:* Free 100, other 80. *Attendance:* Afternoon: general congregation 18; evening: general congregation 96. *Average attendance:* not given. *Signed:* Stephen Adcock, chapel steward, local preacher, Swanwick, nr Alfreton. [HO 129/446/41]

Golden Valley

Primitive Methodist. *Erected:* 1834. Separate and entire, exclusively used. *Sittings:* Free 120, other 50. *Attendance:* Morning: Sunday school 75; afternoon: general congregation 52, Sunday school 75, total 127; evening: general congregation 168. *Average attendance:* Morning: Sunday school 80; afternoon: general congregation 30, Sunday school 70; evening: general congregation 120. *Remarks:* Some scholars where preasant in the morning which were not in the afternoon and some in the afternoon that were not in the morning. *Signed:* John Smith, superintendent, Butterley Park, Alfreton. [HO 129/446/42]

Riddings – Greenhill Lane

Origanal Methodist. *Erected:* 1849. Separate and entire, exclusively used. *Sittings:* Free 170, other none. *Attendance:* Afternoon: general congregation 42; evening: general congregation 70. *Average attendance:* not given. *Signed:* John Armstrong, Manager, Greenhill Lane, Alfreton. [HO 129/446/43]

Riddings

Congregational. *Erected:* 1821. Seperate and entire, exclusively as a place of worship & Sunday school. *Sittings:* Free 250, other 150. *Attendance:* Morning: Sunday school 133; afternoon: general congregation 99, Sunday school 135, total 234; evening: general congregation 142. *Average attendance:* not given. *Signed:* Thomas Colleage, minister, Riddings, Alfreton. [HO 129/446/44]

Alfreton

Particular Baptist. *Erected:* 1813. separate and entire, exclusively used. *Sittings:* Free 204, other 136. *Attendance:* Morning: general congregation 150, Sunday School 107, total 257; afternoon: Sunday school 107; Evening: General congregation 360, Sunday school 40, total 400. *Average attendance:* Sunday scholars 164. *Remarks:* Members 122 in the church fellowship. *Signed:* John Pyer Barnett, minister, Jno Knight, deacon, Riddings, Alfreton. [HO 129/446/45]

Riddings

Wesleyan Methodist. *Erected:* 1817. Rebuilt, enlarged 1838. Separate and entire, exclusively used. *Sittings:* Free 250, other 194. *Attendance:* Morning: general congregation 80, Sunday school 120, total 200; afternoon: Sunday school 135; evening: general congregation 86. *Average attendance:* general congregation 150, Sunday school 200. *Remarks:* Recent Agitation in the Wesleyan Church has reduced the Congregation from 400 and the school from 300 to the numbers herein specified. *Signed:* Joseph Walker, steward, Riddings, Alfreton. [HO 129/446/46]

Somercotes

Wesleyan Methodist. *Erected:* 1849. Separate and entire, exclusively used. *Sittings:* Free 220, other 56. *Attendance:* Afternoon: general congregation 40, Sunday school 128, total 168; evening: general congregation 150, Sunday school 60, total 210. *Average attendance:* Afternoon: general congregation 40, Sunday school 135, total 175; evening: general congregation 180, Sunday school 70, total 250. *Signed:* Bradley Martin, Manager, Birchwood Colliery, Nr Alfreton. [HO 129/446/47]

Wirksworth Sub-District

ASHOVER[1]

Dethick[2]

Church of England. Chapel of an ancient chapelry. *Erected:* Before 1800. *Endowments:* Land £93. *Sittings:* Free 20, other 90, total 110. *Attendance:* Morning: general congregation 60. *Average attendance:* Morning: general congregation 60; afternoon: general congregation 70. *Signed:* Nathan Hubbersty, Incumbent, Wirksworth. [HO 129/446/48]

Ashover

Wesleyan Methodist. Mr Wass's chapel, Lea. *Erected:* A.D. 1839. Separate and entire, exclusively used. *Sittings:* Free 250, other 150. *Attendance:* Morning: Sunday school 70; afternoon: general congregation 150, Sunday school 70, total 220; evening: general congregation 150, Sunday school 25, total 175. *Average attendance:* Morning: Sunday school 70; afternoon: general congregation 150, Sunday school 70, total 220; evening: general congregation 150, Sunday school 25, total 175. *Signed:* Jno F. England, Minister, Wirksworth. [HO 129/446/49]

REPORT OF THE REGISTRAR WITH REFERENCE TO INQUIRIES RELATING TO DETHICK LEA HOLLOWAY
Aug. 21 1852

I have this day (Aug. 21st 1852) been to Holloway and find that in the Wesleyan Reformers Chapel there they have *250* Free sittings in it and none chargeable. I may here also remark the peculiarity of the Township of Dethick, Lea and Holloway having now six different places of worship for a population of 866 as under.[3]

The Established church at Dethick.

---

[1] Population 3,311.

[2] Population, with Lea, 866.

[3] There appears to be a discrepancy here in that the Wesleyan Reform chapel at Holloway is entered twice.

The Wesleyan Chapel at Lea.
The Wesleyan Reformers Chapel at Holloway.
The Unitarian at Lea reopened after being closed 14 years.
Mr Smedley's Chapel at Lea.
The Primitive Methodist Ch. at H.
Wesley Reform – Holloway.

The first of the last three is now open after being closed about 14 years. The other two are quite new and but just completed.

Mr Smedley's Chapel and school is erected entirely at his own cost and not connected with any particular body of Christians. He regularly sends out for several miles round a Tent for Sunday services that will accomodate about 200 persons. He takes the duty himself on these occasions and though he contributes liberally to dissenting places of worship in general yet he does not attach himself to any of them. I am sorry to find that in my reply *last week* the number of Houses stated to be at Rise End in the township of Wirksworth was returned 7 and 6 at the Cole Hills. It should have been 13 at the former and 6 at the latter. A private memorandum of my own has enabled me to correct the statement of the Enumerator for that District. Dated 21st August 1852. Marcellus Peal, Registrar. [HO 129/446/50]

WIRKSWORTH[1]

Church of England. S. Mary, an ancient parish church of Wirksworth. *Erected:* Middleton by Wirksworth.[2] Consecrated 1840, since made a separate district at which place a return can be made. *Endowments:* not given. *Sittings:* Free 200, other 1,000, total 1,200, see letter. *Attendance:* At S. Mary's. Morning: general congregation 500, Sunday school 250, total 760; afternoon: general congregation 650, Sunday school 250, total 900. *Average attendance:* Morning: general congregation 460, Sunday school 230, total 690; afternoon: general congregation 508, Sunday school 220, total 728. *Remarks:* Besides the parish church there are in the same parish of Wirksworth Cromford chapel, Alderwasley chapel and the district chapelry of Middleton. Schools also to each. *Signed:* John Harward, M.A., Vicar of Wirksworth. [HO 129/446/51]

[1] Parish population 7,480, Wirksworth township 3923.

[2] Population 1,012; it is not clear why the incumbent has conflated the entries for the parish church of Wirksworth and the district church of Holy Trinity, Middleton.

Wesleyan Methodist. Chapel Lane. *Erected:* A.D. 1810. Seperate and entire, exclusively. *Sittings:* Free 160, other 200. *Attendance:* Morning: general congregation 130, Sunday school 70, total 200; afternoon: Sunday school 70, evening: general congregation 300. *Average attendance:* about as above. *Signed:* John Fredk England, Wesleyan Minister, Wirksworth. [HO 129/446/52]

General Baptist. *Erected:* 1818. Separate and entire, exclusively used. *Sittings:* Free 260, other 140. *Attendance:* Morning: general congregation 70, Sunday school 100, total 170; afternoon: general congregation 50, Sunday school 120, total 170; evening: general congregation 180. *Average attendance:* not given. *Signed:* Richard Stanion, Baptist minister, Wirksworth. [HO 129/446/53]

Independent. In Colld Well St. *Erected:* 1700. A separate and entire building, exclusively used. *Sittings:* Free 92, other 203, standing 50. *Attendance:* Morning: general congregation 90, Sunday school 113, total 203; evening: general congregation 110. *Average attendance:* General congregation 150, Sunday school 100, total 250. *Signed:* Roger Knowles senior, deacon, Cold Well St, Wirksworth. [HO 129/446/54]

Primitive Methodist. Dale. *Erected:* 1830. Separate and entire, exclusively used. *Sittings:* Free 128, other 100, see letter. *Attendance:* Afternoon: general congregation 110; evening: general congregation 250. *Average attendance:* not given. *Signed:* Robert Taylor, steward, Green Hill, Wirksworth. [HO 129/446/55]

Warm Brook

Primitive Methodist. *Erected:* 1835. Separate and entire, exclusively used. *Sittings:* other 55, standing 130. *Attendance:* Afternoon: general congregation 40; evening: general congregation 53; total 93. *Average attendance:* Afternoon: Sunday school 19. *Signed:* William Walker, Steward, New Bridge, Wirksworth. [HO 129/446/56]

Gorsey Bank

Primitive Methodist. *Erected:* 1846. Separate and entire, exclusively used. *Sittings:* Free 100, other 40. *Attendance:* Morning: Sunday school 56; afternoon: general congregation 120; evening: general congregation 130.

Average attendance: general congregation 140; Sunday school 56, total 196. *Signed:* William Udale, steward, Gorsey Bank, near Wirksworth. [HO 129/446/57]

Millers' Green

Wesleyan Methodist. Preaching room. *Erected:* Uncertain, not separate, not exclusively used. *Sittings:* Free 50. *Attendance:* Afternoon: general congregation 50. *Average attendance:* Afternoon: general congregation 35. *Signed:* Jno. F. England, Minister, Wirksworth. [HO 129/446/58]

Bole Hill

Wesleyan Methodist. Preaching room. *Erected:* uncertain, not separate, not exclusively used. *Sittings:* Free 30. *Attendance:* Afternoon: general congregation 30. *Average attendance:* Afternoon: general congregation 30. *Signed:* Jno. F. England, Minister, Wirksworth. [HO 129/446/59]

Primitive Methodist. *Erected:* 1823. Separate and entire, exclusively used. *Sittings:* Free 75, other 60, standing 30. *Attendance:* Morning: Sunday school 80; afternoon: general congregation 56, Sunday school 74, total 130; evening: general congregation 120. *Average attendance:* General 176, Sunday school 154, total 330. *Signed:* John Slater, Superintendent & steweard, Bole Hill, Wirksworth. [HO 129/446/60]

Longway Bank

Wesleyan Methodist. *Erected:* A.D. 1833. Separate and entire, exclusively used. *Sittings:* 70. *Attendance:* Morning: Sunday school 10; afternoon: general congregation 25, Sunday school 10, total 35; evening: general congregation 25, Sunday school 5, total 30. *Average attendance:* Morning: Sunday school 10; afternoon: general congregation 25, Sunday school 16, total 41; evening: general congregation 25, Sunday school 8, total 33. *Signed:* Jno. F. England, Minister, Wirksworth. [HO 129/446/61]

Alderwasley[1]

Church of England. Chapel. *Erected:* Licensed in lieu of an old chapel previously existing. *Endowments:* Other permanent endowments optional paid by Fras. Hurt Esq. *Sittings:* Free 220, other 33, total 253. *Attendance:* Afternoon: general congregation 140, Sunday school 35, total 175. *Average attendance:* Morning: general congregation 110, Sunday school 40, total 150; afternoon: general congregation 150, Sunday school 40, total 190. *Signed:* N. Hubbersty, Minister, Wirksworth. [HO 129/446/62]

Ashleyhay Bent Chapel[2]

Wesleyan Methodist. *Erected:* A.D. 1811. Separate and entire, exclusively used. *Sittings:* 100 in all. *Attendance:* Morning: general congregation 20; afternoon: general congregation 30. *Average attendance:* Morning: general congregation 25; afternoon: general congregation 35. *Corrected by:* Jno. F. England, Minister, Wirksworth. [HO 129/446/63]

N.B. No 4. This Enumerators List of Schools and Churches has got mislaid but the Chapel herein mentioned [HO 129/446/64] is the only place for which such Return could be made.

Idridgehay[3]

Primitive Methodist. *Erected:* 1846, Room, exclusively used. *Sittings:* Free 70, standing 10. *Attendance:* Morning: general congregation 16; afternoon: general congregation 60; evening: general congregation 60. *Average attendance:* 50. *Signed:* Samuel Melbourne, Leader, Idridgehay, near Wirksworth. [HO 129/446/64]

N.B. No 5. This Enumerators List is mislaid but the return herein [HO 129/446/65] herein is the only place requiring it.

---

[1] Population 400.

[2] Population 271.

[3] Population, with Alton, 222.

DUFFIELD

Shottle[1]

Church of England. *Erected:* Licensed 1840, only a School Room as additional. *Endowments:* not endowed. *Sittings:* about 120. *Attendance:* Afternoon: general congregation 18. *Average attendance:* not given. *Signed:* James P. Deacon, Minister, Turnditch. [HO 129/446/65A]

This list is mislaid but the return herein [HO 129/446/65A] is the only place [66] which could have required it.

Shottle

General Baptist. *Erected:* Upper room exclusively used. *Sittings:* all free. *Attendance:* Morning: Sunday school 60; afternoon: general congregation 115, Sunday school 60. *Average attendance:* not given. *Signed:* Jos. Malin, deacon Lamb House, Shottle. [HO 129/446/66]

[1] Population, with Postern, 467.

ASHBOURNE REGISTRATION DISTRICT

Brailsford Sub-District

ASHBOURNE[1]

Hulland Ward[2]

Primitive Methodist. *Erected:* 1827. Separate and entire, exclusively used. *Sittings:* Free 80, other 16. *Attendance:* Afternoon: general congregation 39; evening: general congregation 42. *Average attendance:* general congregation 50, Sunday school 12. *Signed:* Samuel Bottomley, Minister of the Gospel, Primitive Methodist Chapel House, Belper. [HO 129/447/1]

Cross of Hands

Primitive Methodist. *Erected:* 1831. Separate and entire, exclusively used. *Sittings:* Free 100, other none, standing none. *Attendance:* Afternoon: general congregation 45, Sunday school 11, total 56; evening: general congregation 55. *Average: attendance:* Morning: Sunday school 12; afternoon: general congregation 100; evening: general congregation 100. *Signed:* Samuel Bottomley, minister, Primitive Methodist Chapel House, Belper. [HO 129/447/2]

BRAILSFORD[3]

Church of England. Brailsford Rectory cum Osmaston – called All Saints, in the middle of the parish or township. *Erected:* Consecrated before 1st Jany 1800. *Endowments:* Tithe with Osmaston, gross amount £600, glebe £150. *Sittings:* Free 11, other 281, total 292. *Attendance:* Morning: general congregation 120, Sunday school 48; afternoon: general congregation 73, Sunday school 40. *Average attendance:* not given. *Remarks:* The church is inconveniently situated in a field at half a mile distance from the nearest

---

[1] Parish population 5,087.

[2] Population 369.

[3] Population 708.

house. The outgoings of the living for 2 curates etc. etc. amount to nearly £240 – the *net* amount therefore is £510. *Signed:* Walter Shirley, Rector, Brailsford Rectory. [HO 129/447/3]

Primitive Methodist. *Erected:* 1845. Separate and entire, exclusively used. *Sittings:* Free 87, other 33. *Attendance:* Afternoon: general congregation 40; evening: general congregation 70. *Average attendance:* not given. *Signed:* Henry Brownson, chapel steward, Brailsford, near Derby. [HO 129/447/4]

Wesleyan Methodist. *Erected:* 1821. Separate and entire, exclusively used. *Sittings:* Free 150, other 60. *Attendance:* Afternoon: general congregation 80; evening: general congregation 50. *Average attendance:* not given. *Signed:* Francis Osborne, chapel steward, farmer, Brailsford. [HO 129/447/5]

SUTTON ON THE HILL[1]

Thurvaston[2]

Wesleyan Methodist. *Erected:* 1814. Separate and entire, exclusively used. *Sittings:* Other 45, standing 120. *Attendance:* Morning: Sunday school 45; afternoon: general congregation 150; evening: general congregation 50. *Average attendance:* not given. *Signed:* John Wainwright, chapel steward, farmer, Thurvaston, nr Longford. [HO 129/447/6]

LONGFORD[3]

Church of England. S. Chad. Ancient parish church. *Erected:* Consecrated before 1800. *Endowments:* not given. *Sittings:* Free 232, other 254, total 486. *Attendance:* Morning: general congregation 68, Sunday school 29, total 97; afternoon: general congregation 31, Sunday school 29, total 60. *Average attendance:* not given. *Remarks:* If the account of the gross Income for the year 1850 is required it can be furnished. Tithe & glebe are the sources from which the Income is derived. *Signed:* T.A. Anson, Rector, Longford. [HO 129/447/7]

---

[1] Population 570.

[2] Population, with Osleston, 395.

[3] Parish population 1,162, Longford township 530.

Rodsley[1]

Wesleyan Methodist. *Erected:* about 1825. Separate and entire, exclusively used. *Sittings:* Free 130, other 40. *Attendance:* not given. *Average attendance:* Afternoon: general congregation 80; evening: general congregation 45. *Signed:* Charles Walker, chapel steward, *Signed:* Charles Holmes, Rodsley, Ashbourne. [HO 129/447/8]

Hollington[2]

Primitive Methodist Chappel. *Erected:* 1847. Separate and entire, exclusively used. *Sittings:* Free 86, other 72, standing 21' x 18'. *Attendance:* Morning: general congregation 30; afternoon: general congregation 71; evening: general congregation 120. *Average attendance:* 120. *Signed:* William Williamson, chappel steward, Hollington. [HO 129/447/9]

Alkmonton – Bentley[3]

Wesleyan Methodist. *Erected:* Not separate, not exclusively used. *Sittings:* Free 40. *Attendance:* general congregation 49. *Average attendance:* Morning: general congregation 50. *Remarks:* We are frequently crowded almost to suffocation. The Lord is gracious to us and enlarges our borders. Amen and Amen. About the same number at the afternoon service. *Signed:* Joseph Baker, Cubley, nr Sudbury. [HO 129/447/10]

Alkmonton[4]

Church of England. The church of S. John, Alkmonton, attached to which is the chapelry district of Alkmonton. *Erected:* Consecrated July 27 1848 as an additional church, chiefly at the expense of William Evans M.P. Esq., the inhabitants of the district contributing about £50. Cost Wm Evans Esq. 450, inhabitants £50, total £500. *Endowments:* Endowed by Wm Evans M.P. who invested a certain sum in the three per cent consolidated Bank

---

[1] Population 168.
[2] Population 302.
[3] Population 84.
[4] Population 78.

Annuities producing a yearly stipend of £50 which is paid through the Commissioners or Treasurers of Queen Anne. *Sittings:* Free 120. *Attendance:* Morning and afternoon on alternate Sundays: general congregation 35, Sunday school 5, total 40. *Average attendance:* not given. *Remarks:* I am not quite sure whether under 'Name and desc.' of church' above I have expressed myself sufficiently clearly. The church is called the 'church of S. John' and is the church of a new district chapelry called 'the chapelry district of Alkmonton'. *Signed:* Alpheus Slight, Perpetual curate, Alkmonton, Longford. [HO 129/447/11]

SHIRLEY[1]

Church of England. Ancient parish church. *Erected:* not given. *Endowments:* Tithe £150, glebe £18. *Sittings:* Free 105, other 119, total 224. *Attendance:* Morning: general congregation 85, Sunday school 41, total 126; evening: general congregation 78. *Average attendance:* Morning: general congregation 110, Sunday school 70, total 180; evening: general congregation 170. *Remarks:* The Services are Morning and Evening. *Signed:* E.W. Michell, Vicar of Shirley, Shirley, near Derby. [HO 129/447/12]

Primitive Methists – Wesleyan Methodist. *Erected:* Erected out of dweling house in 1841. Seperate, exclusively used. *Sittings:* Free 38, other 12, standing 10. *Attendance:* Afternoon: general congregation 38; evening: general congregation 39. *Average attendance:* 34. *Remarks:* Superintendent Lee, Belper. This chapel is occupide by the Wesleyan Reformers every Sunday afternoon; by the Primitives in the evening. *Signed:* Joseph Goodall, steward, Shirley, Derby. [HO 129/447/13]

YEAVELEY[2]

Church of England. Trinity church. Church of a District made by order in council under 16 Section of 59 of George 3rd, 3rd Cap. 1 & 4. *Erected:* Consecrated May 1840 in lieu of an old church. *Endowments:* Tithe £20. *Sittings:* Free 74, other 80, total 154. *Attendance:* Afternoon: general congregation 70, Sunday school 32, total 102. *Average attendance:* Morning:

---

[1] Parish population 659, Shirley township 387.

[2] Population 238.

general congregation 60, Sunday school 40, total 100; afternoon: general congregation 75, Sunday school 36, total 101. *Remarks:* The service is at present but once on Sunday alternately morning and afternoon. *Signed:* E.W. Michell, Vicar, Shirley, nr Derby. [HO 129/447/14]

Methodist and Calvinist. *Erected:* 1810. Separate and entire, exclusively used. *Sittings:* Free 90. *Attendance:* Afternoon: general congregation 40; evening: general congregation 40. *Average attendance:* 40. *Signed:* Joseph Allen, Keeper of chapel, Yeavely. [HO 129/447/15]

MUGGINTON

Hulland Ward Intake[1]

Church of England. Intake Chapel. *Erected:* Consecration not known, erectd by Francis Brown, cost by himself. Endowment: Land 17 ac. *Sittings:* all free. *Attendance:* morning and evening no service; afternoon: general congregation 19. *Average attendance:* Morning and evening no service; afternoon: general congregation 20 to 30. *Signed:* John Barton, Curate of Intake, Langley, Nr Derby. [HO 129/447/16]

Mayfield Sub-District

NORBURY[2]

Snelston[3]

Church of England. *Erected:* Consecrated before 1800. *Endowments:* Land 47 acres, tithes, glebe £300, dues & Easter offering 15s. 6d. *Sittings:* Free 75, other 160, total 235. *Attendance:* Morning: general congregation 45, Sunday school 27; afternoon: general congregation 71, Sunday school 29. *Average attendance:* not given. *Signed:* Clement F. Broughton, Rector, Norbury, Ashbourn. [HO 129/447/17]

---

[1] Population 44.

[2] Parish population 475.

[3] Population 389.

ASHBOURNE

Clifton[1]

Church of England. Holy Trinity, the church of the chapelry district of Clifton. The district was assigned on the 6 July 1846 under an Act passed in the 59th year of His late Majesty King George the Third, Section 16. *Erected:* Cons. June 18 1845 as an additional church for the use of the inhabitants of the chapelry district of Clifton. By private benefaction and subscription assisted by a grant of £100 from the Incorporated Society and another of £150 from the Lichfield Diocesan Society for building Churches etc. Cost: £1313 12s. 11d. *Endowments:* House & garden: Assessment under Property Tax £25, other permanent endowment grant from Ecclesiastical Commissioners £50, pews £5, fees about £1. *Sittings:* Free 122, other 96, total 218. *Attendance:* Morning: General congregation 33, Sunday school 35, total 68; afternoon: general congregation 56, Sunday school 35, total 91 [*Comment:* A wet and stormy day.]. *Average attendance:* not given. *Remarks:* Previous to the erection and consecration of Holy Trinity Church there were only 24 sittings in the parish church at Ashbourne appropriated to the use of the inhabitants of the present district of Clifton: as a natural consequence Dissent prevails to a considerable extent. *Signed:* H. Gamble, Incumbent, The Parsonage, Clifton. [HO 129/447/27]

Clifton – Hanging Bridge

Primitive Methodist. *Erected:* 1830. Separate and entire, exclusively used. *Sittings:* Free 64, other 62, standing none. *Attendance:* Morning: general congregation 23; afternoon: general congregation 57, Sunday school 23; evening: general congregation 103. *Average attendance:* not given. *Signed:* William Froggatt, chapel steward, Hanging Bridge, nr Ashbourne. [HO 129/447/28]

Independent. *Erected:* About 1830. Seperate and entire, exclusively used. *Sittings:* 80 & all free. *Attendance:* evening: general congregation 40. *Average attendance:* evening: general congregation 50. *Remarks:* The whole of the sittings in the Chapel are free. *Signed:* James Peach, minister, Ashbourne. [HO 129/447/29]

---

[1] Population 887.

Ashbourne Sub-District

Hulland[1]

Church of England. Christchurch having a consolidated district under the provisions of 1 & 2 Wm IV c. 38. The church stands in Hulland in the parish of Ashbourne, the district includes with Hulland, Biggin in Wirksworth, and the extra-parochial district of Hulland Ward. *Erected:* Licensed for public worship May 13th, consecrated Aug. 29 1838 as a new church. Erected by Private Benefaction & Subscription & principally by T. Borough Esq. of Chetwynd Park, Salop, J. Blackwall Esq. of Blackwall and Miss Downing of Biggin. Diocesan Church Society's Grant £245. Total cost £1,300. *Endowments:* Other permanent endowments £1196 9s. 4d. in Funds, pews £11, fees £3. *Sittings:* Free 100, other 200, total 300. *Attendance:* Morning: general congregation 55, Sunday school 67, total 122; afternoon: general congregation 70, Sunday school 67, total 137. *Average attendance:* not given. *Remarks:* congregation below average March 30th. *Signed:* Charles Evans, perpetual curate of Hulland, Blackwall, Wirksworth. [HO 129/447/30]

Sturston[2]

Wesleyan Methodist. Compton Street. *Erected:* 1822. Separate and entire, exclusively used. *Sittings:* Free 220, other 206. *Attendance:* Morning: general congregation 85, Sunday school 40, total 125; evening: general congregation 110, Sunday school 10, total 120. *Average attendance:* Morning: general congregation 85, Sunday school 40, total 125; evening: general congregation 110, Sunday school 10, total 120. *Signed:* Richard Sergeant, Wesleyan minister, Ashbourne. [HO 129/447/31]

Sturston Sion Chapel (Countess of Huntingdon). *Erected:* 1800. Separate and entire, exclusively used. *Sittings:* Free 100, other 240. *Attendance:* Morning: general congregation 143, Sunday school 90, total 233; afternoon: general congregation 88, Sunday school 90, total 178; evening: general congregation 133. *Average attendance:* Morning: general congregation 150, Sunday school 90, total 240; afternoon: general congregation 90,

[1] Population 219.

[2] Population 664.

Sunday school 90, total 180; evening: general congregation 160. *Remarks:* The chapel is generally considered as belonging to the Countess of Huntingdon's Connection but the form of church government is Independent. *Signed:* Henry Hollis, Minister, Chapel House, Ashbourne. [HO 129/447/32]

Hulland

Primitive Methodist. *Erected:* 1821. Separate and entire, exclusively used. *Sittings:* Free 60, other 44. *Attendance:* not given. *Average attendance:* Morning: general congregation 40; afternoon: Sunday school 10. *Signed:* Joseph Riley, Chapel Steward, Hulland Ward, near Ashbourne. [HO 129/447/33]

Hulland Wardgate

Wesleyan Methodist. *Erected:* 1817. Separate and entire, for place of worship and Sunday school but for no other purpose. *Sittings:* Free 200, other 60, standing 25. *Attendance:* not given. *Average attendance:* Morning: Sunday school 23; afternoon: general congregation 45. *Signed:* Willm Whittaker. Wardgate Wesleyan Chapel, Turnditch, Derbys. [HO 129/447/34]

Ashbourne[1]

Church of England. S. Oswald. *Erected:* not given. *Endowments:* Tithe £52, glebe £4 10s., other permanent endowment £8, total £64 10s., fees £20. *Sittings:* Free 300, other 1,000, total 1,300. *Attendance:* Morning: general congregation 542, Sunday school 204, total 746; afternoon: general congregation 589, Sunday school 206, total 795; evening: general congregation 326, total 326. *Average attendance:* not given. *Signed:* John Rd Errington, Vicar, Ashbourne. [HO 129/447/35]

Church of England. S. Mary's Chapel. *Erected:* Licensed 1845 for the accomodation of the poor, purchased from the Baptists. Cost: £300. *Endowments:* Not endowed. *Sittings:* Free 100, other 100, total 200. *Attendance:* Afternoon: general congregation 105. *Average attendance:* not given. *Remarks:* The service is maintained at the cost of the Vicar being £20 per annm. *Signed:* John Rd Errington, Vicar of Ashbourne. [HO 129/447/36]

---

[1] Population 2,154.

Primitive Methodist Chappel. *Erected:* 1846. Seperate, exclusively used as a place of worship. *Sittings:* Free 80, other 60. *Attendance:* Afternoon: general congregation 50; evening: general congregation 70. *Average attendance:* not given. *Signed:* Brian Wibberley, leader, Market Place, Ashbourne. [HO 129/447/37]

Church of Jesus Christ of Latterday Saints. Club room at the George and Dragon, Market Place, Ashbourne. *Erected:* detached building in the yard, not exclusively used. *Sittings:* all free. *Attendance:* Afternoon: general congregation 12; evening: general congregation 16. *Average attendance:* not given. *Signed:* Wm Chadwick, priest, Offcote, Underwood, Sandy Brook, nr Ashbourne. [HO 129/447/38]

Wesleyan Reformers. *Erected:* Used for public worship 1 year. Separate and entire, exclusively used. *Sittings:* Free 100, other 80. *Attendance:* Morning: general congregation 89; evening: general congregation 145. *Average attendance:* Morning: general congregation 110; evening: general congregation 150. *Remarks:* In addition to the numbers given there are in connection with us in the Ashbourne circuit worshiping in private houses of which no return will be made the following numbers Brailsford 50, Osmaston 40, Bentley 40, Mappleton 30, Mayfield 20. *Signed:* Thomas Coxon, Steward, Ashbourne. [HO 129/447/39]

EDLASTON[1]

Church of England S. James. an ancient parish church. *Erected:* Before 1800. *Endowments:* Tithe £165 4s. 4d., glebe £57 4s. *Sittings:* Free 47, other 98, total 145. *Attendance:* Morning: general congregation 50, Sunday school 21, total 71; evening: general congregation 68. *Average attendance:* not given. *Signed:* Thomas Cupiss, officiating minister, Edlaston Rectory, Ashbourne. [HO 129/447/40]

---

[1] Population 197.

Wyaston

Wesleyan Methodist.[1] *Erected:* Abt 1830. Separate and entire, exclusively used. *Sittings:* Free 100, other 36. No other information given. *Signed:* R. Sergeant, Wesleyan Minister, Ashbourne. [HO 129/447/41]

OSMASTON[2]

Church of England.[3] – annexed to Brailsford. *Erected:* Consecrated 20 June 1845. A very old church was pulled down and rebuilt on nearly the same site under Faculty by Francis Wright Esq. at a cost of about £8,000. *Endowments:* Returned in Brailsford. *Sittings:* Free 70, children 100, other 136, total 306. *Attendance:* Morning: general congregation 113, Sunday school 96, total 209; afternoon: general congregation 111, Sunday school 96, total 207. *Average attendance:* Morning: general congregation 140, Sunday school 96, total 236; afternoon: general congregation 150, Sunday school 96, total 246. *Remarks:* The average number of attendants at church during the last twelve months exceeds the number on March 30th because there was a large work going on in the Parish which is now finished. *Signed:* F. Wright, Churchwarden, Osmaston Manor, Derby. [HO 129/447/42]

Wesleyan Reformers. *Erected:* A separate dwelling house in which Divine Worship is conducted. *Sittings:* Free 60. *Attendance:* Evening: general congregation 40. *Average attendance:* not given. *Remarks:* This Place is Regurly supplyed on sabbath days by Weslayan Methadist Reform Local Preachers. *Signed:* Herbert Baker, local preacher, Osmaston, Ashbourne. [HO 129/447/43]

Wesleyan Methodist. *Erected:* 1827. Separate and entire, exclusively used. *Sittings:* Free 75, other 80. *Attendance:* not given. *Average attendance:* evening: general congregation 30. *Signed:* R. Sergeant, Wesleyan minister. [HO 129/447/44]

---

[1] This chapel is not in the enumerator's list.

[2] Population 366.

[3] The dedication is to S. Martin.

BRADLEY[1]

Church of England. All Saints, an ancient church, the parish is distinct and separate. *Erected:* Consecrated before 1800. *Endowments:* Rent charge £271, glebe land £68, fees 15s. *Sittings:* Free 55, other 145, total 200. *Attendance:* Morning: general congregation 63, Sunday school 35, total 98. *Average attendance:* Morning: general congregation 45 or 50, Sunday school 40, total 85 or 90; afternoon: general congregation 80, Sunday school 45, total 125. *Remarks:* The necessary outgoings from the above amounts are £27 0s. 9d. besides Property Tax. There is only one service which is performed morning and afternoon alternately. It is a scattered population, there is no village. *Signed:* Evan Thomas, curate, Hulland, Ashbourne. [HO 129/447/45]

BRADBOURNE[2]

Atlow[3]

Church of England. ancient parish church. *Erected:* Cons. before 1800. *Endowments:* Land £4, tithe £110, house and small garden let for £2 10s., fees 5s. *Sittings:* Free 35, other 72, total 107. *Attendance:* Afternoon: general congregation 50, Sunday school 13, total 63. *Average attendance:* Morning: general congregation 50, Sunday school 12, total 62; afternoon: general congregation 70, Sunday school 14, total 84. *Remarks:* The number of persons stated to be in the church this afternoon could not be accurately counted, neither can the average number of persons attending the church be accurately stated. The number of Sunday school children also frequently varies. *Signed:* R.R. Vaughtan, Incumbent of Perpetual Curacy, Yeldersley House, Derby. [HO 129/447/46]

KNIVETON[4]

Church of England. Parish church. Perpetual curacy supposed to be an ancient chapelry. *Erected:* Cons. before 1800. *Endowments:* Tithe £25, glebe

---

[1] Population 248.

[2] Parish population 1,230, Bradbourne township 163.

[3] Population 137.

[4] Population 331.

£30, total about £55. *Sittings:* Free 200. *Attendance:* Morning: general congregation 36, Sunday school 10, total 46; afternoon: the afternoon congregation is more than double this number. *Average attendance:* not given. *Remarks:* The services being alternate the numbers given for two Sundays would show more correctly what numbers actually attend the church services. *Signed:* Charles William Richards, officiating minister, Ashbourne. [HO 129/447/47]

Primitive Methodist. *Erected:* 1832. Separate and entire, exclusively used. *Sittings:* Free 80, other 34, standing 20. *Attendance:* Afternoon: general congregation 77, other 31, total 108; evening: general congregation 70. *Average attendance:* Morning: general congregation 80, Sunday school 36, total 116. *Signed:* Samuel Wade, minister, Kniveton, Ashbourne. [HO 129/447/48]

Calton Sub-District

BRADBOURNE

Tissington[1]

Church of England. S. Mary the Virgin. *Erected:* Cons. before 1800. *Endowments:* Tithe £3 10s. other permanent endowment £92 18s. 6d., dues £1, Easter offering 10s. *Sittings:* Free 53, other 110, total 163. *Attendance:* Morning: general congregation 49, Sunday school 24, total 73. *Average attendance:* Morning: general congregation 65, Sunday school 25, total 90; afternoon: general congregation 78, Sunday school 25, total 103. *Remarks:* The service is alternately morning & afternoon; there has also been an alternate service for the last service at a licensed room in the parish. *Signed:* Alleyne Fitzherbert, curate, Tissington, Ashburn. [HO 129/447/50]

Woodeaves Mill

Church of England. Licensed school room. *Erected:* Schoolroom licensed 1841 as an additional place of worship. The room merely lent by the occupier of cotton mill. *Sittings:* Free 45. *Attendance:* Afternoon: general

---

[1] Population 344.

congregation 22, Sunday school 13, total 35. *Average attendance:* Morning: general congregation 12, Sunday school 15, total 27; afternoon: general congregation 12, Sunday school 15, total 27. *Remarks:* Service in this Licensed Room has been alternately with that at the parish church morning and afternoon. *Signed:* Alleyne FitzHerbert, curate, Tissington. [HO 129/447/51]

FENNY BENTLEY[1]

Church of England. S. Mary Magdalene. An ancient parish church. *Erected:* Cons. before 1800. *Endowments:* Total about £125. *Sittings:* Free 72, other 64, total 136. *Attendance:* Afternoon: general congregation 56, Sunday school 34, total 90. *Average attendance:* not given. *Remarks:* The services are alternate morning and afternoon every other Sunday. *Signed:* Charles William Richards, A.B., Officiating minister, Fenny Bentley, Ashbourne. [HO 129/447/52]

Wesleyan Reformers. preaching house. *Erected:* House taken for preaching June 1850, exclusively used. *Sittings:* Free 50. *Attendance:* Afternoon: general congregation 22, Sunday school 11, total 26; evening: general congregation 26. *Average attendance:* general congregation 30, Sunday school 16, total 46. *Signed:* John Redfern, steward, Fenny Bentley, Ashbourne. [HO 129/447/53]

Wesleyan Methodist. *Erected:* 1832. Entire building, exclusively used. *Sittings:* Free 100, other 24. *Attendance:* not given. *Average attendance:* afternoon: general congregation 27. *Signed:* Richd. Sergeant, Wesleyan minister, Ashbourne. [HO 129/447/54]

THORPE[2]

Church of England. S. Leonard. Ancient parish church. *Erected:* Before 1800, probably abt 1100. *Endowments:* Land none, tithe £84 11s. 6d., glebe £59, fees a few shillings. *Sittings:* Free 50, other 80, total 130. *Attendance:* Morning: general congregation 42, Sunday school 31, total 73; afternoon: general congregation 47, Sunday school 16, total 63. *Average attendance:* not

---

[1] Population 290.
[2] Population 188.

given. *Remarks:* Attendance on the 30th March may perhaps be considered below the usual average. *Signed:* Benjn. George Blackden, Rector, Ashbourn, Derbys. [HO 129/447/55]

MAPLETON[1]

Church of England. S. Mary. *Erected:* not given. *Endowments:* Tithe £38, glebe £36, fees 10s., total £74. *Sittings:* Free 45, other 108, total 153. *Attendance:* Afternoon: general congregation 79, Sunday school 16, total 95. *Average attendance:* not given. *Signed:* John Rd Errington, Rector of Mappleton. [HO 129/447/56]

Wesleyan Methodist. *Erected:* Not separate, not exclusively used. *Sittings:* Free 40. *Attendance:* Evening: general congregation 29. *Average attendance:* Evening: general congregation 32. *Remarks:* This place is a private dwelling house occupied by a widow who takes in the preachers and opens her house on Sabbath evening for public worship. It will be seen that we have termed ourselves as Wesleyans and such we consider ourselves to be. It will be right to observe that owing to some arbitrary acts of the Circuit Minister this Society with others in the Circuit has withdrawn from his control and now exist separate from the Conference body. It is supplied only by Local Preachers. *Signed:* William Walters, Junr. Local Preacher, Church St, Ashbourne. [HO 129/447/57]

Hartington Sub-District

PARWICH

Alsop en le Dale[2]

Church of England. Parish church of Allsop en le Dale dedicated to S. Michael. *Erected:* not given. *Endowments:* Land £37, other permanent endowment £8 14s. *Sittings:* Free 26, other 78, total 106. *Attendance:* afternoon: general congregation 52. *Average attendance:* alternate morning and afternoon 60. *Remarks:* Ancient name of the manor and lands Elleshope

---

[1] Population 200.
[2] Population 80.

a berwick of Ashbourne. Possessor when the Survey of Domesday was taken – the King. The number of attendants at divine service is sometimes more than the whole population of the parish. In this place the Reformer Becon took refuge in the Marian persecution. *Signed:* Willm Fisher, Minister, Parwich. [HO 129/447/70]

Parwich[1]

Church of England. S. Peter parish church. *Erected:* not given. *Endowments:* Land £43, tithe £10, other permanent endowment £84. 0s. 10d. *Sittings:* Free 190, other 94, total 284. *Attendance:* Morning: general congregation 81, Sunday school 36, total 117; evening: general congregation 71. *Average attendance:* Morning: general congregation 100, Sunday school 35; alternate with afternoon, evening: general congregation 90. *Remarks:* Ancient name of manor and lands Pevrewic. Possessor when the Survey of Doomsday was taken Colne under the King. One duty alternate morning and afternoon and one service voluntary regularly in the evening. *Signed:* William Fisher, Perpetual curate, Parwich, Ashbourne. [HO 129/447/71]

Wesleyan Methodist. *Erected:* 1850. Separate and entire, exclusively used. *Sittings:* Free 75, other 60. *Attendance:* Morning: Sunday school 22; afternoon: general congregation 32, Sunday school 21, total 53; evening: general congregation 39. *Average attendance:* general congregation 35, Sunday school 22, total 57. *Signed:* Thomas Etherington, trustee, Parwich Ashbourne. [HO 129/447/72]

HARTINGTON[2]

Biggin[3]

Primitive Methodist. *Erected:* 1842. Separate and entire, exclusively used. *Sittings:* Free 39, other 33. *Attendance:* Afternoon: general congregation 12. An exclusive service called a love-feast. *Average attendance:* afternoon 20. *Signed:* William E. Saunders, Superintendant Minister, Fountain St, Leek, Stafford. [HO 129/447/73]

---

[1] Population 493.

[2] Parish population 2,089.

[3] Population 133.

PARWICH

Pike Hall

Wesleyan Methodist. Pike Hall preaching room. *Erected:* uncertain, not separate, not exclusively used. *Sittings:* Free 45. *Attendance:* Afternoon: general congregation 30. *Average attendance:* general congregation 30. *Signed:* Jno. F. England, Minister, Wirksworth. [HO 129/447/74]

HARTINGTON Nether Quarter[1]

Heathcote

Primitive Methodist. *Erected:* 1835. Separate and entire, exclusively used. *Sittings:* Free 100, other 24, standing 150. *Attendance:* Morning: class or members 11; afternoon: 30 to 40; evening: 40 to 50. *Average attendance:* about 45 at each service, Sunday school none. *Remarks:* The Primitive Methodists preach the doctrines of the Church of England as is ascribed in Deed Poll of the Connexion which is enrolled in the Court of Chancery. Heathcote is in the Winster Circuit. *Signed:* Adolphus Frederick Beckerlegge, minister, Winster, Matlock Bath. [HO 129/447/75]

Biggin

Church of England. S. Thomas. *Erected:* Consecrated April 25 1848. Biggin church was built in consequence of the inhabitants being for the most part nearly three miles distant from Hartington. The land was given by the Duke of Devonshire on which the church was built aided by a grant of £200 from the Incorporated Society and £300 from Lichfield Diocesan Society. Cost: Societies £500, Subs. £755, total £1,255. *Endowments:* House and garden free, Land £3, Rent charge £15, other permanent endowment £619 13s. 11d. in 3% Consols £18 4s. 6d., pew rents £6 15s. fees £1, annual donation from the Duke of Devonshire £35. *Sittings:* Free 220, other 80, total 300. *Attendance:* Afternoon: general congregation 67, Sunday school 64, total 131. *Average attendance:* single duty alternately: general congregation 100, Sunday school 75. *Remarks:* All the materials for Building the Church were carted free by the Inhabitants. There is a Parsonage House and

---

[1] Population 436.

Garden for the Minister. *Signed:* Thomas Booth, Perpetual curate, Biggin Parsonage, Ashbourne. [HO 129/447/76]

BRADBOURNE[1]

Ballidon[2]

Church of England. an ancient chapel to Bradbourne church. *Erected:* Cons. before 1800. *Endowments:* modus instead of tithe £11 2s. 9$\frac{1}{2}$d. *Sittings:* Free 8, other 64, total 72. *Attendance:* evening: general congregation 26. *Average attendance:* evening: general congregation 20 to 35. *Remarks:* The service is once a fortnight in the Evening; & there is no school, the children attending Bradbourne school. *Signed:* Augustus Wingman, minister, Bradbourne, Wirksworth. [HO 129/447/77]

Brassington Sub-District

WIRKSWORTH

Middleton by Wirksworth[3]

Church of England. Trinity church. *Erected:* 1839. *Endowments:* not given. *Sittings:* Free 363, other 50, total 413. *Attendance:* Morning: General congregation from 10 to 15; afternoon: from 15 to 25; Sunday school about 50. *Average attendance:* not given. *Signed:* J. Frederic Harward, Incumbent. [HO 129/447/79]

BRADBOURNE[4]

Church of England. All Saints. *Erected:* Cons. before 1800. *Endowments:* Tithe £107 10s., glebe about £4 14s., other permanent endowments

---

[1] Parish population 1,230.

[2] Population 99.

[3] Population 1,012.

[4] Township population 163.

£1 9s. 4d., from Aldwark £1 6s. 10d., & Lea Hall 2s. 6d., fees about £1 2s., total £113 3s. 4d. *Sittings:* Free 80, other 180, total 260. *Attendance:* Afternoon: general congregation 50, Sunday school 8, total 58. *Average attendance:* Morning: general congregation 45, Sunday school 16, total 61; aftenoon: general congregation 60, Sunday school 16, total 76. *Remarks:* One service each Sunday performed alternately morning and afternoon. The interior of the Church was restored and repewed in 1846 at the cost of nearly £300 by subscription & a small rate. The Vicarage house was also enlarged & rendered inhabitable at the sole expense of the present curate at the cost of about £300 in the same year. *Signed:* Augustus Wingman, curate, Bradbourne, Nr. Wirksworth. [HO 129/447/80]

Aldwark

Wesleyan Methodist.[1] *Erected:* A.D. 1829. Separate and entire, exclusively used. *Sittings:* Total 70. *Attendance:* Morning: general congregation 35; afternoon: general congregation 25. *Average attendance:* Morning: general congregation 35; afternoon: general congregation 25. *Signed:* Jno. F. England, minister, Wirksworth. [HO 129/447/81]

Brassington[2]

Church of England. An ancient parish church in the parish of Bradbourne. *Erected:* Cons. before 1800. *Endowments:* Land £24, tithe by impropriator £10, Q. Anne's Bounty £6 10s., Parliamentary Grant £42 7s. 2d., Gross £82 17s. 2d., fees (surplice) about £1 14s. *Sittings:* Free 170, other 145, total 315. *Attendance:* Morning: general congregation 66, Sunday school 43, total 109. *Average attendance:* Morning: general congregation 35, Sunday school 40, total 75; afternoon: general congregation 75, Sunday school 40, total 115. *Remarks:* One service performed each Sunday alternately morning and afernoon; not having been in the habit of counting the number of people I can only guess at the return of the average. *Signed:* Augustus Wingman, minister or curate, Bradbourn. [HO 129/447/82]

---

[1] This may be the same chapel as HO 129/449/82 (p. 193).

[2] Population 729.

Dale End

Independent. *Erected:* 1845. Separate and entire, exclusively used. *Sittings:* Free 160. *Attendance:* Morning: general congregation 17, afternoon: general congregation 52, Sunday school 54, total 106; evening: general congregation 78. *Average attendance:* not given. *Signed:* George Grafftey, minister, Brassington, Nr. Wirksworth. [HO 129/447/83]

Brassington

Primitive Methodist. *Erected:* AD 1834. Separate and entire, exclusively used. *Sittings:* Free 90, other 34, standing 30. *Attendance:* Morning: No morning services, Sunday school 34; afternoon: general congregation 94; evening: general congregation 152, Sunday school 94, total 246. *Average attendance:* Morning: No morning service, Sunday school 40; afternoon: general congregation 80; evening: general congregation 130. *Signed:* Simeon Webster, assistant steward, Brassington, Near Wirksworth. [HO 129/447/84]

CARSINGTON[1]

Church of England. Parish church. Name of saint in honour of whom called unknown: perhaps called after S. Bartholomew or S. Michael.[2] *Erected:* Cons. before 1800. *Endowments:* Land £65 or 70, tithe £109, glebe, Rectory house, fees about 30s. *Sittings:* the gallery free, others appropriated, total about 200. *Attendance:* Afternoon: general congregation 157; evening: prayers only, general congregation 107. *Average attendance:* not given. *Remarks:* The glebe land, house etc. is let for about 65 or 70£: two rooms in the house being reserved for the curate who occupies them. In the return for the Number of Persons attending Divine Service on March 30 1851, both adults and children are included. *Signed:* Robert Picton B.A., curate, Carsington Rectory, Wirksworth. [HO 129/447/85]

---

[1] Population 235.

[2] Present dedication is to S. Margaret.

HOGNASTON[1]

Church of England. S. Bartholomew. It is commonly known by the name of Hognaston church as all village churches are. It is the church of an ancient chapelry in the midst of the village of Hognaston but the parish is a distinct & separate parish. *Erected:* Cons. before 1800. *Endowments:* Land £45, small tythes £7, other permanent endowments £6, fees 10s. = £58 10s. *Sittings:* Free 30, other 120, total 150. *Attendance:* Afternoon: general congregation 48, Sunday school 39, total 87. *Average attendance:* Morning: general congregation 35, Sunday school 30, total 65; afternoon: general congregation 55, Sunday school 30, total 85. *Remarks:* There is only one service each Sunday in morning and afternoon alternately. The glebe land and great tithes are in the hands of a lessee who derives all the benefits of them subject, however, to an annual payment of £6 9s.6d. to the minister. The estimated value of the Glebe and Tythe is, I believe, somewhere about £240. The endowment given in the annexed return £45 is derived from land purchased with grants of money from Queen Anne's Bounty Board and forms no part of the original endowments of the church in Hognaston. The £7 is in round numbers the sum for which the small tithes have been commuted. It is humbly conceived here that a tax of £15 or £20 per cent annually should be levied on all lessees of Church property to be applied exclusively to the support of the minister & for the purposes of Education in connexion with the Church in the parishes to which the property or endowment belongs; in as much as the vested *rights* of the people to such an application of that kind of property are more ancient than those of any Lessee can be nor does it appear that any Lessee could have more right to complain of such an arrangement than the purchaser of stolen property has to demur to the restoration to its right owner of that property which does not equitably belong to him. *Signed:* Evan Thomas, curate, Hulland, Ashbourne. [HO 129/447/87]

Independent. *Erected:* not separate, not exclusively used. *Sittings:* not given. *Attendance:* Morning: general congregation 28. Averge attendance: Morning: general congregation 25. *Signed:* G. Grafftey, Minister, Brassington, near Wirksworth. [HO 129/447/88]

Primitive Methodist. *Erected:* 1827. Separate and entire, exclusively used. *Sittings:* Other 30, standing 25. *Attendance:* afternoon: general

---

[1] Population 299.

congregation 37, evening: general congregation 65. *Average attendance:* not given. *Signed:* John Allsop, chappel steward. [HO 129/447/89]

KIRK IRETON[1]

Church of England. Ancient Parish church. In the early Norman style. *Erected:* not given. *Endowments:* Tithe £315, glebe £102, fees £2. *Sittings:* Free and open forms 60, other 270, total 330. *Attendance:* Morning: general congregation 78, Sunday school 89, total 167; afternoon: general congregation 120, Sunday school 89, total 209. *Average attendance:* Not given. *Remarks:* The day being wet and stormy the number of the afternoon congregation was below the average attendance which is about 140. *Signed:* Robert Gell, Curate, Kirk Ireton, Wirksworth. [HO 129/447/90]

Primitive Methodist. *Erected:* 1836. Separate and entire, exclusively used. *Sittings:* Free 50, other 40, 18' x 12'. *Attendance:* Morning: general congregation 10, Sunday school 40; afternoon: general congregation 30; evening: general congregation 70. *Average attendance:* general congregation 70, Sunday school 40, total 110. *Signed:* James Smith, superintendant, Kirk Ireton, Derby. [HO 129/447/91]

WIRKSWORTH

Ible[2]

Primitive Methodist. *Erected:* 1823. Separate and entire, exclusively used. *Sittings:* 100 all free. *Attendance:* Afternoon: general congregation 31; evening: general congregation 28, total 59. *Average attendance:* general congregation 40. Sunday school none. *Signed:* John Rains, steward, Griff grange, Near Wirksworth. [HO 129/447/92]

---

[1] Parish population 735, Kirk Ireton township 569.

[2] Population 91.

Middleton[1]

Wesleyan Methodist. *Erected:* 1815. enlarged to present size 1821. Separate and entire, exclusively used except Sunday school. *Sittings:* Free 161, other 178, standing none except the aisles. *Attendance:* Morning: Sunday school 120; afternoon: general congregation 72, Sunday school 120, total 192; evening: general congregation 139, total 139. *Average attendance:* Morning: Sunday school 44; afternoon: general congregation 75, Sunday school 105, total 180; evening: general congregation 143. *Remarks:* These remarks and statements are as near as we can possibly come to as correct. *Signed:* Benjamin Clayton, steward, 204 Draper St,[2] Middleton by Wirksworth. [HO 129/447/93]

Independent or Congregational. *Erected:* 1787. Separate and entire, exclusively used. *Sittings:* Free 200, standing none except the aisles. *Attendance:* Afternoon: general congregation 50, Sunday school 60. *Average attendance:* Afternoon: general congregation 60, Sunday school 60, total 120. *Signed:* John Brown, minister, Wirksworth. [HO 129/447/94]

Primitive Methodist. *Erected:* 1846. Separate and entire, exclusively used. *Sittings:* Free 94, other 37, standing none except the aisles. *Attendance:* Afternoon: General congregation 95; evening: general congregation 151. *Average attendance:* Afternoon: General congregation 98; evening: general congregation 130. *Signed:* Joseph Doxey, steward, grocer, No. 89 Middleton by Wirksworth. [HO 129/447/95]

BONSALL[3]

Church of England. S. James. An old parish church. *Erected:* Cannot say (being absent from home). *Endowments:* Tithe £125, glebe £103, fees £4 10s. £620 have been borrowed from Queen Ann's Bounty for the Erection of a new Rectory. *Sittings:* Free 480. *Attendance:* Service numbers not given. *Average attendance:* Morning: general congregation 75, Sunday school 180, total 205; afternoon: general congregation 150, Sunday school 150, total 300. *Remarks:* This paper was forwarded to me in London because the officiating

---

[1] Population 1,012.

[2] *Sic,* although both the house-number and street name seem highly improbable: Benjamin Clayton appears in White's Directory (1857) as a grocer and draper of Middleton.

[3] Population 1,449.

clergyman could not answer the questions – & for this reason I cannot fill up III. *Signed:* E.S. Greville, Rector of Bonsall, near Matlock. [HO 129/447/96]

General Baptist. Yeoman St. *Erected:* 1824. Separate and entire, exclusively used. *Sittings:* Free 250, other 50. *Attendance:* Morning: Sunday school 125; afternoon: general congregation 50; evening: general congregation 57, total 107. *Average attendance:* Morning: Sunday school 131; evening: general congregation 50. *Signed:* John Worthy, deacon, Yeoman St, Bonsall. [HO 129/447/97]

Wesleyan Methodist.[1] preaching room. *Erected:* uncertain, not separate and not exclusively used. *Sittings:* not given. *Attendance:* Evening: general congregation 12. *Average attendance:* Evening: general congregation 14. *Signed:* Jno. F. England, Minister, Wirksworth. [HO 129/447/98]

Wesleyan Methodist.[2] *Erected:* Not separate, not exclusively used. *Sittings:* Free all. *Attendance:* Evening: General congregation 55. *Average attendance:* General congregation 30. *Remarks:* Public Worship closing here this day. Being removed to a more suitable place. *Signed:* Daniel Massey, Manager, Framework knitter, Bonsall. [HO 129/447/99]

Primitive Methodist. High Street. *Erected:* Before 1800. Not separate, not exclusively used. *Sittings:* Free 70, standing 30. *Attendance:* Evening: general congregation 98. *Average attendance:* Evening: general congregation 95. *Signed:* George Samuel Ward, class leader, Bonsall, near Matlock. [HO 129/447/100]

---

[1] See also next entry.

[2] This entry appears to duplicate the preceding one.

CHESTERFIELD REGISTRATION DISTRICT

Ashover Sub-District

ASHOVER[1]

Church of England. All Saints. *Erected:* Parish church founded as is said A.D. 1419. *Endowments:* Tithe £450, glebe £100, Easter offering £10. *Sittings:* Free 98, other 345, total 443. *Attendance:* Morning: general congregation 113; afternoon: general congregation 57. *Average attendance:* not given. *Signed:* Joseph Nodder, rector, Ashover, Chesterfield. [HO 129/448/1]

NORTH WINGFIELD[2]

Clay Cross[3]

Church of England. S. Bartholomew. *Erected:* 1851. *Endowments:* not given. *Sittings:* 450. *Attendance:* not given. *Average attendance:* Morning: general congregation 100, Sunday school 80 to 100; evening:general congregation 300 to 400. Afternoon: Service only once a month for baptisms. *Signed:* J. Oldham, Incumbent, Dec. 5 1851. [HO 129/448/2]

SHIRLAND[4]

Church of England. S. Leonard. *Erected:* not known. *Endowments:* not given. *Sittings:* Free 138, other 239, total 377. *Attendance:* not given. *Average attendance:* Morning: general congregation supposed to be about 250, Sunday school about 60; afternoon: general congregation supposed to be about 160, Sunday school about 60. *Signed:* Chas. H. Ramsden, curate, Shirland, Nov. 26 1851. [HO 129/448/3]

---

[1] Parish population 3,311, Ashover township 2,445.

[2] Parish population 4,351.

[3] Population 2,278.

[4] Parish population 1,268, Shirland township 851.

BRACKENFIELD[1]

Church of England. Holy Trinity. *Erected:* not known suppose above 400 years. *Endowments:* not given. *Sittings:* 100 total. *Attendance:* Not given. *Average attendance:* Morning: general congregation 15, Sunday school 60; afternoon: general congregation 50, Sunday school 60. *Remarks:* Clergyman the Rev. Packer, successor the Rev. J. Rushton Dec. 26 1851. *Signed:* Knowles, clerk. [HO 129/448/4]

MORTON[2]

Church of England. S. Michael.[3] *Erected:* Rebuilt (except the tower) 1850. original not known. *Endowments:* not given. *Sittings:* 200. *Attendance:* Not given. *Average attendance:* Morning: general congregation 40, Sunday school 26; afternoon: general congregation 20, Sunday school 26. *Signed:* Spencer, Morton, Dec. 1851. [HO 129/448/5]

NORTH WINGFIELD

Woodthorpe[4]

Methodist New Connexion. *Erected:* not known, schoolroom used exclusively for school etc. *Sittings:* 150. *Attendance:* evening: general congregation 50. *Average attendance:* Not given. *Signed:* John Berry, builder, Tupton, nr Chesterfield. [HO 129/448/6]

ASHOVER[5]

Wesleyan Methodist.[6] *Erected:* In the year 1807. Separate and entire, exclusively used. *Sittings:* Free 160, other 60. *Attendance:* Afternoon: general congregation 40, Sunday school 120, total 160; evening: general con-

---

[1] Population 399.

[2] Population 257.

[3] The present dedication is to Holy Cross.

[4] Population 267.

[5] Population 2,445.

[6] This is the same chapel as in HO 129/448/13 (p. 145).

gregation 100, Sunday school 20, total 120. *Average attendance:* General congregation 120, Sunday school 100, total 220. *Signed:* John Bassett, steward, printer, Ashover, nr. Chesterfield. [HO 129/448/7]

Primitive Methodist. *Erected:* 1849. Not separate, not exclusively used. *Sittings:* Free 50. *Attendance:* Evening: general congregation 41. *Average attendance:* general congregation 40. *Signed:* Benjamin Bunting, steward, Ashover, nr Chesterfield. [HO 129/448/8]

CRICH

Holloway

Wesleyan Reform. *Erected:* 1818. Separate and entire, exclusively used. *Sittings:* 16 yds x 6 yds, 320 all free. *Attendance:* Morning: Sunday school 101; afternoon: general congregation 71, Sunday school 101, total 172; evening: general congregation 120. *Average attendance:* General congregation 180, Sunday school 120, total 300. *Signed:* Wm Storer, steward of Holloway Chapel, Holloway nr Cromford. [HO 129/448/9]

ASHOVER

Span Carr

Wesleyan Methodist. preaching room. *Erected:* Uncertain, not separate, not exclusively used. *Sittings:* Free 40. *Attendance:* Afternoon: general congregation 20. *Average attendance:* Afternoon: general congregation 25. *Signed:* Jno. F. England, Minister, Wirksworth. [HO 129/448/10]

Upper Town

Wesleyan Methodist. preaching room. *Erected:* Uncertain, not separate, not exclusively used. *Sittings:* Free 40. *Attendance:* Afternoon: general congregation 30. *Average attendance:* Afternoon: general congregation 30. *Signed:* Jno. F. England, Minister, Wirksworth. [HO/129/448/11]

Butterley

Wesleyan Methodist. preaching room. *Erected:* uncertain, not separate, not exclusively used. *Sittings:* Free 30. *Attendance:* Afternoon: general congregation 22. *Average attendance:* Afternoon: general congregation 20. *Signed:* Jno. F. England, Minister, Wirksworth. [HO 129/448/12]

Ashover

Wesleyan Methodist.[1] *Erected:* A.D. 1807. Separate and entire, exclusively used. *Sittings:* Free 150, other 63. *Attendance:* Afternoon: general congregation 40, Sunday school 100, total 140; evening: general congregation 103, Sunday school 30, total 133. *Average attendance:* Afternoon: general congregation 40, Sunday school 100, total 140; evening: general congregation 100, Sunday school 30, total 130. *Signed:* Jno. F. England, Minister, Wirksworth. [HO 129/448/13]

Kelstedge

Wesleyan Methodist. preaching room. *Erected:* Uncertain, not separate, not exclusively used. *Sittings:* Free 30. *Average attendance:* general congregation 20. *Remarks:* On week nights only. *Signed:* Jno. F. England, Minister, Wirksworth. [HO 129/448/14]

Alton

Primitive Methodist. *Erected:* Opened for Religious Worship 1849. Not separate, not exclusively used. *Sittings:* Free 35. *Attendance:* Evening: general congregation 32. *Average attendance:* not given. *Signed:* Elizabeth Heeton, manager, Alton, Ashover [*Replacing* Henry Swift, preacher, *crossed through*]. [HO 129/448/15]

[1] See HO 129/48/7 (p. 143).

Mount Pleasant

Primitive Methodist. *Erected:* 1824. Separate and entire, exclusively used. *Sittings:* Free 180. *Attendance:* Afternoon: general congregation 70. *Average attendance:* General congregation 70. *Signed:* Anthony Hind, steward, tailor, Ashover, Chesterfield. [HO 129/448/16]

Ashover

Primitive Methodist. *Erected:* 15 years. Not separate, not exclusively used. *Sittings:* Free none, other none, standing none. *Attendance:* Morning: General congregation 12 persons. *Average attendance:* not given. *Signed:* Peter Nightingale, steward, Ashover, Chesterfield.[1] [HO 129/448/17]

Moor Grange

Primethodist. Primitive Methodist. *Erected:* 1851. Seperate a place of worship and day school. *Sittings:* not given. *Attendance:* Afternoon: general congregation about 30. *Average attendance:* not given. *Remarks:* Built for Sunday preaching in afternoon and a day school for little children. All free sittings. *Signed:* Nathl. Wheatcroft, Senr, steward, Cromford. [HO 129/448/18]

Whitfield House, Ashover

Primitive Methodist. *Erected:* 3 months. Not separate, not exclusively used. *Sittings:* not given. *Attendance:* Afternoon: general congregation 30. *Average attendance:* Aftenoon: general congregation 35. *Signed:* John Barber, Manager and local preacher, Ashover, nr Chesterfield. [HO 129/448/19]

---

[1] The official signature is unclear and this has been added later in pencil.

CRICH

Wessington[1]

Church of England. The chapel at Wessington was formerly a village school now converted into a place of worship. *Erected:* Licensed in 1841. Consecrated upon the plea of spiritual destitution. Erected and purchased by subscription – cost £130. *Sittings:* Free 100. *Attendance:* Evening: general congregation 65. *Average attendance:* No service in the winter. *Signed:* C.B. Dunn, curate, Crich, Alfreton. [HO 129/448/20]

Wesleyan Methodist.[2] *Erected:* 1847. Separate and entire, exclusively used. *Sittings:* Free 100, other none. *Attendance:* Morning: Sunday school 23; afternoon: Sunday school 23; evening: general congregation 63. *Average attendance:* General congregation 60, Sunday school 25, total 75. *Signed:* Timothy Taylor, Manager, Wessington, Alfreton. [HO 129/448/21]

Washington

Primitive Methodist. *Erected:* 1849. Separate and entire, exclusively used. *Sittings:* Free 100, other none. *Attendance:* Morning: Sunday school 42; afternoon: general congregation 55; evening: general congregation 20. *Average attendance:* General congregation 50, Sunday school 40, total 90. *Signed:* Benjamin Peat, Manager, Washington, Alfreton [HO 129/448/22]

Amber Row

Particular Baptist. School room. *Erected:* About the year 1812. Not separate and entire, exclusively used. *Sittings:* Free 80, other none. *Attendance:* Morning: Sunday school 69; afternoon: general congregation 10, Sunday school 71, total 81; evening: general congregation 42. *Average attendance:* general congregation 55, Sunday school 80, total 135. *Signed:* John Lomas, Manager, Swanwick, Nr Alfreton. [HO 129/448/23]

---

[1] Population 515.

[2] See also HO 129/446/26 (p. 105), which appears to be the same chapel.

SHIRLAND[1]

Wesleyan Methodist Reformed. *Erected:* 1830. Separate and entire, exclusively used. *Sittings:* Free 150. *Attendance:* Morning: Sunday school 105; afternoon: general congregation 35, Sunday school 105; evening: general congregation 103. *Average attendance:* not given. *Signed:* Joseph Allen, Manager, Shirland, Near Alfreton. [HO 129/448/24]

Furnace

Quakers. *Erected:* Before 1800. Separate and entire, exclusively used. *Sittings:* Admeasurement in superficial feet 360, no gallery. No of persons 65. *Attendance:* Morning: 5. *Signed:* Robert Wright, Chesterfield. [HO 129/448/25]

BRACKENFIELD[2]

Weslian Methodist. *Erected:* 1844. Not separate, exclusively used. *Sittings:* Free, other none. *Attendance:* Evening: general congregation 40. *Average attendance:* Evening: general congregation 40. *Signed:* Samuel Hopkinson, steward, Brackenfield, near Alfreton. [HO 129/448/26]

Brackenfield – Woolley Chapel

Primitive Methodist. *Erected:* 1841. Separate and entire, not exclusively used. *Sittings:* Free 200. *Attendance:* Morning: general congregation 14, Sunday school 29, total 43; afternoon: general congregation 60, Sunday school 29, total 89. *Average attendance:* Morning: general congregation 14, Sunday school 30, total 44; evening: general congregation 70, Sunday school 30, total 100. *Signed:* Edward Barker, manager, Woolley, near Alfreton. [HO 129/448/27]

---

[1] Population 851.
[2] Population 399.

Chesterfield Sub-District

NORTH WINGFIELD[1]

Hanley

Methodist New Connexion. *Erected:* about 1800. Separate and entire, exclusively used. *Sittings:* Free 20, other 90, standing none. *Attendance:* per month 180, afternoon 45. *Average attendance:* general congregation 45, Sunday school 22, total 67. *Remarks:* The place of worship above named was built as near *1800* as can be ascertained and has never been used for any purpose than above named. *Signed:* Richd. Hodgson, superintender, Hanley, Nr Chesterfield. [HO 129/448/28]

Clay Cross

Wesleyan Methodist. *Erected:* April 30 1848. Separate and entire, exclusively used. *Sittings:* Free 100, other 100. *Attendance:* Afternoon: general congregation 40, Sunday school 55, total 95; evening: general congregation 50, Sunday school 14, total 64. *Average attendance:* not given. *Signed:* Joseph Peake, steward, carpenter, Clay Cross, Chesterfield. [HO 129/448/29]

North Wingfield[2]

Primitive Methodist. Ebenezer. *Erected:* 1849. Separate and entire, exclusively used. *Sittings:* Free 150, other 100, standing none. *Attendance:* Morning: Sunday school 84; afternoon: general congregation 53, Sunday school 74, total 127; evening: general congregation 106. *Average attendance:* Morning: Sunday school 84; afternoon: general congregation 50, Sunday school 74, total 124; evening: general congregation 150. *Remarks:* The congregation is less tonight than usual. *Signed:* James Shaw, minister, Clay Cross, Near Chesterfield. [HO 129/448/30]

---

[1] Parish population 4,351.

[2] Township population 668.

Clay Lane

Methodist New Connexion. Lion Chapel. *Erected:* 1848. Seperate and entire, exclusively used as a place of worship. *Sittings:* Free 190 to 196, standing 100. *Attendance:* Morning: general congregation 60, Sunday school 144, total 204; evening: general congregation 150. *Average attendance:* Morning: general congregation 70, Sunday school 144; evening: general congregation 230. *Signed:* John Thelwall, Local preacher, grocer, Clay Cross, Nr Chesterfield. [HO 129/448/31]

Pilsley[1]

Wesleyan Methodist. *Erected:* 1843. Separate and entire, exclusively used. *Sittings:* other 18, standing 100. *Attendance:* Morning: Sunday school 41; afternoon: general congregation 16, Sunday school 26, total 42; evening: general congregation 27. *Average attendance:* not given. *Signed:* George Marsden, steward, Astwith, near Chesterfield. [HO 129/448/32]

North Wingfield

Church of England. Ancient parish church dedicated to S. Lawrance. *Erected:* not given. *Endowments:* Tithe £1200, glebe 80 acres. *Sittings:* Free 450. *Attendance:* not given. *Average attendance:* not given. *Remarks:* A new district church has recently been erected at Clay Cross, Parish of North Wingfield. Consecrated 25 January 1851, dedicated to S. Bartholomew. 400 sittings all free. *Signed:* E.W. Lowe, 29 March. [HO 129/448/33]

Wingerworth[2]

Church of England. *Erected:* Unknown, about two centuries years ago. *Endowments:* not given. *Sittings:* Free and appropriated 200. *Average attendance:* General congregation 30, Sunday school 70 (40 boys and 30 girls). Only one service morning and afternoon alternately. *Signed:* Robert Shaw, Registrar, Chesterfield. [HO 129/448/34]

---

[1] Population 403.
[2] Population 463.

Chesterfield

Union Workhouse chapel. *Erected:* 1838. *Sittings:* Free 160. *Attendance:* Morning: 60 of whom 26 are children. *Signed:* Alexander Poole, chaplain of the Union. [HO 129/448/35]

BRAMPTON[1]

Walton[2]

Church of England. Licensed school room in the Ecclesiastical District of S. Thomas' Church, Brampton. *Erected:* 1840. *Sittings:* Free 80. *Attendance:* Afternoon: general congregation 50, Sunday school 40. *Average attendance:* Not given. *Signed:* J.B. Jebb, Incumbent of S. Thomas' Church, Brampton. [HO 129/448/36]

BRAMPTON

Church of England. S. Thomas. *Erected:* 1832. *Endowments:* not given. *Sittings:* Free 100, other 300, total 400. *Attendance:* Morning: general congregation 150, Sunday school 200; afternoon: Sunday school 200; evening: general congregation 80, Sunday school 30 voluntary. *Signed:* J.B. Jebb, Incumbent. [HO 129/448/37]

Old Brampton

Church of England. S. Peter. Parish church. *Erected:* about 3 centuries ago. *Endowments:* not given. *Sittings:* free and appropriated about 500. *Attendance:* Morning: general congregation about 30 in winter and 60 in summer, Sunday school 12. *Signed:* Robert Shaw, Registrar. [HO 129/448/38]

Wesleyan Methodist. *Erected:* 1827. Separate and entire, exclusively used. *Sittings:* Free and others 250 adults. *Attendance:* Morning: general congregation about 80, Sunday school 220, total 300; evening: general con-

---

[1] Population 4,409.

[2] Population 1,114.

gregation about 90. *Average attendance:* not given. *Signed:* Robert Shaw, Registrar. [HO 129/448/39]

Wadshelf

Primitive Methodist. *Erected:* 1834. Seperate and entire, exclusively used. *Sittings:* Free 90, other 30. *Attendance:* Morning: Sunday school 40; afternoon: general congregation 30, Sunday school 40, total 70; evening: general congregation 40. *Average attendance:* not given. *Signed:* Robert Parks, Ebenezer Cottage, Chesterfield. [HO 129/448/40]

Wesleyan Methodist. *Erected:* about 10 years. Separate and entire, exclusively used. *Sittings:* Free 50, other 100. *Attendance:* Afternoon: general congregation 6. *Average attendance:* not given. *Signed:* Alfred F. Abbott, Chesterfield. [HO 129/448/41]

Wesleyan Methodist. Hollins Chapel – the private property of John Drabble, a farmer. *Erected:* 1847. Separate and entire, exclusively used. *Sittings:* 25 ft x 18 ft space. *Attendance:* Afternoon: general congregation 50; evening: general congregation 50. *Average attendance:* not given. *Signed:* Robert Shaw, Registrar, Chesterfield. [HO 129/448/42]

NORTH WINGFIELD

Original Methodists. *Erected:* an inhabited house, not exclusively used. *Sittings:* not given. *Attendance:* Morning: general congregation 6; afternoon: general congregation 18; evening: general congregation 53. *Average attendance:* Morning: general congregation 12; Afternoon: general congregation 20; evening: general congregation 40. *Signed:* Jno Wilson, steward, Ling's Colliery, Nr Chesterfield. [HO 129/448/43]

CHESTERFIELD

Wingerworth[1]

Independent Calvinists. Salem Independent Chapel. *Erected:* 1849. Separate and entire, exclusively used. *Sittings:* Free 112, other 49, standing 72. *Attendance:* Afternoon: general congregation 49, Sunday school 44, total 93; evening: general congregation 57. *Average attendance:* General congregation 75, Sunday school 33, total 108. *Signed:* Jos. Fletcher, minister, Wingerworth Iron Works, Chesterfield. [HO 129/448/44]

Chesterfield[2]

Church of England. S. Mary. *Erected:* Before 1800. *Endowments:* Other permanent endowment £50. *Sittings:* Free 1800, other none. *Attendance:* Morning: general congregation about 580, Sunday school 155, total 735; afternoon: general congregation about 165, Sunday school 155; evening: general congregation about 700, Sunday school none. *Average attendance:* Morning: general congregation 600, Sunday school 160, total 760; afternoon: general congregation about 165, Sunday school 155, total 320; evening: general congregation about 800. *Signed:* George Butt, M.A. vicar, Vicarage, Chesterfield. [HO 129/448/45]

Newbold Lane

Church of England. Trinity church. *Erected:* Consecrated Aug. 29 1838 as an additional church; by voluntary subscription and aid from Diocesan Society. This sum includes 500 guineas for fencing churchyard, [*Following words undecipherable*] some due. Cost: Diocesan Society £500, Private Benefactions etc £4,200, total £4,700. *Endowments:* Tithe, not including cost of collection and rates £32, other permanent endowment £34 7s. 8d, pew rents £54 13s. 3d., fees £12 perhaps. The expenses of the church are about 25£ annually. *Sittings:* Free 333, other 667, total 1,000. *Attendance:* Morning: general congregation 92, Sunday school 166, total 258; afternoon: general congregation 117, Sunday school 118, total 235; evening: general

---

[1] Population 463.

[2] Parish population 13,421, Chesterfield township 7,101.

congregation 68. *Average attendance:* not given. *Remarks:* The above services are attended each of them by different persons. By many in the afternoon not present in morning & by others in evening not present morning or afternoon. *Signed:* Alexander Poole, Incumbent of Trinity Church, Chesterfield. [HO 129/448/46]

Beetwell St

Primitive Methodist. *Erected:* 1848. Separate and entire, exclusively used. *Sittings:* Free 300, other 400, standing none. *Attendance:* Morning: general congregation 205, Sunday school 86; afternoon: Sunday school 104; evening: general congregation 375. *Average attendance:* not given. *Signed:* Robert Parks, minister, Ebenezer Cottage, Chesterfield. [HO 129/448/47]

South Street

Independent. South Place chapel. *Erected:* Before 1800 [*Note added:* Only been occupied as an Independent chapel since 1844.]. Separate and entire, exclusively used. *Sittings:* Free 50, other 180. *Attendance:* Morning: general congregation 69, Sunday school 73, total 142; evening: general congregation 90. *Average attendance:* not given. *Remarks:* Attached to the chapel there is a vestry which will seat 40 people. *Signed:* Francis Hurst, deacon, Abercrombie St, Chesterfield. [HO 129/448/48]

General Baptist. *Erected:* Room now used as a chapel. Not separate, exclusively used. *Sittings:* Free 70. *Attendance:* Morning: Sunday school 24; afternoon: general congregation 20, Sunday school 25, total 45; evening: general congregation 35. *Average attendance:* Morning: Sunday school 30; afternoon: general congregation 20, Sunday school 35; evening: general congregation 30. *Signed:* Ed. Bombroffe, steward, Packers Row, Chesterfield. [HO 129/448/49]

Saltergate

Wesleyan Methodist. *Erected:* Before 1800, enlarged 1821. Separate and entire, exclusively used. *Sittings:* Free 135, other 480, standing none. *Attendance:* not given. *Average attendance:* Morning: general congregation 150, Sunday school 120, total 270; Evening: general congregation 250. *Signed:* William Parker, minister, Saltergate, Chesterfield. [HO 129/448/50]

Elder Yard

Presbyterian or Unitarian. *Erected:* Before 1800 (in 1694). *Sittings:* Free 100, other 200, standing 150. *Attendance:* Morning: general congregation 55, Sunday school 80; evening: general congregation 90. *Average attendance:* Morning: general congregation 80, Sunday school 80; Evening: general congregation 70. *Remarks:* Owing to an oversight on the part of the district officer this Paper was not recd. by me until today (31st); consequently I have put down the *probable* attendance at chapel yesterday. The members of the congregation are Anti-Trinitarian; but they unite in the principle of religious freedom rather than dogma. The chapel was built by a Presbyterian. *Signed:* Thomas Hunter, Minister, Spring Vale, Nr Chesterfield. [HO 129/448/51]

Saltergate

Quakers. *Erected:* Before 1800. Separate and entire, exclusively used. *Sittings:* 44′ long x 22′ wide, total 968′. No gallery, 192 people. *Attendance:* Morning: 24; afternoon: 17. *Average attendance:* Not given. *Signed:* Samuel Bower, Chesterfield. [HO 129/448/52]

Soresby Street

Independent. *Erected:* 1822. Separate and entire, exclusively used. *Sittings:* Free 130, other 436. *Attendance:* Morning: general congregation 143, Sunday school 113, total 256; afternoon: Sunday school 120; evening: general congregation 150. *Average attendance:* not given. *Signed:* William Blandy, Independent Minister, Chesterfield. [HO 129/448/53]

Wesleyan Reformers. preaching room. *Erected:* Separate and entire, exclusively used. *Sittings:* Free 350. *Attendance:* Morning: general congregation 250; evening: general congregation 300. *Average attendance:* 250. *Remarks:* The building is rented by the Committee at 20£ per annum and the preachers are laymen and unpaid. *Signed:* William Edwin Dutton, Secretary of Managing Committee, draper, Chesterfield. [HO 129/448/54]

Soresby Street

Church of Jesus Christ of Latter Day Saints. *Erected:* Can't find out, separate and entire, exclusively used. *Sittings:* Free 120, standing 25. *Attendance:* Morning: general congregation 16; afternoon: general congregation 80; evening: general congregation 100. *Average attendance:* the same. *Remarks:* Number of members belonging the church 192. *Signed:* Isaac Allen, elder, Church Lane, Chesterfield. [HO 129/448/55]

BRAMPTON

Walton[1]

Wesleyan Methodist. *Erected:* not known but before 1800, cottage house, not exclusively used. *Sittings:* all free. *Attendance:* afternoon: general congregation 15. *Average attendance:* not given. *Remarks:* The aforesaid return relates to a meeting of the Wesleyan Methodists in a small house occupied by a labourer of which about fifteen attends on an average every Sunday afternoon. *Signed:* Samuell Hulley, occupier of the house, Walton, Near Chesterfield. [HO 129/448/56]

CHESTERFIELD

Newbold[2]

Wesleyan Methodist. *Erected:* 1842. Separate and entire, exclusively used. *Sittings:* Free 100, other 42, standing none. *Attendance:* Morning: Sunday school 35; afternoon: general congregation 24, Sunday school 20; evening: general congregation 31. *Average attendance:* not given. *Signed:* Thomas Turner, steward, Newbold, Chesterfield. [HO 129/448/57]

Newbold Moor

Primitive Methodist. *Erected:* 1841. Separate and entire, exclusively used. *Sittings:* Free 118, other 82. *Attendance:* afternoon: 140; evening: 121.

---

[1] Population 1,114.

[2] Population, with Dunston, 2,035.

Average attendance: not given. *Signed:* James Moore, steward, Newbold Moor [*Replacing* Whittington, *deleted*], Via Chesterfield. [HO 129/448/58]

Chesterfield Warfe

Primitive Methodist. *Erected:* Before 1800. Separate and entire, a place of worship and a Sunday school. *Sittings:* Free 80. *Attendance:* Afternoon: general congregation 15; evening: general congregation 40. *Average attendance:* General congregation 35; Sunday school 33, total 68. *Signed:* Richard Hollingworth, Steward, Brick Yard, Chesterfield. [HO 129/448/59]

Calow[1]

Primitive Methodist. *Erected:* Not separate, not exclusively used. *Sittings:* standing 90. *Attendance:* Morning: general congregation 10; afternoon: general congregation 36; evening: general congregation 55. *Average attendance:* Morning: general congregation 13; afternoon: general congregation 40; evening: general congregation 40. *Signed:* George Slack (his mark) class leader, farmer, Calow Green. [HO 129/448/60]

Independent. *Erected:* 1837. Separate and entire, exclusively used. *Sittings:* Other 67, standing 186. *Attendance:* Morning: Sunday school 70, 12 teachers, total 82; afternoon: general congregation 50, Sunday school 68. *Average attendance:* not given. *Signed:* Thomas Mason, manager, Devonshire St, Chesterfield. [HO 129/448/61]

Hasland[2]

Church of England. S. Paul. *Erected:* Cons. September 24 1850. New church, by private subscription, cost unknown. *Endowments:* Other permanent endowment not yet determined, pew rents £10. *Sittings:* Free 150, other 50, total 200. *Attendance:* Afternoon: general congregation 100. *Average attendance:* not known. *Signed:* James Stevenson Rice, churchwarden, Hasland, Chesterfield. [HO 129/448/62]

---

[1] Population 571.

[2] Population 1,176.

Hasland Birdholme

Roman Catholic. *Erected:* Not known, part of a dwelling house exclusively used. *Sittings:* Free 90, other 12, standing 25. *Attendance:* Morning: general congregation 120. *Average attendance:* not given. *Signed:* James Austin Eccles, Catholic Priest, Mount Saint Mary's College, Barlboro', Chesterfield. [HO 129/448/63]

Hasland

Primitive Methodist. *Erected:* 1842. Separate and entire, exclusively used. *Sittings:* Free 77, other 73, standing none. *Attendance:* general congregation 100; evening: general congregation 93. *Average attendance:* not given. *Signed:* William Windle, steward, Hasland, Near Chesterfield. [HO 129/448/64]

Brimington[1]

Church of England. The parish church of Brimington, formerly the church of an ancient chapelry dedicated to Saint Michael; but the chapelry was constituted a *parish* and the church a *parish church* by an order in Council dated September 3rd 1844 under 1 & 2 Victoria C. 106, S. 26. *Erected:* Before 1800. *Endowments:* Land £30, glebe £18, other permanent endowment £50, fees £3, aggregate annual amount £101. *Sittings:* Free 365, other 207, total 572. *Attendance:* Morning: general congregation 65, Sunday school 52, total 117; afternoon: general congregation 150, Sunday school 55, total 205. *Average attendance:* Morning: general congregation 50, Sunday school 50, total 100; afternoon: general congregation 130, Sunday school 55, total 185. [Wednesday evening 30][2] *Remarks:* No service on Sunday evening but as there is a weekly service on Wednesday evening in the Church school room I thought it well to enter it as above. The population consists chiefly of colliers and Foundry Men whose habits are very unfavorable to moral and religious influences and to attendance upon public worship. *Signed:* J.K. Marsh, Minister, Brimington Chesterfield. [HO 129/4-48/65]

---

[1] Population 1,103.
[2] This passage is crossed out in a later hand.

Primitive Methodist. *Erected:* 1835. Separate and entire, exclusively used except a day school. *Sittings:* Free 10, other 59, standing 79. *Attendance:* Morning: Sunday school 71; afternoon: general congregation 30, Sunday school 72, total 102; evening: general congregation 90. *Average attendance:* not given. *Signed:* Joseph Ashmore, chapel steward, Brimington Common, Nr Chesterfield. [HO 129/448/66]

Wesleyan Methodist. *Erected:* 1808. Separate and entire, exclusively used. *Sittings:* Free 84, other 100. *Attendance:* not given. *Average attendance:* Afternoon: general congregation 40, Sunday school 50, total 90; evening: general congregation 60. *Signed:* William Parker, Minister, Saltergate, Chesterfield. [HO 129/448/67]

BRAMPTON[1]

Primitive Methodist. *Erected:* 1827. Separate and entire, exclusively used and as a Sabbath school. *Sittings:* Free 200, other 213, standing none. *Attendance:* Morning: general congregation 80, Sunday school 140, total 220; evening: general congregation 214. *Average attendance:* general congregation 200, Sunday school 140, total 340. *Signed:* George Goldsmith, One of the ministers, Brampton, Near Chesterfield. [HO 129/448/68]

Wesleyan Methodist. *Erected:* 1840. Separate and entire, exclusively used. *Sittings:* Free 70, other 42, standing none. *Attendance:* Morning: Sunday school 76; afternoon: general congregation 24, Sunday school 66; evening: general congregation 35. *Average attendance:* Morning: Sunday school 70; afternoon: general congregation 40, Sunday school 70; evening: general congregation 60. *Remarks:* The number of attendants is diminished in consequence of the Wesleyan agitation. *Signed:* George Bingham, steward, Holymoor Side, near Chesterfield. [HO 129/448/69]

Holymoor Side

Primitive Methodist. *Erected:* 1830. Separate and entire, exclusively used. *Sittings:* Free 66, other 24. *Attendance:* Morning: Sunday school 48; afternoon: Sunday school 48; evening: general congregation 50. *Average attendance:* general congregation 50, Sunday school 48. *Signed:* John

[1] Population 4,409.

Hubback, secretary, tailor and draper, Holymoor Side, Chesterfield. [HO 129/448/70]

Cutthorpe

Primitive Methodist. *Erected:* 1837. Separate and entire, exclusively used. *Sittings:* Free 84. *Attendance:* Afternoon: general congregation 35, Sunday school 37, total 72; evening: general congregation 40. *Average attendance:* not given. *Signed:* Geo. Tagg, chapel steward, Cutthorpe, Nr Chesterfield. [HO 129/448/71]

WHITTINGTON[1]

Church of England. *Erected:* Before 1800. Cons. & erection unknown. *Endowments:* Tithe £226 17s., glebe £53 0s. $1^1/_2$d. *Sittings:* Free 30, other 270, total 300. *Attendance:* Morning: general congregation 91, Sunday school 33; afternoon: general congregation 105, Sunday school 23. *Average attendance:* can give no statement. *Remarks:* The church is a very ancient building & supposed to have been built above eight hundred years. *Signed:* Robert Robinson, officiating minister, Whittington, Chesterfield. [HO 129/448/72]

Wesleyan Methodist. *Erected:* 1828. Separate and entire, exclusively used. *Sittings:* Free 50, other 70, standing none. *Attendance:* Morning: general congregation 20, Sunday school 40, total 60; evening: general congregation 45. *Average attendance:* Morning: general congregation 20, Sunday school 40; evening: general congregation 45. *Remarks:* This number is as near as can be ascertained. *Signed:* William Lindley, minister, Chesterfield. [HO 129/448/73]

Primitive Methodist. *Erected:* 1849. Separate and entire, used exclusively as a place of worship & Sunday school. *Sittings:* Free 60, other 20, standing 20. *Attendance:* Afternoon: general congregation 13, Sunday school 27, total 40; evening: general congregation 30, Sunday school 26, total 56. *Average attendance:* Afternoon: general congregation 15, Sunday school 27, total 42; evening: general congregation 20, Sunday school 15,

[1] Population 874.

total 35. *Signed:* Sampson Holland, steward, Whittington, near Chesterfield. [HO 129/448/74]

Bolsover Sub-District

SUTTON CUM DUCKMANTON[1]

Church of England. S. Mary. Sutton ancient parish church. *Erected:* Before 1800. *Endowments:* Tithe £300, glebe £65, fees £12. *Sittings:* Free 60, other 190, total 250. *Attendance:* Morning: general congregation 85, Sunday school 35, total 120; afternoon: general congregation 80, Sunday school 35, total 115. *Average attendance:* Morning: general congregation 80, Sunday school 35, total 115; afternoon: general congregation 85, Sunday school 10, total 95. *Remarks:* The church being situated 2 miles from bulk of the inhabitants is scarcely possible to give an average attend: had Sunday 30th been a wet day not one-fifth perhaps wd have been present – the above is to the best of my belief. NB. *80 communicants* in the parish. Query How can a Dissenter or a non attender at Church *verify* these statements? *Signed:* M.M. Humble, Rector, Sutton Rectory, Chesterfield. [HO 129/448/75]

HEATH[2]

Church of England. All Saints. Ancient parish church. *Erected:* Cons. before 1800. *Endowments:* Tithe £229 4s., glebe £6, total £235 4s. 0d. *Sittings:* other 160. *Attendance:* Morning: general congregation 65, Sunday school 31, total 96. *Average attendance:* not given. *Signed:* Godfrey Arkwright, officiating minister, Heath, Chesterfield. [HO 129/448/76]

BOLSOVER[3]

Church of England. S. Mary. *Erected:* Consecrated 12th century. *Endowments:* Land £67, other permanent endowment £30, fees £10, income

[1] Population 587.

[2] Population 378.

[3] Parish population 1,611, Bolsover township 1,512.

of vicar from 100 to 110£ per annum. *Sittings:* 500 sittings. *Attendance:* not given. *Average attendance:* Morning: General congregation from 70 to 90; afternoon: general congregation from 150 to 190, Sunday school from 70 to 90; total morning from 140 to 170 or 180; afternoon from 220 to 270 or 280. *Remarks:* There are more Sunday scholars on the books. *Signed:* John Hamilton Gray, vicar and of Scarcliffe & Rural Dean of Chesterfield, Bolsover Castle. [HO 129/448/77]

High Street

Congregational or Independent. *Erected:* Before 1800. Separate and entire, exclusively used. *Sittings:* Free 100, other 150. *Attendance:* Morning: Sunday school 58; afternoon: general congregation 46, Sunday school 58, total 104; evening: general congregation 80. *Average attendance:* not given. *Signed:* John Wardley, deacon, Scarcliffe, Nr Mansfield, Notts. [HO 129/448/78]

Wesleyan Methodist. *Erected:* 1826. Separate and entire, exclusively used. *Sittings:* Free 80, other 70, standing none. *Attendance:* Afternoon: general congregation 37, Sunday school 25, total 62; evening: general congregation 53. *Average attendance:* afternoon: general congregation 40, Sunday school 30, total 70; evening: general congregation 55. *Signed:* Jno. Bennett, steward, High St, Bolsover. [HO 129/448/79]

Eckington Sub-District

STAVELEY[1]

Handley

Church of England. Chapel of ease to Staveley church. *Erected:* Licensed 1839 as an additional church for the benefit of an outlying hamlet; Cost: £1146, by the Duke of Devonshire but the late Rector is expected to contribute £300. *Endowments:* not given. *Sittings:* Total about 240. *Attendance:* Afternoon: general congregation 50, Sunday school 38, total 88.

---

[1] Parish population 4,634, Staveley township 3,998.

Average attendance: General congregation 50 to 80; Sunday school about 40. *Remarks:* Better attendance always in summer. *Signed:* J.D. Macfarlane, Rector of Staveley, Nr Chesterfield. [HO 129/448/80]

Staveley

Church of England. S. John. Ancient parish church. *Erected:* Before 1800. *Endowments:* Tithe £619, glebe about £120. *Sittings:* Under 550. *Attendance:* Morning: general congregation about 200, Sunday school 86, total 286; afternoon: general congregation about 150, Sunday school 86, total 236. *Average attendance:* Morning: general congregation 200 to 250, Sunday school about 90; afternoon: general congregation 150 to 200, Sunday school about 90. *Remarks:* Too low an average perhaps, better attendance in summer certainly. Parish upwards of 6,600 acres. Agricultural population lying generally wide of the Parish Church. Mining population here as generally chiefly Methodists. A great part of the mining population is fluctuating. These strangers have no association with the parish church nor indeed with any place of worship. *Signed:* J.D. Macfarlane, Rector, Staveley. [HO 129/448/81]

Woodthorpe

Church of England. Almshouse chapel. Ancient erection. *Erected:* Before 1800. *Endowments:* The reader is endowed with £8 per annum. *Sittings:* about 100. *Attendance:* No service. Chapel just rebuilt and not reopened yet. *Average attendance:* Morning: general congregation about 70 to 80, Sunday school 50, total about 120. *Remarks:* The chapel has just been rebuilt at the cost of the Duke of Devonshire whose estate at Staveley is chargeable with the support of the almshouses etc. *Signed:* J.D. Macfarlane, Rector, Staveley, Nr Chesterfield. [HO 129/448/82]

Handley

Wesleyan Methodist. *Erected:* 1796. Separate and entire, exclusively used. *Sittings:* Free 130, other 44, standing 50. *Attendance:* Morning: general congregation 30, Sunday school 30, total 60; evening: general congregation 100. *Average attendance:* not given. *Signed:* Aaron Bates, chapel steward, Handley, nr Chesterfield. [HO 129/448/83]

Staveley

Wesleyan Methodist. *Erected:* 1849 on site of a former one erected in 1826. Separate and entire, exclusively used. *Sittings:* Free 200, other 280. *Attendance:* Morning: general congregation 82, Sunday school 156; evening: general congregation 206, Sunday school 30. *Average attendance:* Morning: general congregation 140, Sunday school 90; afternoon: Sunday school 80; evening: general congregation 260. *Signed:* Benjamin Fox, Chapel steward, Staveley, nr Chesterfield. [HO 129/448/84]

ECKINGTON[1]

Church of England. S. Peter and S. Paul. *Erected:* Before 1800. *Endowments:* Tithe £280, glebe £535 11s. 8d., fees £5. *Sittings:* Free 270, other 872, total 1,142. *Attendance:* Morning: general congregation 240, Sunday school 131; afternoon: general congregation 192, Sunday school 152, total 344. *Average attendance:* not given. *Remarks:* I have deducted from Total of Endowment £300 payable yearly to the Incumbent of Ridgway by Order in Council. And £5 payable to the organist by Eckington Enclosure Act. Nothing on account of my Rents and Tithe, Assistant Curate or Property Tax. *Signed:* Edmd. Bucknall Estcourt, Rector, Eckington Rectory, Chesterfield. [HO 129/448/85]

Ridgeway

Church of England. S. John. This church is the church of a district constituted a separate parish for ecclesiastical purposes by an order of council dated June 10th 1843. *Erected:* 1843. *Endowments:* Tithe £280. *Sittings:* Free 324, other 250, total 574. See letter. *Attendance:* Morning: general congregation 50, Sunday school 56, total 106; afternoon: general congregation 60, Sunday school 73, total 133. *Average attendance:* not given. *Signed:* John Owen Picton, curate, Ridgway, Chesterfield. [HO 129/448/86]

---

[1] Population 4,958.

Eckington

Wesleyan Methodist. *Erected:* 1807. Separate and entire, exclusively used. *Sittings:* Free 200, other 100. *Attendance:* Morning: general congregation 34, Sunday school 20, total 54; evening: general congregation 87. *Average attendance:* Morning: 60; evening: 80. *Signed:* Joshua Chapman, steward, Eckington, nr Chesterfield. [HO 129/448/87]

Chapel Street

Wesleyan Methodist Association. *Erected:* 1836. Separate and entire, exclusively used. *Sittings:* Free 100, other 80, standing none. *Attendance:* Morning: general congregation 34, Sunday school 52, total 86; afternoon: no public service; evening: general congregation 106. *Average attendance:* Morning: general congregation 40, Sunday school 60; evening: general congregation 145. *Signed:* W.E. Harrison, elder, nail manufacturer, Eckington. [HO 129/448/88]

Roman Catholic. Church of the Immaculate Conception. *Erected:* About 1845. Separate and entire, exclusively used. *Sittings:* Free about 50, other about 160. *Attendance:* Morning: general congregation about 200; afternoon: general congregation about 100. *Average attendance:* not given. *Signed:* John Baron, Catholic priest, Mount S. Mary, Chesterfield. [HO 129/448/89]

Renishaw Ironworks

Wesleyan Reformers. Chappel and school in one. *Erected:* 1850. Separate and entire, chappel and Sunday school exclusively. *Sittings:* all free. 150. See letter. *Attendance:* afternoon: general congregation 70; evening: general congregation 40. *Average attendance:* not given. *Signed:* John Hadfield, superintendant, Eckington, Chesterfield. [HO 129/448/90]

Mosborough

Wesleyan Methodist. *Erected:* 1839. Separate and entire, exclusively with Sunday school underneath. *Sittings:* Free 80, Sittings provided 66, standing none. *Attendance:* Afternoon: general congregation 45, Sunday school 51, total 96; evening: general congregation 64. *Average attendance:* Afternoon: general congregation 60, Sunday school 70; evening: general congregation 80. *Signed:* Thomas Hutton, steward, Mosbro', near Eckington. [HO 129/448/91]

Eckington

Primitive Methodist. *Erected:* 1830. Separate and entire, exclusively used. *Sittings:* Free 70, other 50, standing none. *Attendance:* Morning: Sunday school 57; afternoon: general congregation 40, Sunday school 65, total 105; evening: general congregation 110. *Average attendance:* not given. *Signed:* John Rose, chapel steward, carpenter, Mosbro', nr Eckington. [HO 129/448/92]

Birdfield

Primitive Methodist. *Erected:* Before 1800. A room in a large house, not exclusively used. *Sittings:* All free 40. *Attendance:* Afternoon: general congregation 30, evening: general congregation 35. *Average attendance:* not given. *Signed:* John Turner, steward, Highlane, nr Chesterfield. [HO 129/448/93]

Ridgeway

Wesleyan Methodist. *Erected:* 1806. Separate and entire, exclusively used. *Sittings:* Free 110, other 90. *Attendance:* Afternoon: general congregation 73, Sunday school 36, total 109; evening: general congregation 81. *Average attendance:* not given. *Signed:* William Webster, steward, Highlane, nr Chesterfield. [HO 129/448/94]

KILLAMARSH[1]

Church of England. S. Giles. *Erected:* The parish church of Killamarsh; probably built by the Normans; formerly held along with the Rectory of Eckington now separate. *Endowments:* Land £160, tithe £200, fees £2 10s., other sources £4 4s. *Sittings:* Free 13, other 216, total 229. *Attendance:* Morning: general congregation 73, Sunday school 110, total 183; afternoon:

[1] Population 1,070.

general congregation 76, Sunday school 82, total 158. *Average attendance:* not given. *Remarks:* The *morning* number includes the attendants at *two* services at $1/_2$ past 8 and at 11. The average of the year would be at least 200, instead of 183. Under 'Sunday scholars' all children are included. One Sunday school only assembles in the afternoon. The general congregation is *adults*. *Signed:* E.H. Smith, perpetual curate, Killamarsh, nr Chesterfield. [HO 129/448/95]

Independent or Congregationalists. *Erected:* In the autumn of 1848. Separate and entire. No, we conduct our day school in the same building. *Sittings:* Free 50, standing 20. *Attendance:* Afternoon: general congregation 20, Sunday school 10, total 30; evening: general congregation 30, Sunday school 8, total 38. *Average attendance:* Afternoon: general congregation 15, Sunday school 28, total 43; evening: general congregation 40, Sunday school 15, total 55. *Remarks:* Building: much too small either as a Place of Worship, Sunday School or Day School. *Signed:* Edwin Webster, Manager, Killamarsh, nr Eckington. [HO 129/448/96]

Dronfield Sub-District

DRONFIELD[1]

Holmesfield[2]

Church of England. S. Swithen. *Erected:* 1826 (re-erected). *Sittings:* Free 21, other 229, total 250. *Attendance:* Morning: general congregation 12, Sunday school 30; afternoon: general congregation 70, Sunday school 30; evening: no service. *Average attendance:* Not given. *Signed:* Thomas Hirst, Perpetual Curate, Dronfield, Sheffield. [HO 129/448/97]

---

[1] Parish population 5,321, Dronfield township 2,469.

[2] Population 520.

Dronfield

Church of England. S. John Baptist. A Parish Church 132 feet long, & a spire of the same height. Had formerly a chantry & was appropriated to Beauchief Abbey. The Vicarage is in the gift of the Crown. The Church of Dronfield was given to Beaucheif Abbey by Sir Hy de Brailsford time of Edwd I & was appropriated to it in 1399. Thomas Gomfrey, Rector died Oct. 1399. Wm Cocks vicar 1534. The Church Registers begin 1560, Pop'n nearly 4000, vicarage endowed in AD 1405. *Erected:* Before 1800. *Endowments:* not given. *Sittings:* Free 1200. *Attendance:* Morning: general congregation 50, Sunday school 33 boys, 12 girls, total 97; afternoon: general congregation 140, Sunday school 33 boys, 14 girls, total 187. *Average attendance:* Morning: general congregation 30 to 50, Sunday school 40b. 13g, total 83; afternoon: general congregation 80 to 100, Sunday school 40b. 13g. total 183. *Remarks:* The winter congregations are very small – the church being cold and damp. *Signed:* Willm. Conyngham Ussher, curate, Dronfield. [HO 129/448/98]

Woodhus

Wesleyan Methodist. *Erected:* 1848. Separate and entire, a Place of Worship and Sunday school. *Sittings:* Free 70, other 50. *Attendance:* Morning: Sunday school 57; afternoon: general congregation 60, Sunday school 48, total 108; evening: general congregation 75. *Average attendance:* not given. James Bennett, Trustee & steward, Dronfield Woodhouse. [HO 129/448/99]

Dronfield

Independent. *Erected:* 1812. Separate and entire, exclusively used. *Sittings:* Free 50, other 200. *Attendance:* Morning: general congregation 90, Sunday school 60, total 150; afternoon: Sunday school 80; evening: general congregation 160. *Average attendance:* not given. *Signed:* Joseph Mason Calvert, minister, Dronfield. [HO 129/448/100]

Wesleyan Methodist. *Erected:* 1800. Seperate and entire, exclusively used as place of worship except for Sunday school. *Sittings:* 12 yards long by 9 yards wide. Free 110, other 54. *Attendance:* Morning: Sunday school 35; afternoon: general congregation 43, Sunday school 40; evening: general congregation 64. *Average attendance:* Morning: Sunday school 50; afternoon:

general congregation 46, Sunday school 50; evening: general congregation 60. *Signed:* William Booker, steward, Dronfield. [HO 129/448/101]

Unstone[1] – Crow Lane

Wesleyan Methodist. *Erected:* In the year 1847. Separate and entire, exclusively used. *Sittings:* Free 50, other 70, standing occupied by Sunday scholars. *Attendance:* Morning: general congregation 45, Sunday school 50, total 95; afternoon: general congregation 55, Sunday school 56, total 111. *Average attendance:* not given. *Remarks:* I think March 31 *(sic)* about the average congregation when the weather favourable. *Signed:* John Walker, steward, Unstone Mill, Dronfield. [HO 129/448/102]

Holmesfield – Grateful Mill

Wesleyan Methodist. *Erected:* 1833. Separate and entire, exclusively used, Sunday school. *Sittings:* Free 65, other 33. See letter. *Attendance:* Morning: general congregation 40, Sunday school 10, total 50; afternoon: general congregation 50, Sunday school 30, total 80. *Average attendance:* Morning: general congregation 20, Sunday school 25, total 45; afternoon: general congregation 35, Sunday school 30, total 65. *Signed:* George Godber, chapel keeper, Holmesfield, Dronfield. [HO 129/448/103]

Coal Aston[2]

Wesleyan Methodist. *Erected:* 1848. Separate and entire, exclusively used. *Sittings:* Free 70, other 30. *Average attendance:* Afternoon: general congregation 30, Sunday school 40, total 70; evening: general congregation 50. *Signed:* Henry Hardcastle, Coal Aston, Dronfield. [HO 129/448/104]

Primitive Methodist. *Erected:* In 1833. Separate and entire, exclusively used. *Sittings:* Free 70, other 30. *Attendance:* Morning: Sunday school 56; afternoon: general congregation 30, Sunday school 56, total 86; evening: general congregation 65 or 70. *Average attendance:* not given. *Signed:* Francis Oldall, Coal Aston, Nr Dronfield. [HO 129/448/105]

---

[1] Population 776.

[2] Population 421.

Dronfield

Baptist. Meeting House. *Erected:* Separate and entire, exclusively used, except for Sunday school. *Sittings:* Free 76, other 24. *Attendance:* Morning: general congregation 25, Sunday school 64, total 89; afternoon: general congregation 14, Sunday school 85, total 99; evening: general congregation 82. *Average attendance:* not given. *Signed:* Edwin Lowe, Dronfield. [HO 129/448/106]

GREAT BARLOW[1]

Church of England. S. Laurence. *Erected:* Before 1800. *Endowments:* Land £52, other permanent endowment £46. *Sittings:* Free 71, other 301, total 372. *Attendance:* Afternoon: general congregation 146, Sunday school 56. *Average attendance:* Afternoon: general congregation 235, Sunday school 64. Edward Straw, schoolmaster, Barlow, Chesterfield. [HO 129/448/107]

---

[1] Population 636.

BAKEWELL REGISTRATION DISTRICT

PART 1

Bakewell Sub-District

BAKEWELL[1]

Great Longstone[2]

Church of England. S. Giles. Church of an ancient chapelry. *Erected:* Before 1800. *Endowments:* Land £150, other sources £30. *Sittings:* Free about 80, other about 320, total 400. *Attendance:* Very wet. Morning: general congregation 84, Sunday school 80, total 164; afternoon: general congregation 138, Sunday school 81, total 219. *Average attendance:* Morning: general congregation 115, Sunday school 100, total 215; afternoon: general congregation 186, Sunday school 100, total 286. *Remarks:* Living in the gift of the vicar of Bakewell. *Signed:* J.S. Hodson, M.A. Perpetual curate, Parsonage House, Gt. Longstone. [HO 129/449/1]

Bakewell

Parochial Union chapel. *Sittings:* Free 120. *Endowments:* Other sources £30. *Attendance:* Morning: general congregation 72. *Average attendance:* Morning: general congregation 72. *Signed:* Thomas Hirst, Chaplain, Chantry House, Bakewell. [HO 129/449/2]

Over Haddon[3]

Church of England. *Erected:* School room licensed for Divine Worship July 30 1840 as a place of worship for the township of Over Haddon additional to the Parish Church of Bakewell. By Private Benefaction and subscription. *Sittings:* About 30 or 40 persons can assemble. There are

---

[1] Parish population 9,897.

[2] Population 564.

[3] Population, with Nether Haddon, 235.

moveable benches and all free. *Attendance:* Service has been performed during the summer months generally on Thursday evening. *Remarks:* The incumbent having 3 duties viz. 2 at Bakewell and one at Rowsley on Sundays service has been performed during the summer months on Thursday evenings or afternoon, never on Sundays. *Signed:* Hubert Kestell Cornish, vicar. [HO 129/449/3]

Bakewell – Ashford Lane

General Baptist. *Erected:* Supposed about 1770. Separate and entire, not used but standing void & no services performed therein. *Sittings:* 100. *Remarks:* The chapel has been closed about 4 years. *Signed:* George Birley, one of the persuasion, Ashford, near Bakewell. [HO 129/449/4]

Ashford[1]

Unitarian. Cliff End. *Erected:* Rebuilt in the year 1841. Separate and entire, exclusively used. *Sittings:* Free 160. *Attendance:* Evening: general congregation 20. Joseph Smith, One of the congregation, Ashford, near Bakewell. [HO 129/449/5]

Bakewell[2]

Congregational or Independent. *Erected:* 1844. Separate and entire, exclusively used. *Sittings:* Free 100, other 300, standing aisles & pulpit pew, total 400. *Attendance:* Morning: general congregation 63, Sunday school 75, total 138; afternoon: Sunday school 75; evening: general congregation 91, Sunday school 10, total 101. *Average attendance:* Morning: general congregation 75, Sunday school 90, total 165; afternoon: Sunday school 90; evening: general congregation 100, Sunday school 10, total 110. *Remarks:* General sickness has affected the attendance today both in the congregation & in the School. *Signed:* Joseph Spencer, minister, Bakewell. [HO 129/449/6]

---

[1] Population 777.

[2] Population 2,217.

Wesleyan Methodist. *Erected:* 1799. Separate and entire, exclusively used. *Sittings:* Free 70, other 150, see letter, standing not any except in the aisles. *Attendance:* Morning: general congregation 75, Sunday school 45, total 120; evening: general congregation 130. *Average attendance:* Morning: general congregation 70, Sunday school 55, total 125; evening: general congregation 130. *Signed:* Moses Rayner, one of the ministers, Bakewell. [HO 129/449/7]

Froggatt[1]

Wesleyan Methodist. *Erected:* 1832. Separate and entire, exclusively used. *Sittings:* Free 100, standing not any excepting aisles. *Attendance:* Afternoon: general congregation 45; evening: general congregation 25. *Average attendance:* Afternoon: general congregation 50; evening: general congregation 25. *Signed:* Moses Rayner, Minister, Bakewell. [HO 129/449/8]

Calver[2]

Church of England. A large room above a stable. *Erected:* Licensed 1844 for divine service according to the rites of the C. of E. *Sittings:* Free 200. *Attendance:* Afternoon: general congregation 50, Sunday school 50, total 100. *Average attendance:* Afternoon: general congregation 50, Sunday school 50, total 100. *Signed:* A. Auriol Barker, minister, Baslow, Chesterfield. [HO 129/449/9]

Hassop[3]

Roman Catholic. All Saints chappell. *Erected:* about 1822. Separate and entire, exclusively used. *Sittings:* Free 200, standing 30. *Attendance:* Morning: general congregation 140, afternoon: from 30 to 60, no evening service. *Average attendance:* general congregation 120 to 180; no Sunday school. *Signed:* John Jones, Roman Catholic priest, Hassop, Bakewell. [HO 129/449/10]

---

[1] Population 135.

[2] Population 621.

[3] Population 95.

Great Longstone[1]

Wesleyan Methodist. *Erected:* 1844. Separate and entire, exclusively used. *Sittings:* Free 60, other 40, standing not any. *Attendance:* Evening: general congregation 50, Sunday school 10, total 60. *Average attendance:* Evening: general congregation 50, Sunday school 10, total 60. *Signed:* Moses Rayner, Minister, Bakewell. [HO 129/449/11]

Little Longstone[2]

Independent or Congregational. *Erected:* 1844. Separate and entire, exclusively used. *Sittings:* Free 60, other 58 standing aisles and around the pulpit. *Attendance:* Afternoon: general congregation 31; evening: no service. *Average attendance:* Morning: general congregation 28; afternoon: general congregation 36; no Sunday school. *Remarks:* Morning service every alternate Sunday; & afternoon every Sunday. *Signed:* Joseph Spencer, Minister, Bakewell. [HO 129/449/12]

Ashford

Church of England. Holy Trinity. *Erected:* Church of an ancient chapelry. Cons. before 1800. *Endowments:* Land £87 1s. 6d., glebe £4 10s. other permanent endowment £11 18s. 6d., fees £1. *Sittings:* Free 164, other 300, total 464. *Attendance:* Morning: general congregation 98, Sunday school 94, total 192; evening: general congregation 134, Sunday school 83, total 217. *Average attendance:* Morning: general congregation 120, Sunday school 110, total 230; evening: general congregation 190, Sunday school 110, total 300. *Remarks:* Sunday March 30th was a very unfavourable day. These numbers represent as nearly as possible the average number of attendants, morning and evening. *Signed:* W.F. Boyd, minister, Ashford, Nr Bakewell. [HO 129/449/13]

Wesleyan Methodist. *Erected:* 1830. Separate and entire, exclusively used. *Sittings:* Free 45, other 48. *Attendance:* Afternoon: general congregation 27, Sunday school 37, (average number 48) total 64. *Average attend-*

---

[1] Population, with Holme, 564.
[2] Population 154.

ance: not given. *Signed:* George Oldfield, chapel steward, Geo. Oldfield & Co. Ashford Marble Works. [HO 129/449/14]

Sheldon[1]

Church of England. S. Michael. A chapel of ease, a perpetual curacy in the parish of Bakewell. *Erected:* Before 1800. *Endowments:* Glebe land £75 per an., fees 5s. *Sittings:* Free 20, other 100, total 120. *Attendance:* Morning: general congregation 11, Sunday school 31, total 42. *Average attendance:* Afternoon: general congregation 30, Sunday school 35, total 65. *Remarks:* There is one service every Sunday performed alternately Morning & Evening and the average number attending the Evening services about 30 adults & from 30 to 40 children. *Signed:* James Coates, incumbent, Near Bakewell. [HO 129/449/15]

Primitive Methodist. *Erected:* 1848. Separate and entire, exclusively used. *Sittings:* Free 24, other 44. *Attendance:* Afternoon: general congregation 20; evening: general congregation 40. *Average attendance:* general congregation 60. *Signed:* Levi Brocklehurst, steward, Sheldon. [HO 129/449/16]

Taddington[2]

Church of England. church or chapel. *Erected:* Before 1800. *Endowments:* Land £85, fees £2, other sources Parsonage house. *Sittings:* Free 30, other 200, total 230. *Attendance:* I never count the numbers. Evening no service. *Average attendance:* Not counted. *Remarks:* In addition to the endowments above mentioned there is a chert quarry on the land out of the proceeds of which the expense of building the Parsonage was partly paid. This quarry produced from 1838 to 1844 £253 4s. 7d. Since 1844 the Incumbent has only received 4£ 2s.6d. *Signed:* Richard Heighway Kirby, Perpetual curate, Taddington. [HO 129/449/17]

[1] Population 197.
[2] Population, with Priestcliffe, 460.

Rowsley[1]

Church of England. *Erected:* Cons. July 31 1841, licensed in lieu of a church or chapel. The room is used for a school during the week and licensed for Divine Service on Sundays. Erected by the Duke of Rutland at his sole expence. Cost not known. *Sittings:* Free about 180. *Attendance:* Evening: general congregation 44, Sunday school 15. *Average attendance:* Evening: general congregation 20, Sunday school 10, total 30. *Remarks:* There is no endowment of any kind but the Duke of Rutland is pleased to make an annual payment in consideration of the services of the present Incumbent. *Signed:* Hubert Kestell Cornish, officiating minister, Bakewell. [HO 129/449/18]

Taddington[2]

Weslian Methodist. *Erected:* 1833. Separate and entire, exclusively used. *Sittings:* Free 38, other 40, standing 20. *Attendance:* Afternoon: general congregation 15, Sunday school 32, total 47; evening: general congregation 55. *Average attendance:* not given. *Signed:* Robert Broom, chapel steward Priestcliff, Taddington. [HO 129/449/19]

Primitive Methodist. *Erected:* 1843. Separate and entire, exclusively used. *Sittings:* Free 50, other 50, standing 20. *Attendance:* Afternoon: Sunday school 21; evening: general congregation 33, total 47. *Average attendance:* not given. *Signed:* Ralph Bagshaw, trustee, Taddington, Nr Bakewell. [HO 129/449/20]

Chelmorton[3]

Church of England. Supposed to be dedicated to S. John Baptist. The church of an ancient chapelry, parish of Bakewell & supposed to have been built A.D. 1111. *Erected:* Cons. before 1800. *Endowments:* Land Annual Rent £73, dues very trifling. *Sittings:* Free 20, other 342, total 362. *Attendance:* Afternoon: general congregation 68, Sunday school 22, total 90. *Average attendance:* Afternoon: general congregation 130, Sunday school 40,

[1] Population 265.
[2] Population 460.
[3] Population 238.

total 170. *Remarks:* Surplice Fees, about £1 per Annum on an Average. Average number of attendants at church during the summer months last year 150 adults. *Signed:* James Coates, 'minister', near Bakewell. [HO 129/449/21]

Primitive Methodist. *Erected:* Before 1800. Separate and entire, used exclusively as a place of worship. *Sittings:* Free 95. *Attendance:* Morning: general congregation 4.[1] *Average attendance:* Morning: general congregation 4, Sunday school none. *Remarks:* Primitive Methodism nearly extinct. There is very rarely any service and is always thinly attended: the Inhabitants prefering the Established Church. *Signed:* Joseph Hodgkinson, Manager, Chelmorton, near Bakewell. [HO 129/449/22]

Flagg[2]

Primitive Methodist. *Erected:* 1839. Separate and entire, exclusively used. *Sittings:* Free 90. *Attendance:* Morning: Sunday school 14; afternoon: general congregation 40, Sunday school 16, total 56; evening: general congregation 50. *Average attendance:* General congregation 40, Sunday school 16, total 56. *Remarks:* The Capple is attended by one traveling preacher and other local preachers according to there appointments. There are 2 sermons each Sunday and one weeknight preaching once every fortnight. *Signed:* Thomas Hodgkinson, superintendent of the school, George Skidmore, trustee of the above Place of Worship, Flagg. Near Bakewell. [HO 129/449/23]

Unitarian. *Erected:* 1839. Separate and entire, exclusively used. *Sittings:* Free 130. *Attendance:* Morning: Sunday school 30, afternoon: general congregation 20, Sunday school 30, total 50. *Average attendance:* not given. *Signed:* William Sutherland, minister, Flagg, near Bakewell. [HO 129/449/24]

---

[1] The figures are partly obliterated and the number could be read as 40 in each case, but is unlikely to be so in view of the comments.

[2] Population 239.

Monyash[1]

Church of England. S. Leonard. The church of an ancient chapelry. *Erected:* Cons. before 1800. *Endowments:* Land £60, other permanent endowments £40. *Sittings:* Free 70, other 150, total 220. *Attendance:* Morning: general congregation 32, Sunday school 40, total 72; evening: general congregation 80. *Average attendance:* Morning: general congregation 40, Sunday school 50, total 90; afternoon: general congregation 60, Sunday school 50, total 110; evening: general congregation 80. *Signed:* Henry C. Smith, minister, Monyash. [HO 129/449/25]

Quakers. *Erected:* Before 1800. Separate and entire, exclusively used. *Sittings:* Admeasurement: Floor 348, Persons 65; galleries 180, Persons 25, totals 528′ 90 persons. *Average attendance:* Morning: general congregation 21. *Signed:* John Bowman, Manager, Monyash. [HO 129/449/26]

Primitive Methodist. *Erected:* 1835. Separate and entire, exclusively used. *Sittings:* Free 100, other 48, standing 150. *Attendance:* Morning: general congregation class 27, Sunday school 56, total 83; afternoon: general congregation 40, Sunday school 56, total 96; evening: general congregation 60. *Signed:* Adolphus Frederick Beckerlegge, licensed minister, Winster, Matlock Bath. [HO 129/449/27]

Over Haddon

Primative Methodist. *Erected:* Not separate, exclusively used. *Sittings:* Free 40. *Attendance:* Afternoon: general congregation 14; evening: general congregation 16. *Average attendance:* general congregation about 20. *Remarks:* Tenant who granted the loan of part of a Dwelling House is about to quit on the 6th April. Whether the next Tenant will allow to be continued as a Place of Worship or not I do not know. *Signed:* William Mellor, deacon, Over Haddon, Nr Bakewell. [HO 129/449/28]

Congregational or Independent. *Erected:* Before 1800. Not separate, not exclusively used. *Sittings:* Free 20, standing 20. *Attendance:* not given. *Average attendance:* during twelve months general congregation 10, no Sunday school. *Remarks:* Divine Service conducted here during the week,

[1] Population 473.

never on the Sabbath Day. *Signed:* Joseph Spencer, minister, Bakewell. [HO 129/449/29]

YOULGREAVE

Middleton

Independent. *Erected:* 1826. Separate and entire, exclusively used. *Sittings:* Free 40, other 95, standing 50. *Attendance:* Morning: general congregation 40, Sunday school 13, total 53; afternoon: general congregation 42, Sunday school 13, total 55. *Average attendance:* Morning: general congregation 50 to 55, Sunday school 14; total 64 to 69. *Signed:* George Boden, Minister, Middleton by Youlgreave. [HO 129/449/30]

BAKEWELL

Rowsley

Independent. *Erected:* Since 1800. A dwelling house, not exclusively used. *Sittings:* Free 40. *Attendance:* not given. *Average attendance:* general congregation 30, no Sunday school. *Remarks:* Divine service is conducted here during the week and not during the Sabbath on Sunday. *Signed:* Joseph Spencer, minister, Bakewell. [HO 129/449/31]

Beeley[1]

Church of England. Chapelry in the parish of Bakewell. *Erected:* Cons. before 1800. *Endowments:* Land £33, other permanent endowment £16, fees £5, dues £5. *Sittings:* 400 see letter. *Attendance:* Afternoon: general congregation 61, Sunday school 31, total 92. *Average attendance:* not given. *Signed:* Edward Synge, curate, Baslow. [HO 129/449/32]

Wesleyan Methodist. *Erected:* 1808. Separate and entire, exclusively used, a place of worship except Sunday School. *Sittings:* Free 40, other 60. *Attendance:* Morning: Sunday school 18; afternoon: general congregation 30,

[1] Population 372.

Sunday school 18; evening: general congregation 30. *Average attendance:* not given. *Signed:* William Huntton, manager, Bakewell. [HO 129/449/33]

Primitive Methodist. *Erected:* Before 1800. Not separate, not exclusively used. *Sittings:* Free all. *Attendance:* Evening: general congregation 50. *Average attendance:* not given. *Remarks:* The reason I put all free sittings and none other is because it is so for we worship the Lord in a low thatched house – some of the people sit on forms, some on chairs, some on the sopha some on the table, some on the slopstone and some stand behind the door. *Signed:* Peter Bond, manager, Mrs Higgs, Beeley, Bakewell. [HO 129/449/34]

Baslow[1]

Church of England. Christchurch.[2] Chapelry in the parish of Bakewell. *Erected:* Cons. before 1800. *Endowments:* Land £30, other permanent endowment £33, fees £10, dues £10, other sources £20. *Sittings:* Other 400. *Attendance:* Morning: general congregation 116; evening: general congregation 141. *Average attendance:* Morning: general congregation 150; evening: general congregation 150. *Signed:* Edward Synge, officiating minister, Baslow. [HO 129/449/35]

Wesleyan Methodist. *Erected:* 1796. Separate and entire, exclusively used. *Sittings:* Free 94, other 91. *Attendance:* Morning: Sunday school 51; afternoon: general congregation 101; evening: general congregation 80. *Average attendance:* not given. *Signed:* Wm. Shillito, chapel steward, Baslow. [HO 129/449/36]

EDENSOR[3]

Church of England. *Erected:* Before 1800. *Endowments:* From the Duke of Devonshire £300. *Sittings:* about 200. Forms for 60 or 70 children. *Attendance:* Morning: general congregation 157, Sunday school 54, total 211. *Average attendance:* not given. *Signed:* Henry J. Ellison, Vicar, Edensor. [HO 129/449/37]

---

[1] Population 834.

[2] Now dedicated to S. Anne.

[3] Parish population 685, Edensor township 346.

Pilsley[1]

Church of England. Licensed School Room. *Erected:* Licensed in Novr. 1849. In the village of Pilsley being distant more than a mile from the Parish Church. Erected by the Duke of Devonshire. Cost: Private Benefaction between £600 and £700. *Endowments:* not given. *Sittings:* Free 125, children 40, total 165. *Attendance:* Afternoon: general congregation 144, Sunday school 12, total 156. *Average attendance:* not given. *Remarks:* The Sunday school at Pilsley being composed of children mostly under 8 yrs of age, only 12 of them attend divine service. The other children are included in general congregation. *Signed:* Henry J. Ellison, Vicar of Edensor, Bakewell. [HO 129/449/38]

Wesleyan Methodist. Preaching room. *Erected:* Cannot state. An upper room exclusively used, underneath used for farming purposes. *Sittings:* All free. standing place filled with benches. *Attendance:* Evening: general congregation 80, Sunday school 20, total 100. *Average attendance:* Evening: general congregation 85, Sunday school 20, total 105. *Remarks:* An upper room – below is used for farming purposes. *Signed:* Thomas Derry, Wesleyan minister, Bakewell. [HO 129/449/39]

YOULGREAVE[2]

Church of England. All Saints. Ancient parish church. *Erected:* Cons. before 1800. *Endowments:* Land £180, tithe £20, glebe £20, fees £5. *Sittings:* Free 60, other 700, total 760. *Attendance:* Morning: general congregation 84, Sunday school 120, total 204; afternoon: general congregation 120, Sunday school 120, total 240. *Average attendance:* not given. *Signed:* Robert M. Milne, vicar, Youlgreave, Bakewell. [HO 129/449/40]

Wesleyan Methodist. *Erected:* 1807. Separate and entire, exclusively used. *Sittings:* Free 84, other 168, standing not any excepting the aisles. *Attendance:* Afternoon: general congregation 70, Sunday school 60, total 130; evening: general congregation 80, Sunday school 20, total 100. *Average attendance:* Afternoon: general congregation 75, Sunday school 65, total 140; evening: general congregation 70, Sunday school 30, total 100. *Signed:* Moses Rayner, Wesleyan Minister, Bakewell. [HO 129/449/41]

---

[1] Population 339.

[2] Parish population 3,764, Youlgreave township 1,194.

Primitive Methodist. *Erected:* 1823. Separate and entire, exclusively used. *Sittings:* Free 110, other 60. *Attendance:* Afternoon: general congregation 108, Sunday school 36, total 144; evening: general congregation 140, Sunday school 40, total 180. *Average attendance:* not given. *Signed:* Humphrey Shimwell, steward, Youlgreave, near Bakewell. [HO 129/449/42]

Stanton[1]

Church of England. Private chapel licensed by the Bp. of the Diocese. *Erected:* Licensed 1839. The parish church being two miles distant this was erected by the Founder for his own and the accomodation of his tenantry and others. Erected by William Pole Thornhill at his own cost and by whom the Minister is paid. *Endowments:* Stipend £50. *Sittings:* Free 200, other 20, total 220. *Attendance:* Morning: general congregation 60. *Average attendance:* Morning: general congregation 60; afternoon 120. *Remarks:* There is only a single service in this chapel morning and afternoon *alternately* and the afternoon congregation usually doubles or more than doubles the morning. *Signed:* John Fisher Garrett, B.A. officiating minister, Elton parsonage, Matlock. [HO 129/449/43]

Stanton Hillside

Wesleyan Methodist. *Erected:* 1833. Dwelling house, not separate, not exclusively used. *Sittings:* Free. *Attendance:* Afternoon: general congregation 20. *Average attendance:* not given. *Signed:* Benjamin Burrs, Wesleyan Methodist Local preacher, grocer, Stanton Hillside, Winster, Matlock. [HO 129/449/44]

Stanton

Wesleyan Methodist. *Erected:* 1829. Separate and entire, place of worship and Sunday school. *Sittings:* Free 48 yds superficial, other pews let 15 yds. *Attendance:* Average Morning: general congregation 80, Sunday school 78, total 158. *Average attendance:* Morning: general congregation 80, Sunday school 78, total 158. *Remarks:* Number of persons attending Divine Service on Sunday March 30 70, congregation will average 80 Persons.

---

[1] Population 705.

Space occupied for Public Worship about 63 superficial yards. Space occupied for Sunday school is about 30 yd superficial. *Signed:* Benjamin Broomhead, Trustee, leader and steward, Stanton, Bakewell. [HO 129/449/45]

Stanton Hillside

Primitive Methodist. *Erected:* In the year 1821 or 1822. Separate and entire, exclusively used. *Sittings:* Free all, 100 see letter. *Attendance:* Morning: Sunday school 52; afternoon: general congregation 80; evening: general congregation 70; total 202. *Average attendance:* Morning: Sunday school 50; afternoon: general congregation 70; evening: general congregation 70; total 190. Samuel Dakin, chapel steward, Birchover, Matlock Bath. [HO 129/449/46]

Middleton by Youlgreave[1]

Primitive Methodist. *Erected:* 1850. Separate and entire, exclusively used. *Sittings:* Free 55, other 32. *Attendance:* Morning: Sunday school 36; afternoon: general congregation 65; evening: general congregation 80. *Average attendance:* not given. *Signed:* Francis Pursglove, Manager, Middleton by Youlgreave, Bakewell. [HO 129/449/47]

HARTINGTON[2]

Earl Sterndale

Church of England. Chapel of Earl Sterndale in Parish of Hartington. *Erected:* Uncertain when consecrated. The chapel was rebuilt and re-opened by the Lord Bishop of Lichfield in 1830. Erected by the Parishioners – Parochial Rate £1,400. *Endowments:* tithe not regd., glebe to be answd. *Sittings:* Free 103, other 213, total 316. *Attendance:* Afternoon: general congregation 62, Sunday school 15. *Average attendance:* Morning: general congregation 45; afternoon: general congregation 80, Sunday school 25. *Remarks:* Earl Sterndale chapel when rebuilt was enlarged to accomodate a

---

[1] Population, with Smerrill, 276.

[2] Parish population 2,089.

hamlet containing 400 inhabitants situated four miles distant none of whom have been in the habit of attending it. *Signed:* William Buckwell, Incumbent, Buxton. [HO 129/449/48]

Matlock Sub-District

YOULGREAVE

Winster[1]

Church of England. S. John. *Erected:* Before 1800. *Endowments:* Land £95, fees in 1850 £5 2s. 4d., Easter offering £12. *Sittings:* Free 294, other 295, total 589. *Attendance:* Morning: general congregation 26, Sunday school 8, total 34; afternoon: general congregation 66. *Average attendance:* Morning: general congregation 50, Sunday school 12, total 62; afternoon: general congregation 70. *Remarks:* The greater portion of the Inhabitants of Winster are professed Dissenters and certain influential persons prevent the children from attending the Church Sunday School and Established Church Service. *Signed:* William Dyke, Perpetual Curate. [HO 129/449/50]

Church of England. *Erected:* Licensed room in the chapelry of Winster, July 1850. In the private occupation of Mr Henry A. Norman. To allow more than nineteen persons to assemble for Divine Worship. *Sittings:* Free about 110. *Attendance:* Morning: Sunday school 80; evening: general congregation 100. *Average attendance:* not given. *Signed:* Henry A. Norman, Reader, Winster. [HO 129/449/51]

Wesleyan Reformed.[2] *Erected:* Domestic place of worship, not exclusively used. *Sittings:* Free 50. *Attendance:* Afternoon: general congregation 25; evening: general congregation 26. *Average attendance:* It has not been in being 12 months. 30 per month. *Signed:* Robert Searle, Local Preacher, Matlock Bridge. [HO 129/449/52]

Primitive Methodist. *Erected:* Enlarged in 1850. Separate and entire, exclusively used. *Sittings:* Free 100, other 80, standing 300. *Attendance:* Morning: class meeting 30; afternoon: general congregation 170 or 180;

---

[1] Population 928.

[2] This entry has been crossed through.

evening: general congregation 200 or 300. *Average attendance:* general congregation 12,000. *Remarks:* The Primitive Methodist Connexion preaches the doctrines of the Church of England as asserted in the Deed Poll of Connexion enrolled in the Court of Chancery. See the printed copy sold by Holliday, Sutton Street, Commercial Road, Georges, East London. *Signed:* Adolphus Frederick Beckerlegge, Licensed Conference Minister, Winster, Matlock Bank. [HO 129/449/53]

Youlgreave

Wesleyan Methodist. *Erected:* 1837. Separate and entire, exclusively used. *Sittings:* Free 105, other 84. *Attendance:* Afternoon: general congregation 48; evening: general congregation 53. *Average attendance:* Afternoon: general congregation 80; evening: general congregation 80. Samuel Swindell, steward, butcher, Winster. [HO 129/449/54]

Elton[1]

Church of England. All Saints. Church of an ancient chapelry. *Erected:* Cons. before 1800. *Endowments:* Land £62 16s., other permanent endowment dividends from Q. Anne's Bounty £6 15s. 8d., fees £2, Easter offering not collected. *Sittings:* Free 22, other 245, total 267. *Attendance:* Afternoon: general congregation 96, Sunday school 25, total 121. *Average attendance:* Morning: general congregation 20, Sunday school 30, total 50; afternoon: general congregation 60, Sunday school 30, total 90. *Remarks:* Elton chapel was rebuilt in 1808 upon the ancient foundations by the Inhabitants. The cost £1500 was raised by Rate & Briefs & private subscription. *Signed:* J.F. Garrett, B.A., perpetual curate. Elton Parsonage, Matlock. [HO 129/449/55]

Wesleyan Methodist. *Erected:* In 1831 on ground procured for the purpose not previously occupied for that purpose. Chapel over Sunday school. Exclusively for a place of worship with Sunday School underneath. *Sittings:* 27 feet by 16 feet. Free 70, other 32. *Attendance:* Evening: general congregation 60. *Average attendance:* Afternoon: general congregation 10, Sunday school 40; evening: general congregation 55. *Remarks:* The Chapel and Premises made over to Wesleyan Methodist Connexion and Enrolled in Chancery. Service every Sunday evening, and every alternate Sunday

---

[1] Population 545.

afternoon. *Signed:* Rev. Rayner, Wesleyan Minister in the Bakewell Circuit, Joseph Lygo, chapel steward and trustee, school-master & shopkeeper, Elton, Matlock. [HO 129/449/56]

Primitive Methodist. *Erected:* 1843. Separate and entire, exclusively used. *Sittings:* Free 54, other 40, standing 20 persons. *Attendance:* Morning: class meeting 16; afternoon: general congregation 30; evening: general congregation 60. *Average attendance:* Morning: class meeting 16; afternoon: general congregation 30; evening: general congregation 60 throughout the year. *Remarks:* Class meeting for Christian religious experience: praises and prayer. Elton in the Winster Circuit. *Signed:* Adolphus Frederick Beckerlegge, Conference Minister, Winster, Matlock Bath. [HO 129/449/57]

Birchover[1]

Church of England. An ancient donative chapel. *Erected:* Cons. before 1800. *Endowments:* Other permanent endowment £20. *Sittings:* Free 80, other 20, total 100. *Attendance:* not given. *Average attendance:* not given. *Remarks:* This chapel is endowed as above for the performance of Divine Service once every month. The present practice is to give one regular service every Sunday from Easter to Michaelmas. During the winter months when the chapel is considered too damp to assemble in a weekly lecture is given in a cottage. *Signed:* J.F. Garrett, Officiating minister, Elton Parsonage, nr Matlock. [HO 129/449/57A]

DARLEY,[2] NORTH AND SOUTH

Church of England. *Erected:* not known. *Endowments:* not given. *Sittings:* Free 0, other 402. *Attendance:* Morning: general congregation 250, Sunday school 100, total 350; afternoon: general congregation 200, Sunday school 100, total 300. *Average attendance:* Morning: general congregation 250, Sunday school 100, total 350; afternoon: general congregation 200, Sunday school 100, total 350. *Remarks:* The above return is only a rough guess as in no other way (without sufficient notice) could a correct return have been made. The Church however is well attended but the great fault of the accomodation is the appropriation of large seats to large houses whether

[1] Population 78.

[2] Parish population 1,932, Darley township 1,375.

there is a family large enough to occupy them or not while no free provision is made for the poor. *Signed:* Daniel Vawdrey, rector, Darley Rectory, Matlock. [HO 129/449/58]

Upper Hackney

Primitive Methodist. *Erected:* 1848. Separate and entire, exclusively used. *Sittings:* Free 67, other 36. *Attendance:* Afternoon: general congregation 51, Sunday school 40, total 91. *Average attendance:* not given. *Signed:* Benjamin Parks, steward, Upper Hackney, Near Matlock. [HO 129/449/59]

Twodales

Wesleyan Methodist. *Erected:* 1827. Separate and entire, exclusively used. *Sittings:* Free 70, other 66. *Attendance:* Afternoon: general congregation 29; evening: general congregation 22. *Average attendance:* Morning: Sunday school 60; afternoon: general congregation 45, Sunday school 60; evening: general congregation 40. *Signed:* John Young, steward, Darley, Nr Matlock. [HO 129/449/60]

Wensley and Snitterton[1]

Church of England. S. Mary. *Erected:* about 10 years. *Endowments:* Not given. *Sittings:* Free 240. *Attendance:* not given. *Average attendance:* Morning: general congregation 20, Sunday school 10; afternoon: general congregation 24. *Signed:* Sampson Roe, registrar. [HO 129/449/60A]

Wensley

Wesleyan Methodist. *Erected:* About A.D. 1830. Separate and entire, exclusively used. *Sittings:* Free 40, other 60. *Attendance:* Morning: general congregation about 30, Sunday school 40; afternoon: Sunday school 40; evening: general congregation about 60, Sunday school 20. *Average attendance:* Morning: general congregation 30, Sunday school 40; afternoon:

---

[1] Population 557.

Sunday school 40; evening: general congregation 60, Sunday school 20. *Signed:* John Alsop, a Trustee, Wensley, Nr Matlock. [HO 129/449/61]

Snitterton

Wesleyan Reformers. *Erected:* Preaching room, separate and entire, exclusively used. *Sittings:* Free 50. *Attendance:* Afternoon: general congregation 25. *Average attendance:* Morning: general congregation 25. *Signed:* William Yeomans, Local Preacher, farmer, Snitterton. [HO 129/449/62]

Wensley – Darley Bridge

Wesleyan Reformers. *Erected:* Before 1800. dwelling house, not exclusively used. *Sittings:* Free 40. *Attendance:* Evening: general congregation 35. *Average attendance:* Morning: general congregation 30. *Signed:* Thomas Yeomans, class leader, farmer, Warren Carr, Near Wensley. [HO 129/449/63]

MATLOCK[1]

Church of England. Parish church *Erected:* Before 1800. *Endowments:* Rent charge, tithe £335, glebe about £50, amount of other sources varying each year. *Sittings:* Free none, other 420. *Attendance:* Morning: general congregation 145, Sunday school 130, total 275; afternoon: general congregation 143, Sunday school 130, total 273. *Average attendance:* Morning: general congregation 300, Sunday school 150, total 350; afternoon: general congregation 300, Sunday school 130, total 350. *Remarks:* The average number of attendants is not by any enumeration which has been kept but is taken in round numbers at a rough guess. *Signed:* W.R. Melville, Rector of Matlock. The Rectory, Matlock. [HO 129/449/64]

---

[1] Population 4,010.

Matlock Bath

Church of England. Holy Trinity. Perpetual curacy with a district under 1&2 Wm IV C. 38. *Erected:* Consecrated Oct. 1842 as an additional church. By Private Subscription and Benefactions. Cost £2,400. *Endowments:* Other permanent endowment £31 15s. 8d., pews £65. *Sittings:* Free 150, other 300, total 450. *Attendance:* Morning: General congregation 154, Sunday school 46, total 200; afternoon: general congregation 146, Sunday school 46, total 192, Evening: only during the summer. *Average attendance:* Morning: general congregation 350, Sunday school 50, total 400; afternoon: general congregation 200, Sunday school 50, total 250; evening: general congregation 350. *Remarks:* The attendance during the summer months is fully double the number of the winter congregation in consequence of the large number of visitors frequenting this Watering place. *Signed:* William Gibbs Barker, Incumbent, Parsonage, Matlock Bath. [HO 129/449/65]

Scarthin Nick

Primitive Methodist. Preaching room. *Erected:* Feby. 10 1850. Not separate, exclusively used. *Sittings:* Free 150, other 42, standing 50. *Attendance:* Afternoon: general congregation 120, Sunday school school 32, total 152; evening: general congregation 140, Sunday school 20, total 160. *Average attendance:* Afternoon: general congregation 150, Sunday school 32, total 182; evening: general congregation 200, Sunday school 20, total 220. *Remarks:* The congregation attending the evening service at this Room has been often so large that every *sitting* & the Standing Room has been occupied. George Farnsworth, Manager, Chapel Hill, Matlock. [HO 129/449/66]

Matlock Bath[1]

Wesleyan Methodist. *Erected:* 1809. Not a seperate Building, a Day School under it belonging to another party. Worship and Sunday school. *Sittings:* Free 310, other 224, standing 50. *Attendance:* Morning: general congregation 100, Sunday school 100, total 200; afternoon: Sunday school 90; evening: general congregation 120, Sunday school 20, total 140. *Average attendance:* Morning: general congregation 100, Sunday school 100, total

---

[1] Replacing 'Cromford', crossed out.

200; afternoon: Sunday school 90; evening: general congregation 120, Sunday school 20, total 140. *Signed:* W.B. Dennis, Wesleyan Minister, Cromford. [HO 129/449/67]

Matlock Bridge

Wesleyan Methodist. *Erected:* 1840. Separate and entire, exclusively used. *Sittings:* Free 150, other 100. *Attendance:* Afternoon: general congregation 40, Sunday school 44, total 84. *Average attendance:* not given. Joseph Hodgkinson, trustee and chapel steward, grocer, Matlock Bath. [HO 129/449/68]

Primitive Methodist. *Erected:* 1838. Separate and entire, not exclusively used. *Sittings:* Free 120, other 50, standing 60. *Attendance:* Morning: Sunday school 95; afternoon: general congregation 69, Sunday school 90, total 159; evening: no service. *Average attendance:* Evening: general congregation. [March 23 160][1] *Signed:* James Hawley, Local Preacher, Matlock Bank. [HO 129/449/69]

Wesleyan Reformers. Preaching room. *Erected:* Opened for Religious Worship March 2 1851. Not separate, exclusively used. *Sittings:* Free 130, other 16, standing 50. *Attendance:* Afternoon: general congregation 72; evening: general congregation 140. *Average attendance:* Morning: general congregation 90. *Signed:* Jno. Cardin, steward, carpenter, Matlock Bridge. [HO 129/449/70]

Independent Congregational Dissenters. *Erected:* September 1848. Separate and entire, exclusively used. *Sittings:* Free 80, other 170. *Attendance:* Morning: general congregation 93, Sunday school 92, total 185; afternoon: Sunday school 94; evening: general congregation 174. *Average attendance:* Morning: general congregation 92, Sunday school 90, total 182; afternoon: Sunday school 90; evening: general congregation 190, Sunday school 20, total 210. *Signed:* John Whewell, Minister, Matlock [HO 129/449/71]

Primitive Methodist. *Erected:* May 1st 1823. Separate and entire, exclusively used. *Sittings:* Free 25, other 90, standing 20. *Attendance:* Morning: general congregation 19; afternoon: general congregation 114;

---

[1] This passage is crossed through.

evening: general congregation 175. *Average attendance:* about 90. *Remarks:* March 30 1851 was our anuel missionary meeting makes the attendance larger than usual. *Signed:* Thomas Carline, Seat Letter, Local Preacher, Hatter, Starkholmes, Matlock Bridge. [HO 129/449/72]

Matlock Bath

Independent or Congregational. Glenorchy chapel. *Erected:* About 1777. Separate and entire, exclusively as a place of worship. *Sittings:* Free 100, other 250. *Attendance:* Morning: general congregation 90, Sunday school 60, total 150; afternoon: general congregation 20; evening: general congregation 180, Sunday school 20, total 200. *Average attendance:* Morning: general congregation 90, Sunday school 60, total 150; afternoon: general congregation 20; evening: general congregation 200. *Signed:* J.M. Newnes, minister, Matlock Bank. [HO 129/449/73]

Wesleyan Methodist. *Erected:* Not separate, exclusively used. *Sittings:* Free 50, other 30. *Attendance:* Evening: general congregation 40. *Average attendance:* Evening: general congregation 40. *Signed:* W.B. Dennis, Wesleyan minister, Cromford. [HO 129/449/74]

TANSLEY[1]

Church of England. Holy Trinity. District chapelry. *Erected:* Consecrated Sept. 18 1840 as an additional church; by subscription £900. *Endowments:* Other permanent endowment £103 3s. 10d, pews £3, fees £1 10s., other £1 5s. *Sittings:* Free 153, other 110, total 263. *Attendance:* Morning: general congregation 65, Sunday school 108, total 173; afternoon: general congregation 89, Sunday school 103, total 192. *Average attendance:* not given. *Remarks:* Under the head of permanent endowment the Income Tax is deducted. The £3 return as arising from pew rents is the average surplus paid to the minister after the expenses of clerk etc have been deducted. The £1 5s. the annual value of the churchyard & adjoining piece of land. There is also a house and garden valued at £20. *Signed:* Melville Holmes, minister, Tansley, Matlock. [HO 129/449/75]

[1] Population 593.

Wesleyan Methodist.[1] *Erected:* Before 1800. Separate and entire, exclusively used. *Sittings:* Free 150, other 120. *Attendance:* Morning: Sunday school 50; afternoon: general congregation 20, Sunday school 50; evening: general congregation 20. *Average attendance:* not given. *Remarks:* The former average actual congregation of grown up people was 50 but has lessened within the last few months through agitation in the Society. *Signed:* William Peters Hackett, acting as steward, Tansley Mills, Nr Matlock. [HO 129/449/76]

Wesleyan Reformers. *Erected:* 1850. Room not separate, exclusively used. *Sittings:* Free 100. *Attendance:* afternoon general congregation 40; evening: general congregation 40. *Average attendance:* not given. *Signed:* Joseph Slack, manager, farmer, Tansley. [HO 129/449/77]

WIRKSWORTH[2]

Cromford[3]

Church of England. S. Mary. *Erected:* Perpetual Curacy built and endowed in 1797. Cons. before 1800. *Endowments:* Land £41, other permanent endowment £50, other sources £96 15s. 8d. *Sittings:* Free 70, other 304, exclusive of seats for scholars. *Attendance:* Morning: general congregation 133, Sunday school 191, total 324; afternoon: general congregation 115, Sunday school 188, total 303. *Average attendance:* not given. *Signed:* Robert Jones, Perpetual Curate, Cromford. [HO 129/449/78]

Wesleyan Reformers. *Erected:* Before 1800. Not separate, not exclusively used. *Sittings:* Free 50, standing 60. *Attendance:* Afternoon: general congregation 50. *Average attendance:* Morning: general congregation 50. *Remarks:* Dweling house. *Signed:* Anthony Britland, steward, Cromford. [HO 129/449/79]

Wesleyan Mithouist Reformers. *Erected:* 1830. Not separate, not exclusively used. *Sittings:* Free 150. *Attendance:* Morning: general congrega-

---

[1] Compare with HO 129/446/17 (p. 104): the double entry implies two Wesleyan chapels in Tansley.

[2] Parish population 7,480.

[3] Population 1,190.

tion 100; evening: general congregation 200. *Average attendance:* not given. *Signed:* Wm. Housley, steward, Cromford. [HO 129/449/80]

General Baptist. Meeting Room or Marts Club Room. *Erected:* Before 1800. Not separate, not exclusively used. *Sittings:* all free, standing 100 persons. *Attendance:* Afternoon: general congregation 30; evening: general congregation 30. *Average attendance:* Afternoon: general congregation 30; evening: general congregation 30, Sunday school none. *Remarks:* The Room has of late been occupied in morning by Reform Wesleyan Methodist Denomination and the attendance has been about 50 on an average. *Signed:* Samuel Bown, Assistant Deacon, Market Place, Cromford. [HO 129/449/81]

BRADBOURNE[1]

Aldwark[2]

Wesleyan Methodist. preaching room.[3] *Erected:* 1829. Not separate, exclusively used. *Sittings:* Free 70. *Attendance:* Afternoon: general congregation 37; evening: general congregation 25. *Average attendance:* Morning: general congregation 30. *Signed:* B.S. Buxton, steward, Aldwark, nr Winster. [HO 129/449/82]

---

[1] Parish population 1,230.

[2] Population 79.

[3] Compare with HO 129/447/81 (p. 136): although there are minor differences these appear to be duplicate returns.

PART 2

Tideswell Sub-District

STONEY MIDDLETON[1]

Presbyterian. *Erected:* Separate and entire, exclusively used. *Attendance:* Morning: general congregation 7; no Sunday school. *Signed:* Josiah Payne, Registrar, Tideswell. [HO 129/449/1]

HOPE[2]

Great Hucklow[3]

Unitarian. *Erected:* About 1799. Separate and entire, exclusively used. *Sittings:* not given. *Attendance:* Afternoon: general congregation 20, no Sunday school. *Signed:* Josiah Payne, registrar, Tideswell. [HO 129/449/2]

Bradwell[4] – Smithy Hill

Unitarian. *Erected:* Separate and entire, exclusively used. *Sittings:* all free. *Attendance:* Evening: general congregation 25. *Signed:* Josiah Payne, registrar, Tideswell. [HO 129/449/3]

STONEY MIDDLETON

Church of England. S. Martyn. Chapel to Hathersage with its own district. *Erected:* Consecrated before 1800. *Endowments:* Land £19, other permanent endowment, £82, fees £2. *Sittings:* Other 300. *Attendance:* Morning: general congregation 20, Sunday school 62, total 82; afternoon: general congregation 94, Sunday school 67, total 161. *Average attendance:* Morning: general congregation 25, Sunday school 62, total 87; afternoon:

---

[1] Population 593.
[2] Parish population 4,604.
[3] Population 232.
[4] Population 1,334.

general congregation 120, Sunday school 70, total 190. *Remarks:* March 30th very stormy. No pews are free. The scholars are accomodated in the vacant spaces. *Signed:* Urban Smith, minister, Stoney Middleton, nr Bakewell. [HO 129/449/4]

HATHERSAGE[1]

Church of England. S. Michael. An ancient parish church. *Erected:* Consecrated before 1800. *Endowments:* Land £118, tithe £9 15s., glebe £3 5s., fees £5 10s., Easter offering £2. *Sittings:* Other 270. *Attendance:* Morning: general congregation 60, Sunday school 78, total 138; afternoon: general congregation 115, Sunday school 84, total 199. *Average attendance:* Morning: general congregation 80, Sunday school 100, total 180; afternoon: general congregation 200, Sunday school 100, total 300. *Remarks:* The small attendance at church on Sunday 30th March was owing to severity of the weather. *Signed:* Henry Cottingham, Minister, Hathersage, nr Bakewell. [HO 129/449/5]

Roman Catholic chapel. *Erected:* About 190 years ago. Separate and entire, exclusively used. *Sittings:* totally free. *Attendance:* [The implication of the figures given is unclear: 150 is entered above the first column, 120 written across Morning attendance, afternoon 'very few' and evening 'none'.] *Average attendance:* About 25. *Remarks:* one of the oldest chapels in England, – once unroofed by a gang of Ruffians – urged by their no-popery zeal – something like what at present animates the soul of Lord John Russell. *Signed:* Benjamin Hulme, Catholic priest, Hathersage, N. Bakewell. [HO 129/449/6]

Wesleyan Methodist. *Erected* 1807. Separate and entire, exclusively used. *Sittings:* Free 200, other 158. *Attendance:* Morning: general congregation 60, Sunday school 36, total 96; evening: general congregation 80. *Average attendance:* not given. *Signed:* Joseph Robt Cocken, steward, Hathersage. [HO 129/449/7]

---

[1] Parish population 2,106, Hathersage township 832.

EYAM[1]

Grindleford Bridge – Eyam Woodlands[2]

Wesleyan Methodist. *Erected:* Before 1800. Separate and entire, exclusively used. *Sittings:* Free 54, other 46. *Attendance:* Morning: general congregation 29, Sunday school 42, total 71; afternoon: general congregation 43, Sunday school 45, total 88; evening: general congregation 16. *Average attendance:* Morning: general congregation 50, Sunday school 45, total 95; afternoon: general congregation 50, Sunday school 45, total 95; evening: general congregation 40. *Remarks:* An unusually slender attendance this day in consequence of the weather being stormy and the district stragling. The night service is a prayer meeting. *Signed:* Joseph Andrew, steward, Grindleford Bridge. [HO 129/449/8]

Foolow[3]

Wesleyan. *Erected:* About the year of our Lord 1810. Separate and entire, exclusively used. *Sittings:* Free 80, other 40, standing not any excepting aisles. *Attendance:* Afternoon: general congregation 35, Sunday school 45, total 80; evening: general congregation 50. *Average attendance:* Afternoon: general congregation 45, Sunday school 50, total 95; evening: general congregation 60. *Signed:* Moses Rayner, Wesleyan Minister, Bakewell. [HO 129/449/9]

Eyam[4]

Church of England. *Erected:* not given. *Endowments:* not given. *Sittings:* 440 see letter. *Attendance:* Morning: general congregation 42, Sunday school 68, total 110; afternoon: general congregation 111, Sunday school 79, total 190. *Average attendance:* not given. *Signed:* Thomas Allnutt, stipendiary curate, Eyam, near Bakewell. [HO 129/449/10]

---

[1] Parish population 1,580.

[2] Population 275.

[3] Population 226.

[4] Township population 1,079.

Wesleyan. *Erected:* Before 1800. Separate and entire, exclusively used. *Sittings:* Free 130, other 70, standing none, 11 yds x 8 yds dementions. *Attendance:* Afternoon: general congregation 55; evening: general congregation 71. *Average attendance:* Morning: Sunday school 46; afternoon: general congregation 20/75; evening: general congregation 71. *Remarks:* This chaple has connected with it a Sunday school 46 scholars. *Signed:* Thomas Ball, local preacher. [HO 129/449/11]

STONEY MIDDLETON

Wesleyan Methodist.[1] *Erected:* 1827. Separate and entire, exclusively used. *Sittings:* Free 100, other 80, standing none. *Attendance:* Morning: general congregation 35, Sunday school 60, total 95; afternoon: Sunday school 70; evening: general congregation 120. *Average attendance:* not given. *Signed:* Samuel Hereman, officiating preacher, Benjamin Cooper, sturerd, Stoney Middleton, near Bakewell. [HO 129/449/12]

HOPE

Great Hucklow

Wesleyan Methodist. *Erected:* 1806. Separate and entire, exclusively used. *Sittings:* not given. *Attendance:* Morning: general congregation 90, Sunday school 70 on an average. *Average attendance:* not given. *Signed:* George Chapman, Local preacher and trustee, Great Hucklow. [HO 129/449/13]

Little Hucklow[2]

Sunday school room – denomination nil. *Erected:* 1815. Entire Sunday school ocatienaly used as a place of worship. *Sittings:* All free. Afternoon: general congregation 40, Sunday school 30, total 70. *Average attendance:* not given. *Remarks:* Open to Prodestants if they please to give us a sermon. Under no religious denomination. It belongs to Freeholders within the

---

[1] Almost certainly a Wesleyan Reform congregation. Samuel Hereman was a Reform preacher of some note.

[2] Population 235.

Township of Little Hucklow. *Signed:* Richard Chapman, Little Hucklow, Near Tideswell. [HO 129/449/14]

Bradwell

Primitive Methodist. Bethel. *Erected:* 1846. Separate and entire, exclusively used. *Sittings:* Free 480, other 120. *Attendance:* Afternoon: 250; evening: 400. *Average attendance:* not given. *Remarks:* The 226 scholars taught by 34 gratuitous teachers. *Signed:* John Judson, Minister, Bradwell, Near Castleton. [HO 129/449/15]

Church of England. The Bradwell church. Evening service as a kind of chapel of ease to the Parish of Hope. *Erected:* Licensed about the year 1845. Licensed as an additional church. By private subscription for a Sunday school and town's meetings but licensed as a place of worship pro tem. Cost unknown. *Endowments:* The Additional Curates Aid Society grants £80 which with £20 from the vicar makes £100. *Sittings:* Free 200. *Attendance:* Evening: general congregation about 125. *Average attendance:* Evening: general congregation about 140. *Signed:* John Clarke, minister, Bradwell, Bakewell. [HO 129/449/16]

Wesleyan Methodist. *Erected:* 1807. Separate and entire, exclusively used. *Sittings:* Free 300, other 242. *Attendance:* Morning: general congregation 60, Sunday school 126, total 186; evening: general congregation 240. *Average attendance:* Morning: general congregation 100, Sunday school 136, total 236; evening: general congregation 240. *Signed:* David Cornforth, minister, Bradwell, near Bakewell. [HO 129/449/17]

BAKEWELL

Great Longstone[1] – Wardlow[2]

Church of England. School room. *Erected:* Licensed 1840–3. Erected by private subscription. *Endowments:* none. *Sittings:* Free 64. *Attendance:* No returns given. *Remarks:* No service regularly; used as Sunday school for 50.

---

[1] Population 564.

[2] The township of Wardlow was partly in Bakewell parish (population 65) and partly in Hope (126).

Signed: Jas. S. Hodson, P. Curate of Longstone, Longstone Parsonage, Bakewell. [HO 129/449/18]

HOPE

Abney[1]

Wesleyan Methodist. *Erected:* 1812. Separate. A Place of Worship exempt For Sunday school, Yes. *Sittings:* Free all, 90 see letter. Standing 64. *Attendance:* afternoon: general congregation 17. *Average attendance:* Afternoon: general congregation 21, Sunday school 22, total 43. *Remarks:* Chappel built by subscription. *Signed:* Thomas Bagshaw, Chappel Stewart, Abney. [HO 129/449/19]

TIDESWELL[2]

Litton[3]

Wesleyan Methodist. *Erected:* 1834. Separate and entire, exclusively used. *Sittings:* Free 100, other 94. *Attendance:* Afternoon: general congregation 81, Sunday school 100, total 181; evening: general congregation 74. *Average attendance:* not given. *Signed:* David Cornforth, Minister, Bradwell. [HO 129/449/20]

Litton – Cressbrook

Wesleyan Methodist. *Erected:* 1836. Not separate, not exclusively used. *Sittings:* Free 70. *Attendance:* Morning: 44; evening: 57. *Average attendance:* not given. *Signed:* Nicholas Palfreyman, class leader. Cressbrook, Nr Bakewell. [HO 129/449/21]

---

[1] Population 99.

[2] Parish population 3,411.

[3] Population 945.

Litton

Primitive Methodist. *Erected:* Before 1800. dwelling house, not separate, not exclusively used. *Sittings:* not given. *Attendance:* Morning: General congregation 27; afternoon: general congregation 66. *Average attendance:* not given. *Signed:* George Bennett, Local preacher, Tideswell. [HO 129/449/22]

Litton Slack

Primitive Methodist. In a dwelling house. *Erected:* 1809. dwelling house not separate, not exclusively used. *Sittings:* Free 40. *Attendance:* Afternoon: 28. *Average attendance:* Afternoon: general congregation 30. *Signed:* William Birkin, leader, Litton Slack. [HO 129/449/23]

Litton New Houses

Wesleyan Methodist. *Erected:* 1826. In a dwelling house, not separate, not exclusively used. *Sittings:* Free 60. *Attendance:* Evening: general congregation 52. *Average attendance:* Evening: general congregation 49. *Remarks:* A Wesleyan Methodists preaching House for the accomodation of parties residing at Litton Slack in the parish of Tideswell. *Signed:* James Warhurst, Leader, Litton Slack, Near Bakewell. [HO 129/449/24]

Tideswell[1]

Church of England. S. John Baptist. Ancient parish church. *Erected:* Consecrated before 1800. *Endowments:* not given. *Sittings:* Free 1200. *Attendance:* Morning: general congregation 18, Sunday school 79, total 97; afternoon: general congregation 72, Sunday school 110, total 182; evening: general congregation 100. *Average attendance:* Morning: general congregation 35, Sunday school 50, total 85; afternoon: general congregation 150, Sunday school 110, total 260; evening: general congregation 160. *Signed:* John Kynaston, M.A., vicar of Tideswell, Tideswell Vicarage. [HO 129/449/25]

---

[1] Township population 2035.

Tideswell Ash Lane

Independent or Congregational. *Erected:* 1844. Separate and entire, exclusively used. *Sittings:* Free 100, other 140, standing a space of this description is supplied with moveable seats on occasion and might hold from 50 to 60. *Attendance:* Afternoon: general congregation 74, Sunday school 110, total 184; evening: general congregation 170. Average attendance during four months last past: Afternoon: general congregation 70, Sunday school 110, total 180; evening: general congregation 220. *Remarks:* Under the chapel is a large school-room in which the Sunday school is held. The number of Sunday scholars on the book is about 145. The very little ones are generally dismissed before the commencement of the afternoon service. 170 might be regarded as the average number attending on Sunday evenings for the 12 months last past but the attendance has been greater during the winter season and the lower part of col. VIII is used to express that fact. *Signed:* James Rennie, minister, Tideswell. [HO 129/449/26]

Tideswell

Primitive Methodist. *Erected:* 1843. Separate and entire, exclusively used. *Sittings:* Free 140, other 56. *Attendance:* Afternoon: general congregation 33, Sunday school 125, total 158; evening: general congregation 130. *Average attendance:* not given. *Signed:* William Wilkinson, minister, Bakewell. [HO 129/449/27]

Wesleyan Methodist. *Erected:* 1818. Separate and entire, exclusively used. *Sittings:* Free 70, other 82. *Attendance:* Afternoon: general congregation 40, Sunday school 80, total 120; evening: general congregation 60. *Average attendance:* Afternoon: general congregation 40, Sunday school 80, total 120; evening: general congregation 60, total 90. *Signed:* Thomas Bramwell, Local Preacher, Tideswell. [HO 129/449/28]

Roman Catholic. *Erected:* about 1830. Separate and entire, exclusively used. *Sittings:* all free, standing 140. *Attendance:* Morning: general congregation 25. *Average attendance:* Morning: about 25; evening: about 25; no Sunday school. *Remarks:* Service only occasionally about once every 6 weeks done by the Catholic Priest from Hathersage. *Signed:* Benjamin Hulme, Catholic Priest, Hathersage, Nr Bakewell. [HO 129/449/29]

Litton Slack

Wesleyan Methodist. *Erected:* not known, dwelling house. *Sittings:* not given. *Attendance:* Evening: general congregation 52. *Average attendance:* Evening: general congregation 44. *Remarks:* Divine Service once a fortnight held in a dwelling house for the accomodation of the people at Litton Slack. *Signed:* James Warhurst, Class Leader, Litton Slack, near Tideswell. [HO 129/449/30]

HOPE

Wardlow[1]

Wesleyan Methodist. *Erected:* not separate, not exclusively used. *Sittings:* Free 30. See letter. *Attendance:* Afternoon: general congregation 30. *Average attendance:* not given. *Signed:* D. Cornforth, Minister. [HO 129/449/31]

---

[1] Population in Hope 126, in Bakewell 65.

CHAPEL-EN-LE-FRITH
REGISTRATION DISTRICT

Buxton Sub-District

BAKEWELL

Buxton[1]

Church of England. S. John. *Endowments:* not given. *Sittings:* Free 80, other 460, total 540. *Attendance:* not given. *Average attendance:* Morning: average 400, Sunday school 84; afternoon: 300; evening no service. *Signed:* Joseph Vernon, Registrar. [HO 129/450/1]

HARTINGTON[2]

Hartington Upper Quarter[3]

Wesleyan and Primitive Methodist. Brand Top School. *Erected:* 1831. Separate and entire, used for a day & Sunday school. *Sittings* all free. *Attendance:* Morning: Sunday school 47; afternoon: general congregation 35, Sunday school 40, total 75. *Average attendance:* Morning: Sunday school 50; afternoon: general congregation 50, Sunday school 40, total 90. *Remarks:* The Wesleyan Methodists and Primitive Methodists preach every Sunday alternately. *Signed:* William Ashmore, School Master, Brand Top School, near Buxton. [HO 129/450/2]

FAIRFIELD[4]

Church of England. S. Peter. *Endowments:* Land £40, fees £5. *Sittings:* Free 155, other 210. *Attendance:* not given. *Signed:* Geo. Mounsey, Curate of Fairfield, Fairfield, nr Buxton. [HO 129/450/3]

---

[1] Population 1,235.

[2] Parish population 2,089.

[3] Population 893.

[4] Population 574

BAKEWELL

Buxton

Wesleyan Methodist. *Erected:* 1849. Separate and entire, exclusively used. *Sittings:* Free 118, other 310. *Attendance:* Morning: general congregation 88, Sunday school 78, total 166; evening: general congregation 173. *Average attendance:* Morning: general congregation 130, Sunday school 80, total 210; evening: general congregation 240. *Signed:* John Clayton, Chapel steward, Terrace Road, Buxton. [HO 129/450/4]

FAIRFIELD

Wesleyan Methodist. *Erected:* 1844. Separate and entire, exclusively used. *Sittings:* Free all 120. *Attendance:* Evening: general congregation 62. *Average attendance:* not given. *Signed:* George Bennett, Trustee, Fairfield, Nr Buxton. [HO 129/450/5]

Chapel-en-le-Frith Sub-District

CHAPEL-EN-LE-FRITH[1]

Bradshaw Edge[2]

Church of England. S. Thomas the ancient parish church. *Erected:* Before 1800. *Endowments:* The nett annual income is about £150. *Sittings:* Free 70, other 705, total 775. *Attendance:* Morning: general congregation 138, Sunday school 20, total 158; afternoon: general congregation 217, Sunday school 116, total 333. *Average attendance:* Morning: general congregation 200, Sunday school 20, total 220; afternoon: general congregation 350, Sunday school 130, total 480. *Signed:* George Hall, Incumbent, Chapel en le Frith, nr Stockport. [HO 129/450/6]

---

[1] Parish population 3,214.

[2] Population 1,891

TIDESWELL

Wormhill[1]

Church of England. S. Margaret's chapel. Ancient having registers as old as 1620 and before that time but lost. *Erected:* Consecrated before 1800. (the chapel is said to be 400 years old). By private individuals. *Endowments:* Glebe, land £237, fees 10s. *Sittings:* Free none, other 250. *Attendance:* Morning: general congregation about 25, Sunday school 27, total 52; afternoon: general congregation 73, Sunday school 26, total 99. *Average attendance:* Morning: general congregation 29, Sunday school 28, total 57; afternoon: general congregation 95, Sunday school 28, total 123. *Remarks:* Ten years ago value of the perpetual curacy was £270 & surplice fees. *Signed:* Augustus A. Bagshawe, perpetual curate, Wormhill Parsonage, nr Tideswell. [HO 129/450/7]

PEAK FOREST[2]

Church of England. Free chapel of Peak Forest. *Erected:* 1657. Consecrated before 1800. *Endowments:* Annual money payment. *Sittings:* Free about 40, other 138, total 178. *Attendance:* 32. Sunday scholars not attending from great severity of weather. *Average attendance:* Morning: general congregation sometimes more sometimes less, about 100 generally, Sunday school 81. *Signed:* Henry Barrow Chine, Minister, Tideswell. [HO 129/450/8]

CASTLETON[3]

Castleton

Church of England. S. Edmund. Ancient parish church of Castleton. *Erected:* consecrated before 1800. *Endowments:* Glebe letting for 72£, $^1/_3$ of tithe amounting to £75, also $^1/_3$ of lead tithe amounting to about 20£ but uncertain, fees about £2 10s. on an average, Easter offering and small tithes compounded for 10£, deduction from the above to the amount of 10£.

---

[1] Population 369.

[2] Population 596.

[3] Parish population 1,333, Castleton township 867.

Sittings: Free none, other about 350 but *all appropriated* to tenements. *Attendance:* not given. *Average attendance:* Morning: general congregation about 40; afternoon: general congregation 130 to 150, Sunday school 100, total 230 to 250. *Remarks:* It is impossible to give more than a loose average. The above approximates to the truth. In the middle of summer the average is something more; particularly in the morning. *Signed:* Charles Cecil Bates, Vicar of Castleton, near Bakewell. [HO 129/450/9]

Edale[1]

Church of England. Trinity Church. Chapel of ease under Castleton. *Erected:* Consecrated before 1800. *Endowments:* Land £121. *Sittings:* Free 40, other 220, total 260. *Attendance:* Morning: general congregation 38, Sunday school 25, total 63; afternoon: general congregation 90, Sunday school 25, total 115. *Average attendance:* Morning: general congregation 80, Sunday school 55, total 135; afternoon: general congregation 130, Sunday school 55, total 185. *Remarks:* Sunday March 30 being a very stormy day, the congregations were unusually small. *Signed:* G.H. Spurrier, Incumbent, Edale, Castleton. [HO 129/450/10]

HOPE

Hope[2]

Church of England. S. Peter. *Erected:* not known. *Endowments:* Land £28, tithe £244, other permanent endowment £33, fees £20, Easter offering £10. *Sittings:* Free none, other 500. *Attendance:* Morning: general congregation 150; afternoon general congregation 50. *Average attendance:* Morning: general congregation 120; afternoon: general congregation 55. *Signed:* Wilmot Cave Browne Cave, vicar, Hope Vicarage, Bakewell. [HO 129/450/11]

---

[1] Population 466
[2] Township population 429.

HATHERSAGE[1]

Derwent[2]

Church of England. *Erected:* about 1660, before 1800. *Endowments:* unknown. *Sittings:* Free none, other 125. *Attendance:* afternoon: general congregation 40. *Average attendance:* unknown. *Remarks:* There is only service once a day and as the clergyman was away from home and is likely to be so for some time no return could be procured. [*Unsigned*] [HO 129/450/12]

Bamford[3]

Church of England Licensed Schoolroom. *Erected:* Licensed about the year 1845. From the fact of Bamford containing a population of 300 souls and being three miles from the Parish Church of Hathersage. Grant from Privy Council and private contributions. Cost: Grant £62 10s., Private benefactions £313, total £375 10s. *Endowments:* not given. *Sittings:* Free 30, other 110, total 140. *Attendance:* Morning: general congregation 40, Sunday school 35, total 75; evening: general congregation 81, Sunday school 47, total 128. *Average attendance:* Morning: general congregation 45, Sunday school 30, total 75; evening: general congregation 90, Sunday school 40, total 130. *Signed:* Percy Clarke, minister, Hathersage, Nr Bakewell. [HO 129/450/13]

CHAPEL-EN-LE-FRITH

Combs Edge[4]

Wesleyan Methodist. Rye Flatt chapel. *Erected:* Before 1800. Not separate, not exclusively used. *Sittings:* Free 60, other 6, standing 40. *Attendance:* afternoon: general congregation 39. *Average attendance:* Afternoon: general congregation 40. *Remarks:* The Building being Private Property the Upper Room alone is used exclusively as a Place of Worship.

---

[1] Population 2,106.

[2] Population 137.

[3] Population 323.

[4] Population 346.

The remainder being occupied as an Appurtenance belonging to adjoining Farm. *Signed:* B. Jackson, owner, Combs, Chapel en le Frith. [HO 129/450/14]

Bradshaw[1]

Primitive Methodist. School and preaching room. *Erected:* About 1847. Separate and entire, exclusively used. *Sittings:* All free, standing 150. *Attendance:* Morning: Sunday school 68; afternoon: general congregation 35, Sunday school 80, total 115; evening: general congregation 140. *Average attendance:* not given. *Signed:* Isaac Stringfellow, steward, draper. [HO 129/450/15]

Whitehough

Primitive Methodist. *Erected:* 1840. Separate and entire, chapel and Sunday school. *Sittings:* Free 200, other none. *Attendance:* Afternoon: general congregation 50; evening: general congregation 107. *Average attendance:* Morning: General congregation 70, Sunday school 100. *Remarks:* The general congregation will average 70 at each service. *Signed:* William Porritt, superintendent, Whitehough, Chapel en le Frith. [HO 129/450/16]

Chapel-en-le-Frith

Wesleyan Methodist. *Erected:* 1780. Separate and entire, exclusively used. *Sittings:* Free 150, other 186. *Attendance:* Afternoon: general congregation 115, Sunday school 70, total 185; evening: general congregation 160. *Average attendance:* Afternoon: general congregation 140, Sunday school 100, total 240; evening: general congregation 180. *Remarks:* The Free Sittings are forms which will hold 50 adults and 100 Sunday scholars. *Signed:* Peter Kirk, chapel steward, Iron Founder, Chapel en le Frith. [HO 129/450/17]

---

[1] Population 1,891.

Bowden Edge[1] – Barmore Clough

General Baptist. Preaching room. *Erected:* 1841. Separate and entire, exclusively used. *Sittings:* Free 150. *Attendance:* Afternoon: general congregation 27, Sunday school 15, total 42. *Average attendance:* not given. *Signed:* Isaac Hallam, Officiating Minister, Sittinglowe, Nr Chapel en le Frith. [HO 129/450/18]

CASTLETON

Castleton

Wesleyan Methodist. *Erected:* 1809. Separate and entire, exclusively used. *Sittings:* Free 136, other 91. The whole space is occupied either with Pews or Forms. *Attendance:* Afternoon: general congregation 75, Sunday school 69, total 144; evening: general congregation 145. *Remarks:* This statement shews as nearly as possible the *average* number of persons who attend the chapel. The Sunday scholars do not attend the evening service. *Signed:* Micah Pym, steward, Castleton. [HO 129/450/19]

Town Head

Primitive Methodist. *Erected:* 1833. Separate and entire, exclusively used as a Place of Worship and a Sunday School. *Sittings:* Free 90, other none, standing 150. *Attendance:* Morning: general congregation 9; afternoon: general congregation 15; evening: general congregation 62; Sunday school none. *Average attendance:* General congregation 19256 *(sic)*, Sunday school none. *Remarks:* The morning service general average 6, afternoon 12, evening 150. Wednesdays the average 16. *Signed:* John Butler, class leader, Primitive Methodist, Farmer & Cattle Dealer. [HO 129/450/20]

Edale

Wesleyan Methodist. *Erected:* 1811. Separate and entire, exclusively used. *Sittings:* Free 90, other 88. *Attendance:* Morning: general congregation 25, Sunday school 18; afternoon: general congregation 65. *Average*

---

[1] Population 977.

attendance: not given. *Remarks:* NB. This was returned at the proper time but several figures having been misplaced it is desired to substitute the present *amended* form. *Signed:* T. Rowbotham 14 May 1851. Thomas Rowbotham, steward, Grindsbrook, Nr Castleton. [HO 129/450/21]

HOPE

Hope[1]

Wesleyan Methodist. *Erected:* 1835. Separate and entire, exclusively used. *Sittings:* Free 120, other 86. *Attendance:* afternoon: general congregation 40, Sunday school 58, total 90; evening: general congregation 110. *Average attendance:* not given. *Signed:* Jonathan Longden, Trustee and Steward, Hope. [HO 129/450/22]

Gillot Hay

Wesleyan Methodist. *Erected:* Not separate, not exclusively used. See letter. *Sittings:* Free 30. See letter. *Attendance:* Morning: general congregation 26. *Average attendance:* not given. *Remarks:* Omitted to be taken on 30 March. *Signed:* D. Cornforth, Wesleyan Minister, Bradwell, May 10. [HO 129/450/23]

Hag Lee

Wesleyan Methodist. *Erected:* Not separate, not exclusively used. *Sittings:* Free 30. See letter. *Attendance:* Afternoon: general congregation 20. *Average attendance:* not given. *Remarks:* Not taken on 30 March. *Signed:* D. Cornforth, Wesleyan Minister, May 10. [HO 129/450/24]

Marebottom

Wesleyan Methodist. *Erected:* Not separate, not exclusively used. See letter. *Sittings:* Free 30. See letter. *Attendance:* Afternoon: General congregation 25. *Signed:* D. Cornforth, Minister, 10 May. [HO 129/450/25]

---

[1] Population 429.

GLOSSOP[1]

Whaley Bridge

Wesleyan Methodist. *Erected:* 1821. Separate and entire, exclusively used. *Sittings:* Free 290, other 120. *Attendance:* Morning: general congregation 64, Sunday school 195, total 259; evening: general congregation 138. *Average attendance:* Morning: general congregation 75, Sunday school 270, total 345; evening: general congregation 150. *Signed:* Thos. A. Rayner, Wesleyan Minister, Buxton. [HO 129/450/26]

HOPE

Fernilee[2]

Wesleyan Methodist. *Erected:* 1844. Separate and entire, exclusively used. *Sittings:* Free 70, other none. *Attendance:* not given. *Average attendance:* Afternoon: general congregation 50, Sunday school 38, total 88; evening: general congregation 70. *Signed:* Jon. Jodrall, steward, Fernilee, Buxton. [HO 129/450/27]

Thornhill[3]

Primitive Methodist. Mount Zion. *Erected:* 1849. Separate and entire, exclusively used. *Sittings:* Free 60, other 40. *Attendance:* Evening: general congregation 36. *Average attendance:* Afternoon: general congregation 80; evening: general congregation 45. *Remarks:* Our services are Sunday afternoon and Sunday morning alternately. The afternoon service will average about 80 persons, the morning about 45. *Signed:* John Bocking Darwent, Manager, Thornhill, Nr Hope. [HO 129/450/28]

Wesleyan Methodist. *Erected:* 1822. Not separate, exclusively used as a Sunday School. *Sittings:* Free 98. *Attendance:* Afternoon: general congregation 80; evening: general congregation 50. *Average attendance:* Afternoon: general congregation 80; evening: general congregation 50.

---

[1] Parish population 28,625.

[2] Population 651.

[3] Population 131.

Remarks: This is the same room as is returned as the Sunday school. *Signed:* Elias Littlewood, Manager, Thornhill, Near Hope. [HO 129/450/29]

HATHERSAGE

Ashopton

Wesleyan Methodist. *Erected:* 1840. Separate and entire, exclusively used as a Place of Worship and Sunday School. *Sittings:* Free 50, other 56, standing none. *Attendance:* Morning: Sunday school 30; afternoon: general congregation 60; evening: general congregation 65, 75. *Average attendance:* Morning: Sunday school 30; afternoon: general congregation 60; evening: general congregation 65. *Signed:* William Walker, chapel steward, Derwent, Derbys. [HO 129/450/30]

Bamford[1]

Methodist. *Erected:* 1821. Separate and entire, exclusively used. *Sittings:* All free. *Attendance:* Afternoon: general congregation 45. *Average attendance:* Afternoon: general congregation 50. *Signed:* Samuel Ibbotson, steward, Bamford. [HO 129/450/31]

GLOSSOP

Chinley[2]

Wesleyan Methodist. *Erected:* About 1805. Separate and entire, exclusively used. *Sittings:* Free 24, other 176. *Attendance:* Morning: general congregation 24; afternoon: general congregation 20, Sunday school 60, total 80. *Average attendance:* Morning: general congregation 120, Sunday school 60, total 180; afternoon: general congregation 60, Sunday school 60, total 120. *Remarks:* The township of Chinley consisting of only scattered houses and the day being stormy the congregation was not so large as usual. *Signed:* Ralph Harrison, steward, Chinley, near Chapel en le Frith. [HO 129/450/32]

---

[1] Population 323.

[2] Population, with Bugsworth and Brownside, 1,138.

Bugsworth

Independent. School room. *Erected:* 1826. Separate and entire, exclusively used. *Sittings:* Free 110. *Attendance:* Evening: general congregation 19. *Average attendance:* Evening: general congregation 30. *Signed:* Ebenr. Glossop, minister, Chinley, Chapel en le Frith. [HO 129/450/33]

Chinley

Independent. New Chapel. *Erected:* Before 1800 in the year 1711. Separate and entire, exclusively used. *Sittings:* Free 56, other 309. *Attendance:* Morning: general congregation 19, Sunday school 24, total 43; afternoon: general congregation 31, Sunday school 39, total 70. *Average attendance:* Morning: general congregation 50, Sunday school 30, total 80; afternoon: general congregation 100, Sunday school 45, total 145. *Remarks:* Chinley is not a town or a village but a Hamlet. Most of the congregation come from a distance. The day was stormy and the Congregations much fewer than usual. *Signed:* Ebenr. Glossop, Minister, Chinley, near Chapel en le Frith. [HO 129/450/34]

Bugsworth

Primitive Methodist. Chapel and Sunday school. *Erected:* 1841. Seporate chapel and Sunday school. *Sittings:* Free 200. *Attendance:* Morning: Sunday school 28; afternoon: general congregation 10, Sunday school 26, total 36; evening: general congregation 46. *Average attendance:* not given. *Signed:* John Morten, superentendant, Bugsworth, Nr Whaley Bridge. [HO 129/450/35]

PEAK FOREST

Wesleyan Methodist. *Erected:* Not separate, not exclusively used. *Sittings:* Free 110, other 90. See letter. *Attendance:* Afternoon: general congregation 80. *Average attendance:* not given. *Remarks:* omitted to be taken on 30 March. *Signed:* D. Cornforth, Minister, May 10. [HO 129/450/36]

HAYFIELD REGISTRATION DISTRICT

Glossop Sub-District

GLOSSOP[1]

Glossop

Church of England. All Saints. *Erected:* Consecrated before 1800 by the late Lord Bishop of Lichfield, by public subscription and rates. *Endowments:* Glebe, vicarage, other permanent endowment derived from other sources probable amt from three to four hundred pounds. *Sittings:* Free 260, other 740, total 1000. *Attendance:* Morning: general congregation 200, Sunday school 74, total 274; afternoon: general congregation 470, Sunday school 90, total 560, evening no service. *Average attendance:* Morning: 274; afternoon: 560. *Remarks:* the remarks made above are, to the best of my knowledge, truly correct. *Signed:* John Stone, curate. [HO 129/451/1]

Wesleyan Methodist. *Erected:* 1812. Separate and entire, exclusively used. *Sittings:* Free 180, other 420. *Attendance:* Morning: general congregation 220, Sunday school 186, total 548; afternoon: general congregation 350, Sunday school 198, total 548; evening: general congregation 200. *Average attendance:* not given. *Remarks:* The attendance is about the same during the 12 Calendar Months. *Signed:* John Raby, minister, Glossop. [HO 129/451/2]

Wesleyan Methodist Association. Tabernacle. *Erected:* 1836. Separate and entire, exclusively used. *Sittings:* Free 34, other 162, free space or room for standing 100. *Attendance:* Morning: general congregation 90, Sunday school 146, total 236; afternoon: general congregation 150, Sunday school 146, total 296; evening: general congregation 130, Sunday school 40, total 170. *Average attendance:* General congregation 175, Sunday school 150. *Signed:* John Linney,Trustee, grocer, Rose Green, Glossop. [HO 129/451/3]

---

[1] Parish population 28,625, Glossop township 5,467.

Hassop[1] Howardtown

Wesleyan Methodist. *Erected:* 1844. Separate and entire, exclusively used. *Sittings:* Free 200, other 250. *Attendance:* Morning: general congregation 200, Sunday school 250, total 450; afternoon: general congregation 250, Sunday school 250, total 500; evening: general congregation 180. *Remarks:* The attendance is about the same during the 12 Calendar Months. *Signed:* John Raby, Minister, Glossop. [HO 129/451/4]

Glossop

Roman Catholic. All Saints chapel. *Erected:* 1839. Separate and entire, exclusively used. *Sittings:* Will seat 500 easily. All seats free, standing room in the aisles. *Attendance:* Morning: general congregation 400, Sunday school 250, total 600; afternoon: general congregation 200. *Average attendance:* general congregation about 800, Sunday school about 300, rather more, total 1,100. [*Added note:* I put this as the gross amount of the congregation. I should say that during the last twelve months the average number wd vary from 500 to 700.] Remarks: Average number varies – 600 to 700. *Signed:* Theodore Fauvel, Catholic priest, Royle House, Glossop. [HO 129/451/5]

Padfield[2]

Wesleyan Methodist. *Erected:* 1828. Separate and entire, exclusively used. *Sittings:* Free 112, other 92. *Attendance:* Morning: general congregation 60, Sunday school 100, total 160; afternoon: Sunday school 100; evening: general congregation 132. *Remarks:* The attendance is about the same during the 12 Calendar Months. *Signed:* Robert Downs, Trustee. [*Signature very faint*]. [HO 129/451/6]

Independent. *Erected:* 1828. Separate and entire, exclusively used. *Sittings:* Free 200. *Attendance:* Morning: Sunday school 24; afternoon: Sunday school 24; evening: general congregation 60. *Average attendance:* Morning: Sunday school 24; afternoon: Sunday school 24; evening: general congregation 55. *Remarks:* The chapel was built by voluntary contributions

---

[1] *Sic; recte* Glossop.

[2] Population 2,051.

and cost not less than £300. *Signed:* Robert George Milne, Minister, Tintwhistle, Near Mottram, Cheshire. [HO 129/451/7]

Whitfield[1]

Primitive Methodist. Mount Zion. *Erected:* 1844. Chapel, Sunday and Day Schools. *Sittings:* Free 200, other 108, standing none. *Attendance:* General congregation 150, Sunday school 125, total 275. *Average attendance:* General congregation 150, Sunday school 125, total 275. *Remarks:* We could do with more room to accomodate our scholars. *Signed:* Elijah Stott, chapel steward, Waterside, Nr Mottram. [HO 129/451/8]

Hadfield[2]

Wesleyan Methodist. *Erected:* 1804 Separate and entire, exclusively used. *Sittings:* Free 200, other 310. *Attendance:* Morning: general congregation 140, Sunday school 150, total 290; afternoon: general congregation 212, Sunday school 166, total 378. *Remarks:* The attendance is about the same during the 12 Calendar Months. *Signed:* William Swindells, society steward, Hadfield, Mottram. [HO 129/451/9]

Whitfield

Church of England S. James. A new parish constituted under 6 & 7 Vic. c. 37. *Erected:* Consecrated Sept. 8 1846 as an additional church. By grants from Ch. Commissioners, 'Incorporated' & Diocesan Societies & voluntary contributions. Cost £4,200. *Endowments:* not given. *Sittings:* Free 525, other 500, total 1025. See letter. *Attendance:* Morning: general congregation 234, Sunday school 270, total 504; afternoon: general congregation 242, Sunday school 272, total 514; evening: general congregation 120. *Average attendance:* not given. *Signed:* John Teague, Perpetual Curate, Glossop. [HO 129/451/10]

---

[1] Population 4,774.

[2] Population 1,989.

Littlemoor, Whitfield

Independent. *Erected:* 1811. Separate and entire, exclusively used as a place of worship. *Sittings:* Free 100, other 900. *Attendance:* Morning: general congregation 323, Sunday school 298, total 621; afternoon: general congregation 402, Sunday school 304, total 706; evening: not a general service. *Average attendance:* average 520 at one time. *Remarks:* In the 900 sittings appropriated are included 30 to persons not able to pay for them, 40 to singers and 210 to scholars. In the 100 not appropriated are only about 40 are strictly free for strangers. The others are such as may be let being in pews or part let now. Sickness and death in families and a wet day caused the attendance on March 30th to be below the average. The number of sittings let is 620 which are chiefly occupied exclusive of sittings for the poor, for singers & for children. *Signed:* Thomas Atkin, minister, Littlemoor, Glossop. [HO 129/451/11]

Whitfield

Wesleyan Methodist. *Erected:* 1812. Separate and entire, exclusively used. *Sittings:* Free 80, other 140. *Attendance:* Morning: general congregation 80, Sunday school 140 average. *Average attendance:* Morning: general congregation 80, Sunday school 140. *Signed:* John Bennett, chapel steward, Whitfield, near Glossop. [HO 129/451/12]

Green Vale

Primitive Methodist. *Erected:* 1835. Separate and entire, exclusively used. *Sittings:* Free 500. other 273. *Attendance:* Afternoon: general congregation 200, Sunday school 370; evening: general congregation 250. *Average attendance:* Afternoon: general congregation 220, Sunday school 360, total 580. *Signed:* John Newton, seceratry, Milltown, Glossop. [HO 129/451/13]

Charlesworth[1]

Church of England. S. John the Evangelist. A cruciform building in the Early English style. A newly constituted parish under Sir Robert Peel's Act, 6&7 Vict. ch. 37. In the centre of the parish in the township and close to the village of Charlesworth. *Erected:* Cons. on the 8th October 1849 as an additional church, the old Parish church being between 3 to 4 miles distant. Erected by the present incumbent (Goodwin Purcell) who itinerated thro England and by personal appeals to the Nobility and Gentry succeeded in raising £1450 and by written appeal £227, [Total] £1677. No charge was made against subscription for travelling expenses which at times exceeded £2 in a day. Cost: Church Building Commission £250, Incorporated Society £180, Diocesan Extension Society £600, Private Sub. etc £2707. *Endowments:* Other permanent endowment £150, pew rents yearly £10 10s., fees £1, Easter offering unsettled. *Sittings:* Free 242, other 242, total 484. *Attendance:* Morning: general congregation about 100, Sunday school 140, total 240; afternoon: general congregation about 130, Sunday school 160, total 290; evening: a catechmetical taken in the School. *Average attendance:* The congregation has been rather better. *Remarks:* The church in this place seems to have neglected her duty for the last half century or more, consequently on my appointment to this parish I had but a very few churchgoers but am happy to say that church feeling is increasing fast. I beg also to observe that the above income of £161 10s. p. anm is much reduced by the expenses of the church which I pay myself entirely, in addition to the expence of public worship. The other expence is necessary external things having been over £30 a year since its construction. It has always been my wish to avoid taking numbers on the Sabbath Day nor have I wished anyone else to do so. *Signed:* Goodwin Purcell, Incumbent, Charlesworth. [HO 129/451/14]

Particular Baptist. *Erected:* 1835. Separate and entire, exclusively used except for the Sunday school. *Sittings:* Free 72, other 176. *Attendance:* Morning: general congregation 100, Sunday school 54; afternoon: general congregation 200. *Average attendance:* not given. *Remarks:* We, the Particular Baptists at Charlesworth had a Room for Religious Worship from 1825–35 when the Chaple was Built. *Signed:* George Beard, minister, Charlesworth, nr Glossop. [HO 129/451/15]

---

[1] Population 1,714.

Independent. S. Mary Magdalene Chaple. *Erected:* Before 1800. Separate and entire, exclusively used. *Sittings:* Free 100, other 800. *Attendance:* Morning: general congregation 194, Sunday school 143, total 337; afternoon: general congregation 286, Sunday school 175, total 461; evening: general congregation 200. *Average attendance:* Morning: general congregation 200, Sunday school 180, total 380; afternoon: general congregation 320, Sunday school 200, total 520; evening: general congegation 200. *Remarks:* The 30 March was very stormy which along with other local circumstances materially affected the congregation. The average attendance I believe to be correct. *Signed:* Robert Wilson, minister, Charlesworth, Glossop. [HO 129/451/16]

Lee Head

Primitive Methodist. Mount Pleasant Chapel. *Erected:* 1843. Separate and entire, exclusively used. *Sittings:* Free 100, other 60. *Attendance:* Morning: Sunday school 38; afternoon: general congregation 50; evening: no service. *Average attendance:* Morning: Sunday school 44; afternoon: general congregation 50, Sunday school 44, total 94; evening: general congregation 50. *Remarks:* School given up on account of a Particular Service in the Chapel. Service given up at night on account of Particular Service at the Wesleyan Chapel Chisworth. *Signed:* Charles Jubb, steward, Charlesworth, near Glossop. [HO 129/451/17]

Wesleyan Methodist. New Gorte Chapel. *Erected:* 1835. Separate and entire, exclusively used. *Sittings:* Free 32, other 48. *Attendance:* Morning: Sunday school 52; afternoon: general congregation 60, Sunday school 52, total 122; evening: general congregation 40, Sunday school 30, total 70. *Average attendance:* not given. Jno. Clayton, Jnr., Glossop, Nr Manchester. [HO 129/451/18]

Chisworth[1]

Wesleyan Methodist. *Erected:* 1834. Separate and entire, exclusively used. *Sittings:* Free 208, other 112, space 16 x 10 yds. *Attendance:* Afternoon: general congregation 165, Sunday school 69, total 234; evening: general congregation 189, Sunday school 104, total 293. *Average attendance:*

---

[1] Population 555.

Afternoon: general congregation 100, Sunday school 150, total 250. *Signed:* James Clayton, superintendent, Coal Agent, Chisworth, Nr Glossop. [HO 129/451/19]

Marple Bridge

Independent. *Erected:* Before 1800. A.D. 1716. Separate and entire, exclusively used. *Sittings:* Free 225, other 225, standing none. *Attendance:* Morning: general congregation 108, Sunday school 100, total 208; afternoon: general congregation 196, Sunday school 101, total 297. *Average attendance:* Morning: general congregation 137, Sunday school 120, total 257; afternoon: general congregation 234, Sunday school 125, total 359. *Remarks:* Sunday March 30 1851 was exceedingly stormy and unpropitious. The congregation come from a circuit of several miles in breadth round the chapel. The attendance was consequently diminished and our average in the last nine months is given in addition to the actual attendance. *Signed:* Thos. Gill Potter, Minister, Marple Bridge. [HO 129/451/20]

Ludworth[1]

Primitive Methodist. Compstall Road. *Erected:* In the year of our Lord 1833. Separate and entire, exclusively used. *Sittings:* Free 180, other 72. *Attendance:* Morning: Sunday school 104; afternoon: general congregation 70, Sunday school 108, total 178; evening: general congregation 108. [*Average attendance:* General congregation 12360, Sunday school 10460, total 22320: *Crossed through*] *Signed:* Joseph Chappell, Chapl steweard, Compstall Bridge, Baacum, Nr Stockport. [HO 129/451/21]

---

[1] Population 1,578.

Hayfield Sub-District

Hayfield[1]

Church of England. S. Matthew. It was founded in 1386 and rebuilt by the inhabitants in 1819. It is the church of an ancient chapelry reckoned to be in the Parish of Glossop but wholly or in part independent thereof. *Erected:* Consecrated before 1800. Rebuilt by the inhabitants by subscription and benefactions 1819 and an additional plot of Burial Ground consecrated about 1821. Cost: £2,500. *Endowments:* Land £83, pews £15, fees £8 Nett £106. *Sittings:* Free sittings on forms for Sunday scholars 120, other 630, total 750. *Attendance:* Morning: general congregation and Sunday school 185; afternoon: general congregation and Sunday school 320; evening: general congregation about 227. *Average attendance:* Morning: general congregation and Sunday school 246; afternoon: general congregation and Sunday school 480; evening: general congregation 303. These averages are so much greater than the attendance on the 30th March 1851 because that was a very wet and stormy Day in the High Peak of Derbyshire. *Remarks:* The Sunday scholars cannot be reckoned apart from the congregation because they do not sit alone but many of them in the Pews among the congregation. I have answered the above Questions under a strong *Protest.* I consider them impertinent and inquisitorial. *The Census Act does not authorize their being put.* If asked at all they ought to have been sought through the Bishop. Having, however, nothing to conceal (for the Protestant Church of England has nothing to conceal) I have *voluntarily* given the answers to the best of my knowledge & ability. *Signed:* Samuel Walsh, M.A., Incumbent, Hayfield. [HO 129/451/22]

Wesleyan Methodist Association. *Erected:* Before 1800. Not separate, not exclusively used. *Sittings:* Free 220. *Attendance:* Morning: general congregation 30, Sunday school 115, total 145; evening: general congregation 104, Sunday school 30, total 134. *Average attendance:* Morning: general congregation 53, Sunday school 141, total 194; evening: general congregation 142, Sunday school 53, total 195. *Signed:* Robert Turner, Steward, Cotton Band Manufacturer, Hayfield, Nr Stockport. [HO 129/451/23]

Wesleyan Methodist. *Erected:* Before 1800. Separate and entire, exclusively used. *Sittings:* Free 200, other 178. *Attendance:* Afternoon:

---

[1] Population 1,757.

general congregation 76, Sunday school 45, total 121; evening: general congregation 76. *Average attendance:* not given. *Signed:* David Taylor, steward, Hayfield. [HO 129/451/24]

Independent. Meeting House. *Erected:* Occupied since 1849. Erected 1837 and occupied by the Wesleyan Association Methodists till 1849. Used as a place of Public Worship and Sunday school and as a private day school during the week. *Sittings:* Free 400, standing none except the aisle. *Attendance:* Evening: general congregation 32. *Average attendance:* General congregation 25, Sunday school 6. *Signed:* Edward Bond, Superintendant, Hayfield. [HO 129/451/25]

New Mills

Primitive Methodist. *Erected:* 1827. Separate and entire, exclusively used. *Sittings:* Free 171, other 179. *Attendance:* Morning: general congregation 60, Sunday school 180, total 240; evening: general congregation 200. *Average attendance:* Morning: General congregation 60, Sunday school 180, total 240; evening: general congregation 200. *Signed:* George Stansfield, Superintendant Minister, New Mills. [HO 129/451/26]

Primitive Methodist. Schoolroom. *Erected:* Not separate, not exclusively used. *Sittings:* all free. *Attendance:* Afternoon: 14; evening: 28. *Average attendance:* general congregation 40, Sunday school 38. *Remarks:* We are now erecting a new chapel at this place to serve as a Place of Worship & Sunday school. The size 8 yds x 9 yds. *Signed:* John Charlesworth, Sunday School Secretary, Little Hayfield. [HO 129/451/27]

Church of England. S. George. A district Chapelry of New Mills. *Erected:* Consecrated 1831. By Parliamentary grants, & other sources. Cost: £3,500. *Endowments:* Other permanent endowment £144. *Sittings:* 1000 *Attendance:* Not given. *Average attendance:* Morning: general congregation and Sunday school 150; afternoon: general congregation and Sunday school 200. *Remarks:* The attendance is small, the inhabitants being chiefly Dissenters. I have answered the above questions altho' I consider them to be useless and impertinent. They ought to have been asked through the Diocesan. *Signed:* John Rigg, M.A. Oxon., incumbent, New Mills, Stockport. [HO 129/451/28]

Wesleyan Methodist. *Erected:* Before 1800. Separate and entire, exclusively used. *Sittings:* Free 90, other 500, standing 100. *Attendance:*

Morning: general congregation 214, Sunday school 137, total 351; evening: general congregation 267. *Average attendance:* Morning: general congregation 300, Sunday school 200, total 500; evening: general congregation 340. *Signed:* John Connon, Minister, New Mills. [HO 129/451/29]

Low Leighton (in the hamlet of Ollersett)

Quakers *Erected:* Before 1800, say about the year 1717. Separate and entire, exclusively used. *Sittings:* Floor: 34 x 18 = 612 150 persons; Galleries: 12ft 6 x 18 = 225, 50 persons. Total 837, 200 persons. *Attendance:* Morning: general congregation 18; afternoon: general congregation 14. *Average attendance:* The computed average in attendance for the last 12 months is about 20 morning and 18 afternoon. *Signed:* John P. Milner, No 7 Hall Street or 59 Hillgate, Stockport. [HO 129/451/30]

Mellor[1]

Church of England. S. Thomas Perpetual curacy. *Erected:* Consecrated in the reign of King Stephen. *Endowments:* Land £68, other permanent endowment £19, pews £14, fees and dues £21. *Sittings:* Free none, Other 658, children's gallery excluded. *Attendance:* Morning: General congregation 20 to 30, Sunday school none; afternoon: general congregation 165, Sunday school 176, total 341. *Average attendance:* Morning: 40 to 60, Sunday school none; afternoon: general congregation 200 to 400, Sunday school 216, total 616. *Remarks:* Church on a hill distant from the general congregation and Sunday school. The roads in winter almost impassable. Many of the congregation 2 miles from the church. *Signed:* Mattw. Freeman, Perpetual Curate, Mellor, Stockport. [HO 129/451/31]

Primitive Methodist. *Erected:* In the year 1827. Separate and entire, exclusively used. *Sittings:* Free 190, other 60. *Attendance:* Afternoon: general congregation 35, Sunday school 47, total 82; evening: general congregation 100. *Average attendance:* Afternoon: general congregation 70, Sunday school 69, total 139; evening: general congregation 80. *Signed:* John Middleton, Chapel Steward, Sycamore Cottage, Mellor. [HO 129/451/32]

[1] Population 1,777.

Wesleyan Methodist Association. Newhouse Hill Chappell. *Erected:* 1844. Seperate and entire, exclusively used. *Sittings:* Free 232, other 90, standing none. *Attendance:* Morning: general congregation 40, Sunday school 89, total 129; evening: general congregation 45, Sunday school 20, total 65. *Average attendance:* Morning: general congregation 95, Sunday school 100, total 195; evening: general congregation 95, Sunday school 20, total 115. *Signed:* Thomas Sayer, Chappel Steward, Mellor, Nr Stockport. [HO 129/451/33]

Disley

Church of England. S. Mary. Church of an Ancient Chapelry. *Erected:* Consecrated before 1800. *Endowments:* Other permanent endowment £16, pews £22, fees £15, other sources £53 18s. *Sittings:* Free 500, other 400. *Attendance:* Morning: general congregation 65, Sunday school 205, total 270; afternoon: general congregation 105, Sunday school 228, total 333. *Average attendance:* Morning: general congregation 100, Sunday school 250, total 360; afternoon: general congregation 270, Sunday school 300, total 570. *Remarks:* Disley is an extensive chapelry and March 30th being a stormy day the congregations were unusually small. There are 2 other places of Worship within the chapelry. *Signed:* Noble Wilson, perpetual curate, Disley. [HO 129/451/34]

New Mills (Hamlet of Whitle)

Independent. Providence Chapel. *Erected:* 1823. Separate and entire, exclusively used. *Sittings:* Free 60, other 400, standing none. *Attendance:* Morning: general congregation 65, Sunday school 30, total 95; evening: general congregation 79. *Average attendance:* Morning: general congregation 160, Sunday school 100, total 260; evening: general congregation 120, Sunday school 20, total 140. *Signed:* Samuel Simon. minister, New Mills, Nr Stockport. [HO 129/451/35]

Roman Catholic. Church of the Annunciation. *Erected:* 1844. Entire and separate from any other building. Exclusively a Catholic church. Sunday school taught in the Isles. *Sittings:* All seats free. All the poor have seats but pay nothing. A collection is taken on Sundays from *such* as please to pay. 294 See letter. *Attendance:* Morning: general congregation 144, Sunday school 97, total 241; afternoon: general congregation 7, Sunday school 67, total 74; evening: general congregation 87, Sunday school 36, total 123.

Average attendance: Morning: general congregation from 150 to 200, Sunday school from 80 to 100, total 230 to 300; afternoon: general congregation from 6 to 12, Sunday school from 60 to 75, total from 66 to 87; evening: general congregation 70 to 80, Sunday school 35 to 50, total 105 to 150. *Signed:* John Joseph Collins, priest & Catholic pastor, New Mills. [HO 129/451/36]

Mount Pleasant

Wesleyan Methodist Association. *Erected:* 1838. Seperate building for Chapel and Sunday school. *Sittings:* Free school place, other 150 in pews. *Attendance:* Morning: general congregation 70, Sunday school 60. *Average attendance:* not given. *Remarks:* In consequence of the heavy rains on the 30th our number of scholars were generally fewer than what attend generally, many of them having to come at some distance. *Signed:* Benjamin Glazebrook, Minister, New Mills. [HO 129/451/37]

Disley

Wesleyan Methodist. *Erected:* Before 1810. Three cottages as Place of Worship and a Sunday school. *Sittings:* Free 200 all, room for 40 to stand besides the 200 free sittings. *Attendance:* Evening: general congregation 140, Sunday school 109. *Average attendance:* Afternoon: 140; evening: 150. *Signed:* Archibald Vickers, steward, Disley. [HO 129/451/38]

Wesleyan Methodist. Nookole School. *Erected:* 1822. Not separate and entire, used also as a private Day School. *Sittings:* Free 150. *Attendance:* Afternoon: general congregation 29, Sunday school 75, total 104. *Average attendance:* Afternoon: general congregation 24, Sunday school 100, total 124. *Signed:* John Connon, Minister, New Mills. [HO 129/451/39]

ECCLESHALL-BIERLOW
REGISTRATION DISTRICT

Upper Hallam Sub-District

DRONFIELD

Dore[1]

Church of England. Christchurch. *Erected:* 1828 in lieu of an old chapel which was too small by grant from Church Building Society, by Parochial Rate, by subscription from Gentlemen freeholders. Cost £1000. *Endowments:* Not given. *Sittings:* Free 294, other 274, total 568. *Attendance:* no details given. *Signed:* John J.F. Aldred, incumbent, Dore. [HO 129/507/10]

Totley[2]

Wesleyan Methodist. *Erected:* 1848. Separate and entire, exclusively used. *Sittings:* Free 12, other 36, standing 100. *Attendance:* Morning: general congregation 15, Sunday school 34, total 51; afternoon: general congregation 52, Sunday school 41, total 93. *Average attendance:* Afternoon: general congregation 60, Sunday school 50, total 110. *Remarks:* Summer morning and night and attendance like average. *Signed:* James Newbould, Superintendent of the Sabbath School field in Totley. [HO 129/507/11]

Norton Sub-District

Beauchief Abbey (Extra-parochial)[3]

Church of England. An abbey church dedicated to S. Thomas a Beckett in an extra-parochial liberty free from ecclesiastical jurisdiction. *Erected:* 1183. *Endowments:* Donative. *Sittings:* 100. *Attendance:* Morning: general

---

[1] Population 574.
[2] Population 403.
[3] Population 133.

congregation 20, Sunday school 15, total 35. *Average attendance:* Morning: general congregation 30, Sunday school 20, total 50; afternoon: general congregation 60, Sunday school 20, total 80. *Remarks:* The service is alternately morning and afternoon. *Signed:* John Cockerton, M.A., Chaplain, Abbey church, Grammar School, Dronfield. [HO 129/507/13]

NORTON[1]

Church of England. S. James. Ancient parish church. *Erected:* about 350 years ago. *Endowments:* Tithe £20, glebe £217, fees £6. *Sittings:* Free 70, other 450, total 520. *Attendance:* Morning: general congregation 126, Sunday school 52, total 178; afternoon: general congregation 166, Sunday school 60, total 226. *Average attendance:* not given. *Signed:* Henry Hollingsworth Pearson, Vicar, Norton, Nr Sheffield. [HO 129/507/8]

[1] Population 1,856.

ROTHERHAM REGISTRATION DISTRICT

Beighton Sub-District

BEIGHTON[1]

Church of England. S. Mary. *Erected:* Cons. before 1800. *Endowments:* not given. *Sittings:* Total from 350–400. *Attendance:* Morning: general congregation and Sunday school 164; afternoon: general congregation and Sunday school 128. *Average attendance:* Morning: general congregation 140, Sunday school 40, total 180; evening: general congregation 60, Sunday school 60, total 120. *Signed:* Thomas Erskine, M.A., Vicar, Beighton Vicarage. [HO 129/509/2]

Wesleyan Methodist. *Erected:* 1849. Separate and entire, exclusively used. *Sittings:* Free 100, other 43. *Attendance:* Afternoon: general congregation 30; evening: general congregation 40. *Average attendance:* not given. *Signed:* John Hardwick, Beighton, steward. [HO 129/509/3]

Hackenthorpe

Wesleyan Methodist. *Erected:* 1830. Separate and entire, exclusively used. *Sittings:* Free 70, other 65. *Attendance:* Morning: Sunday school 46; afternoon: general congregation 80, Sunday school 46, total 126; evening: general congregation 96. *Average attendance:* Morning: Sunday school 46; afternoon: general congregation 74, Sunday school 46, total 120; evening: general congregation 86. *Signed:* Paul Davies, Trustee and Steward, Hackenthorpe. [HO 129/509/4]

---

[1] Population 1.123.

INDEX OF PERSONS AND PLACES

Places are indexed under the parishes used by K. Cameron, *Place-Names of Derbyshire* (Cambridge, 1959); counties are given only for parishes outside Derbyshire.